FLAS

SOUND

Drawn by P. S. Willats, 1917
A COOK DRAWING WATER FROM A SPRING
This billet overlooked the Souchez Valley and Vimy Ridge

FLASH SPOTTERS

AND

SOUND RANGERS

HOW THEY LIVED, WORKED
AND FOUGHT IN THE GREAT WAR

COMPILED BY

John R. Innes

Illustrated

The Naval & Military Press Ltd

Published by

The Naval & Military Press Ltd

Unit 5 Riverside, Brambleside
Bellbrook Industrial Estate
Uckfield, East Sussex
TN22 1QQ England

Tel: +44 (0)1825 749494

www.naval-military-press.com
www.nmarchive.com

CONTENTS

Flash Spotters & Sound Rangers

LIST OF ILLUSTRATIONS

PROLOGUE

". . . they shall not be found where parables
are spoken.

"But they will maintain the state of the world,
and all their desire is in the work of their craft."

ECCLESIASTICUS

NOTE

THE Flash Spotting Groups and Sound Ranging Sections were detachments of the Field Survey Battalions, R.E.

"Flash Spotting" was a colloquial and semi-official name applied to the detachments engaged on visual observation. At different times they were named Artillery Survey Sections, Artillery Survey Detachments, Observation Sections, and, finally, Observation Groups.

Sound Ranging Sections were always known by that name.

The Field Survey Battalions were first known as the 1st Ranging Section, R.E. Subsequently this Section became the 1st Ranging and Survey Section, R.E. Then came the Topographical Sections, R.E., the Field Survey Companies, R.E., and the Field Survey Battalions, R.E. The Topographical Sections, Field Survey Companies, and Field Survey Battalions were probably best known by their code name, "Maps."

In addition to Flash Spotting and Sound Ranging, there were sections for Administration, Survey (Topo.), Map Drawing, Printing (letterpress and litho.), Map Distribution, Photography, and Air Photo work.

This short explanation may save the uninitiated a certain amount of confusion in reading what follows.

PROLOGUE

Who won the war?

It is not proposed to answer that question here. The purpose of this chapter is to show in some sort of perspective the part played by the Observation Groups and Sound Ranging Sections in achieving victory in the war of 1914–18. In official and other histories there is little or no reference to their work; nevertheless, it is fair to claim that the services rendered by the Groups and Sections were an essential element in the victory, and not a mere "side-show" as one might imagine from the scanty notice that their work has received.

But the Observation Groups and Sound Ranging Sections did not work by themselves. They were detachments or sections of units known as Field Survey Battalions, and, although this book is only designed to tell the story of the Groups and Sections, it will lead to a clearer understanding if, in this chapter, we show how these Battalions worked with the artillery to achieve a triumphant end.

But, first of all, what sort of Battalions were the Field Survey Battalions, R.E? In the pages that follow the reader will learn something of the history of these Battalions, but, for the present, it is enough to say that the need for better maps and different kinds of survey was felt as soon as trench warfare started. Different Sections were formed to deal with different aspects of the problems that had arisen, and it was not long before these Sections were all combined in one unit. These units kept on growing right through the war, and from time to time changes were made in their establishments and the names of the units were changed to meet the altered circumstances.

By 1918, these units had a strength of from eight hundred to a thousand in each, and they became Battalions. The reader who is interested will find these changes set out in a Note facing page 13.

All these Sections came into existence in the war area and, although they still exist in the present Army organization, they are no longer grouped together in an Engineer unit. When the reorganization of the Army took place after the war the Sections that were used entirely for artillery work were handed over to the Royal Artillery and the Field Survey Battalions came to an end. This was the logical thing to do, but those who served with the Battalions cannot but regret that these units are no more.

If the claim is made that it was only proper utilization of the services of the Survey Battalions that made possible the successful attacks of 1918, and that there would not have been so many attacks that missed fire if their work had been not only appreciated but understood earlier, it is made in no spirit of boastfulness, but only to make the reader realize that the influence of these units on the tactical use of the artillery was very much greater than the scanty references to their work in official histories would seem to indicate.

One does not need to be a military expert to realize that surprise is and always has been the most potent weapon in an attack. This is one reason why it is impossible to accept in its entirety the claim that it was the Tanks that alone were responsible for the success of the attack of August 1918. To compare the sixty thousand casualties sustained on the first day of the comparatively unsuccessful battle of the Somme in 1916 with the one thousand casualties incurred in the first day of the successful battle of Amiens in 1918 and attribute the lesser number of casualties to the use of Tanks is to ignore the facts of the case.

But this is what some of the military pundits do. The Tanks were no secret in 1918. If, as it is claimed, they were responsible for the successes at Cambrai, why should the Germans be surprised to find them being used at Amiens? If conditions were otherwise comparable, is it reasonable to suggest that the sight of the Tanks struck such fear into the heart of the enemy that they were only able to hit one man in 1918, as against sixty men in 1916? It should be realised that many of the enemy batteries had been withdrawn far to the rear a week before the attack took place, and it was not the Tanks who found out where these guns were hidden and silenced them. It was the Sound Rangers who discovered where they had gone; the artillery who silenced them; and the Topo. Sections of the Survey Battalions who made it possible for the artillery to hit these targets without previous registration.

If conditions had been favourable no doubt the Air Force would have done their share in locating and destroying these guns. But misty weather prevailed during the critical period when the German guns were being withdrawn and placed in their new positions, and the Sound Rangers were the only people who could and did know where they were. If these guns had remained unlocated, and if our guns had not been able to engage them effectively throughout the day, would the gallant fellows who manned the Tanks have been able to achieve as much as they did?

Nor was Amiens the only place where these things were done. The Earl of Cavan's Despatch dealing with the highly successful attack on the Italian Front in October 1918 shows very clearly how the Survey Battalions were indispensable in preparing for a surprise attack if it were to be successful. (This Despatch is given textually in Chapter 3, p. 75). He tells how the concentration of guns remained silent until zero hour and how "the bombardment and subsequent barrage were excellent." It is, of course, an easy matter to put in the guns and allow them to remain silent, but every gunner knows that if this was the whole story, the "bombardment and subsequent barrage" would have been far from "excellent." Good shooting, particularly in the dark (the bombardment opened at 11.30 p.m.), can ordinarily only be done if the guns have been registered previously, and registration means firing *beforehand* at the target.

What is meant in this Despatch by saying that the guns "remained silent" is that the number of guns that needed to register were so few that the enemy were quite unaware that there was a whole host of new guns concentrated on the front. And it was possible to dispense with all this registering only by using the accurate method of laying provided by the Survey Battalions. In this attack the whole of this preparatory work was done by the 6th Field Survey Company, and the Earl of Cavan gives this work special mention. If it had not been for the services rendered by the 6th Field Survey Company, there must have been so much time and ammunition spent in registering that the enemy would have been warned of the impending attack, as had happened so often before.

These two examples are cited as they show very clearly that these wonderfully successful battles could not have developed as they did if full use had not been made of the services of the Field Survey Battalions. Their part in these battles was an essential one, if the tactics that were employed were to succeed. All arms of the Service had to do their bit, and different people attribute the successes of 1918 to one or another. But it was the Survey Battalions that held the key that unlocked the door to victory.

What was this key?

At Amiens, as we saw, the whole battle-field was shrouded in mist for a week before the attack. The Germans were "windy" and withdrawing their guns to new positions in the rear. How did we get to know this, when we could see nothing clearly beyond the front line? The Sound Rangers found that batteries that were usually active were silent, and they kept on locating the position of new batteries to the rear. If the attack had opened without this information what would have happened? The artillery support must, without doubt, have been very much less effective than it was. Vast quantities of ammunition would have been wasted on empty gun-pits—for two-thirds of our bombardment was directed at the enemy guns—and whole hosts of enemy guns would have been free to retaliate without molestation. Under these circumstances would it have been possible to attack on a wide front and—Tanks, or no Tanks—lose only a thousand men?

But that is only one face of the key. Even if the weather had been clear and all this information had been received from other sources, the attack would either have had to be delayed for several days to allow the guns to register on the new targets, or, if allowed to proceed as planned, the enemy artillery could have retaliated unmolested. But with such an intense concentration of guns this registration would have taken weeks and would have been a regular bombardment. The enemy would have realized that an attack was imminent, and there could have been no element of surprise when the attack was launched, either from the Tanks or the P.B.I. If the attack had taken place without this registration there would have been surprise, but no effective artillery support for either Tanks or infantry. But the Topo. Sections had devised the means of laying the guns on their targets without previous registration, and it was the Topo. Sections that had to make the necessary arrangements for this system of gun laying. So that, without giving away the fact that they were there, the Gunners were able to fire with maximum effect as soon as their fire was needed and not a minute before.

It is futile to speculate on what might or might not have occurred if things had been different, but enough has been said to show that the tactics that proved successful at that and at subsequent attacks were absolutely dependent on the work of the Field Survey Battalions. From Cambrai onwards the tactics employed made necessary—not merely desirable—the use of Survey methods before every full scale attack.

To appreciate properly what the Field Survey Battalions did, it is necessary to go back to 1914. But before doing that it should be made quite clear that nothing that has been said, or that will be said, is to be read as disparagement of other units or formations. From their well-placed Observation Posts, the Survey men were almost privileged spectators of everything that went on along the front. They missed nothing, and no other body of men were so well placed to appreciate the skill and courage of men of other arms of the Service. They saw the infantry advancing steadily to what seemed almost certain death: they watched the Tanks wandering across No-Man's Land—a target for every gun in range: they had a special feeling of pride as they watched the Gunners fire, reload, and relay their guns in all sorts of tight places: and they marvelled at the airmen as they dived and twisted in a cloud of "archies" and still managed to send back their messages by wireless. They had their own bad moments too, but they, at least, will never forget that in the last, as in every other war, it is the man who meets the enemy face to face who decides the issue.

To go back to 1914. Artillery training was based on the assumption that the normal method of shooting would be over "open sights"—that is, much as a man would fire a rifle. The gun layer would look along his sights at a target that he could see from where he was standing. Obviously it was expected that the enemy would do the same thing. Training was largely given up to practising how to get into action quickly and how to get as fast a rate of fire as possible. To use what is now a familiar expression, they practised being "quick on the draw." In a duel where the combatants can see each other, it is a clear advantage to get in the first shot and to shoot more rapidly than the other man.

But the war had not been very long in progress when this was found to be a very expensive process. Any gunners who tried to shoot over open sights were bound to expose themselves to view and become targets for enemy gunners who, because they fired "indirectly," could remain hidden. The game was not worth the candle. The "artillery duel" which had been expected to usher in the big battles came to an abrupt and unexpected end. Direct fire was given up and virtually never used again. This experience was the same for both the Germans and ourselves, and both parties started to dig themselves in. This saved lives and guns, but it had a very serious effect on the future conduct of the war, because, from then till late in 1917, the range of usefulness of the artillery was greatly restricted. For one thing the guns could no longer be laid directly on the target by means of the sights. The best the gunner could do was to get an approximate line and try the effect of a few rounds. This meant sending someone forward to observe where the shots were landing and report back to the battery by phone. But to establish communication between the Observation Posts and the gun and to keep communication open, especially after a move forward, was one of the major difficulties to be overcome in an offensive. On the other hand, when the front was not too busy the gun could be relaid and a few more shots fired and observed, and so on, until the Observer was satisfied that both line and range were correct. The bearing and elevation of the gun were noted and this completed what was known as "registration." But this process was easily spotted by anyone familiar with conditions in the front areas, and the consequence of this was that, just as soon as the gun was in a position to fire effectively at the target, the enemy knew that his concealed position had been spotted and could act accordingly.

Another consequence of this going to ground and hiding behind buildings, etc., was that it became increasingly difficult to know where the hostile batteries were located. Practically the only indication of their position was the flash of the gun when it was fired, and that was difficult to see except at night. Aeroplanes might spot these "flashes" if they happened to be in the air when the gun fired, but a 'plane could only fix the position roughly. The position of many gun pits could be found from air photos, but the photos could not show whether the pits were occupied or empty.

These adverse circumstances inevitably limited the use that could be made of the artillery in a battle. In the first place, in spite of every care and precaution, it ruled out any chance of an artillery surprise. Instead of being able to concentrate the artillery at the rear and rush them up to engage their targets when the battle opened, they had to be put in position some time previously, and they had to open fire to register their battle targets. More guns meant more time, but more time meant more opportunities for the enemy guns to move off to new positions. The more the enemy guns flitted about the less effective became the counter battery work. Very little could be done to keep down the enemy fire. So many of the enemy battery positions were unlocated, and so little was known as to which positions were occupied or empty, that large numbers of the enemy guns were unmolested during an attack.

Consequently, when planning an attack the authorities had no other alternative than to use their artillery largely to destroy the enemy trenches and wire. In the early offensives everything (including all chances of surprise) was sacrificed to destroying trenches and wire. Vast quantities of shells were poured on these leaving little over for the Boche guns, and leaving the gunners tired out when the battle started. The trenches and wire were practically the only points where the gunner could see his target properly, and consequently the only points where he could guarantee results.

Nobody was more aware of the limitations that had been placed on artillery work than the Gunners themselves. First of all there came into being a host of what have been described as "ignorant, but enthusiastic, hostile battery locators." These enthusiasts had a lot to answer for, because, when the Survey Battalions had devised a rapid and reliable system of locating these guns, it took a long time to convince the Gunners that they were not dealing with another body of "enthusiasts." Perhaps a proper pride in the Royal Regiment had a little to do with it. If the Gunners had failed to solve the

problem, how could one expect a solution from outsiders? But perhaps this suspicion is unfounded.

Battery location came later. The first job that the
Surveyors were asked to tackle was to provide some
means whereby the gunner could get the range and
bearing of a known target so that there would be no
unnecessary waste of ammunition in registering. This
was done by fixing the position of the gun itself by careful
survey and supplying the gunner with an accurate map
showing his own position and the position of all his
targets. This specially prepared map was known as an
Artillery Board, owing to the fact that the map was
mounted on a zinc-covered board to prevent shrinkage.

The first Artillery Boards proved so useful that, from
that time forward, every heavy gun was surveyed and
supplied with a board. But the preparation of these
boards entailed the mapping of the enemy trench systems.
This was a task without precedent that would have been
no light problem in times of peace. It was not made any
easier by the fact that the existing French maps were
often out of date and inaccurate. The Survey men,
however, set to work and, with the aid of air photography,
invented a completely new surveying technique, which
enabled them to complete the job by the spring of 1916.

But only limited use could be made of the Artillery
Board, unless all the targets that the gunner wanted
to shoot at were accurately located. Among these targets
not the least important were the German guns. The
Survey men undertook to try and improve hostile battery
location, using sound, as well as sight, for this purpose.
The growth of the sections formed for this job will be
dealt with more fully in the following chapters, so that it
is enough here to say that an organization had been
created by the spring of 1916 that enabled the Survey

men to detect and locate a very large number of hostile batteries.

With nearly all the difficulties that had arisen in 1914 out of the way, it would seem as if the higher command would have been in a position to evolve some new tactical use for the artillery. But the position was this. As long as no attack was preparing the Gunners had a plentiful supply of accurately located targets. From their boards they could measure the range and bearing of these targets, but still they could not lay their guns accurately on these targets without firing some trial rounds—registering. The number of rounds required had been very much reduced by the provision of the Artillery Boards, and this number was still further reduced when the accurate methods of ranging employed by the Observation Groups were used, but still they had to register, and the greater number of guns employed meant that it took even longer than before to carry out this necessary preliminary to an attack, despite all these gains in accuracy.

The system of laying that was, at last, to enable the Gunners to do most of the things that they had hoped to do in 1914 was, it is believed, invented by a Survey officer, but the significance of this discovery was hardly realized at the time, and it was not until Cambrai that it was tested in an attack.

This invaluable discovery came about in this way. The preparations for the battle of the Somme included arrangements for a railway gun to be grought up to fire along the Albert–Bapaume road. This was a long straight road, and a main channel of supply to the German trenches. There was no difficulty in laying the siding roughly in alignment, but how was the gun to be laid——or in non-technical language, pointed at—the road some thirteen miles away in, say, the dark? A solution of this problem was found by providing an accurately surveyed point convenient to the siding from which it was possible to lay a "director" accurately on any required bearing—in this case the line of the Albert–Bapaume road. The gun could then be laid parallel to this bearing, using the ordinary artillery drill for this purpose.

This was the origin of the "Bearing Picket" that afterwards became so familiar to all Gunners, and it was the last stage in providing a system that would restore to the guns their full usefulness in both attack and defence. Once this was realized it became possible to employ any tactical scheme that suited the particular circumstances, instead of having to employ tactics that were limited by the limited use that could be made of the guns.

It is curious to speculate why the revolutionary nature of all these improvements seemed to go unheeded until 1918. One reason was, of course, that the system of Bearing Pickets was not given an extensive trial until Cambrai in 1917. But on the technical side it would seem as though the real significance of the Bearing Picket had not been understood. It must be remembered, however, that the artillery commanders had good reason to distrust unobserved fire. It was not in the British Army only that there was delay and difficulty in winning them over to new methods.

It is not necessary for present purposes to describe Aiming Points and Bearing Pickets, or to go into details of how guns are laid. All the reader need understand is that, when a gun is laid on its target by means of an Aiming Point, it is very necessary to know the bearing of the Aiming Point as well as that of the target. Any errors in bearing to the Aiming Point are multiplied as the range increases, and quite small errors will throw the shot well to one side or another of the target.

Prologue

It was almost by accident that the proper use of the Field Survey Battalions in preparing an attack was discovered. Although Cambrai was the first "Survey" battle it was not made so deliberately. It became so because it was decided to prepare a tactical scheme that would give the Tanks a chance to show what they could do. The whole scheme was prepared to suit the Tanks. It was laid down that there were three prerequisites, if the Tanks were to be successful. (1) No artillery registration. (2) No attempt to destroy obstacles by preliminary bombardment. (3) Artillery to be directed on guns instead of on trenches and wire. Surprise was to be the key to success. Well, the Tanks got their own way, and the British Army, at last, burst right through the enemy lines. Everyone was very pleased and the Tanks were all given a pat on the back and an extra drink of petrol.

If the reader will consider the conditions asked for by the Tank Corps, he will notice that they asked for something that up till then had been held to be impossible. The guns could remain silent before the battle, and they could refrain from shooting at the trenches and wire, and they could fire at the enemy artillery when they knew where the German guns were. But without ranging and registering, they could not guarantee to hit any of these things when the time came. They could only shoot off into the blue. If there was not a reasonable chance of silencing the enemy guns, they might as well have stayed away altogether. Up till now a successful bombardment of trenches or guns had always meant preliminary registration, but the above conditions ruled this out.

There was only one possible way of dealing with this situation, and that was by employing the Survey method of gun laying, and it was decided to try it along the whole battle front. The Survey Battalions supplied all the

Bearing Pickets required and a Survey officer paid a visit to every single battery that was to take part in the battle to explain and make sure that the method was understood. Of course, the Flash Spotters and Sound Rangers carried on as usual, but their results were needed now even more than was usually the case. With a rapid concentration of batteries there was no time for each battery to find targets for itself.

That the results from this form of artillery preparation were successful need not be argued. It was adopted in every subsequent battle and it is still part of the routine training of the Gunner. So that, without decrying the work of any other branch of the Service, the Field Survey Battalions may justly claim a full share in the success of the first days of the battle of Cambrai.

Let us now go up the line and see how the infantry were faring. They had achieved a real "break through," and if there was one thing that everyone—generals, clubmen, and press proprietors—agreed upon at that time, it was that once a "break through" occurred all the rest would be plain sailing, but up the line the troops had an uneasy feeling that things were much as before. Then came the German counter-attack that practically wiped out all the gains of the first few days.

The only real distinction between Cambrai and the battles that preceded it was that the initial success was greater and the enemy counter-attack more successful. The same old thing, but more movement. Surprise was undoubtedly the factor that gave us the big initial success. The Tanks were a surprise, of sorts, at that time, but the artillery bombardment without previous registration was, without a doubt, a bigger surprise. Gun laying by Survey methods had never been tested on this scale before, and if it had failed it is pretty certain that the attack would have broken down and the Gunners would have had to take the blame. Survey methods would have been discredited, but it is only right to point out that it would probably have been the Gunners who would have been attacked for listening to "theorists." But neither the Tanks nor the guns could keep the attack going or prevent the successful counter-attack, and the cause of this does not seem far to seek, because it is common to all the attacks of 1915, 1916, and 1917.

The initial successes were gained under the cover of intense artillery fire with the guns all firing on "registered" targets. That is to say the fire was accurate, and this gave an initial impetus which carried the line forward for a few days, but as soon as the advance got beyond the support of the guns it received a check; the enemy could steady his line and get up his reinforcements of men and guns. Meantime, all our guns had to be brought up into new positions, and when they got there they found themselves working under much the same conditions as those that had caused so much trouble in 1914. That is, very few visible targets, and no proper means of laying their guns on such targets as were known. Consequently, very little *effective* artillery support for infantry or anyone else. When an attack succeeded there always came a time when the infantry had to wait on the artillery to come up. This gave the enemy a chance to rally and get himself dug in. When our own guns got up they had to fire "blind." There was no time to register. The enemy were really in a position of advantage.

The reader who has studied the details of the different attacks from 1914 onwards may say that all this is to ignore the many chances that affected the course of these battles and that were independent of artillery work. What about the hold-up of the line at Flesquières at the battle of Cambrai? What about the mud at Passchendaele? And so on. But we are not concerned here with *why* the advances were held up. What concerns us is that once these advances were checked it was found to be impossible to set the line going again without artillery preparation and support which took months to organize. This is the one feature that was common to all attacks—British or German—prior to and even after the battle of Cambrai. Even when the Germans had been driven right beyond their prepared defence lines nothing in the nature of a continuous advance was possible without artillery. The line had first to be broken by a series of sledgehammer blows at different points, and it was the Survey Battalions that made it possible to deal these blows rapidly the one after the other, and leave the enemy no time to prepare new defence lines.

Now if we return to the battle of Amiens in 1918, we find that all the preparations were carried out in exactly the same way as at Cambrai, and that for the first few days the attack developed much as it did at Cambrai. But after that there was a radical change in tactics. To all intents and purposes the battle was broken off and every effort made to consolidate the gains. Local attacks kept the enemy guessing as to what was happening, and compelled him to use up his reserves. Meanwhile the Sound Rangers and Flash Spotters were busy locating the enemy gun positions and the Topo. men—now that the guns were not required to register—were fixing the position of our own guns and supplying them with Artillery Boards, so that the attack could be renewed under the same favourable conditions with the least possible delay.

But no further attempts were made to advance immediately on this front. All the time, however, the Survey

Prologue

Battalions were making the necessary arrangements for other attacks elsewhere. As soon as it was clear that the front had "stabilized" in front of Amiens, all the guns that were not required for defensive purposes were withdrawn to the new front north of the Ancre. Arriving there they found everything ready for them; an Artillery Board with their own position plotted and a plentiful supply of properly located targets: and a Bearing Picket conveniently placed from which they could lay their guns on their chosen targets. Within a few hours of arriving at their battle position they were ready to engage the enemy positions effectively. And so, before the enemy realized that one battle was finished, another surprise was sprung on him. The same policy was pursued as before. The attack was only carried forward so long as effective artillery support was possible. After that the gains were consolidated and a new attack launched from a part of the front where all preparations had been made previously. The time that elapsed between one attack and the one that succeeded it was conditioned only by the time required to move the attacking forces from one point to another. All the preparatory work—thanks to the Survey Battalions—was done long before the attacking troops arrived on the site.

As a sidelight on these impressions it is worth while studying the German attack of March 1918. Three German Armies took part in this attack, but only one succeeded in breaking through. This Army planned the attack on Survey lines, whereas the other two used the traditional methods of artillery preparation. Surprise certainly gave the initial impulse for the break through, although in view of the public controversy that has been waged over this battle, it is hardly necessary to add that it was not a complete surprise. What was significant about the German attack was that the Army which used artillery methods similar to ours at Cambrai got through, whilst the others did not, and this even though the attack was not the complete surprise of ours at Cambrai.

But where this attack differed from the British attack was in the action taken after the initial success. At Cambrai the attack was held up to enable the guns to catch up and give support. There were not sufficient infantry reinforcements to prevent this hold-up. At St. Quentin the Germans pressed on with relays of fresh troops regardless of their artillery. At first success seemed to justify this course, because the other Armies on the right, who had to wait for the artillery in the usual way, could make very little progress. But once the British infantry got a chance to close the gaps in the line, the initiative passed to the Allies again. The Allies could choose where the stand should be made and, fighting on their own ground, the artillery could be employed effectively. The German infantry having gone ahead so fast and so far had no effective artillery support, and so the advance was stayed.

The argument of this chapter may be summarized in this way. In conditions such as those of the last war artillery could only be used *effectively* if they had (1) good maps, (2) their own position accurately located, (3) the position of enemy guns accurately located, and (4) means of laying their guns accurately on these targets without previous registration. All these facilities were provided by the Field Survey Battalions, R.E.—(1) by the Map Sections, (2) by the Topo. Sections, (3) by the Observation Groups and Sound Ranging Sections, (4) by the Topo. Sections. When full use was made of these facilities it was possible to effect surprise, reduce casualties, and attack as often as required. Preliminary arrangements for an attack could be made in a very short time, and the attacking forces did not require to be on the ground until actually needed. This was the basis of the successful "push" in 1918, and this is the basis for claiming that the work done by the Field Survey Battalions is worth recording and that it merits proper consideration.

The reader will realize that, although the Field Survey Battalions, and in particular the Observation Groups and Sound Ranging Sections, may seem to have taken a very small part in the battles of the Great War, their work had an importance that was out of all proportion to their numbers. This chapter has been written in no spirit of self-glorification. Obviously to treat the subject adequately would require a volume and would be out of place in a book designed to deal with men more than things, so the reader will be troubled with no more matters of high policy.

BOOK I

"Enterprise is an endless process of trial and improvement."

J. L. GARVIN

HOW THE OBSERVATION GROUPS AND SOUND RANGING SECTIONS CAME TO BE FORMED

As this book is meant to illustrate the everyday life of the officers and men in the Flash Spotting Groups and Sound Ranging Sections, and is not, in any sense of the word, a "History," or even a record of work, the different phases in the growth of the Groups and Sections from 1914 till their disbandment after the Armistice will only be touched on very lightly. Not that the subject is without interest, but because it is too big, if properly dealt with, to receive proper treatment in a book of this sort.

But the Groups and Sections were distinctly "unconventional" units, and to understand much of what follows, the different chances and changes that brought them into being and kept them ever growing in size and usefulness must be understood.

The Groups and Sections were "unconventional" units, both in respect of the actual form of organization that developed, and in respect of the way in which they were run. This was due to the nature of the task they were called upon to tackle, and also due to the type of officers and men who were employed on the job. These were not recruited haphazard, but had to satisfy educational tests, and undergo a period of probation before they were taken on "the strength."

So, in this, and the next few chapters, it is proposed to set out a few of the landmarks, and in a general way indicate some of the considerations that influenced the growth of the organization.

When the B.E.F. landed in France in 1914, there was

only one officer in the whole force who was employed on duties in any way related to surveying. He was the staff officer (G.S.O. 3) on the Topographical Sub-Section of the General Staff, known officially as I(c), but more commonly as "Maps, G.H.Q." He was assisted by one clerk, and there was another officer and clerk on the Lines of Communication. Around this nucleus grew the organizations that came to be known as the Field Survey Battalions, and which, at the time of the Armistice, must have mustered over five thousand souls all told. It was to these Battalions that the Observation Groups (Flash Spotters) and the Sound Rangers belonged. The Groups and Sections probably comprised rather more than two-thirds of the whole, but he would be a bold man who would dare to suggest which of the many functions of the Field Survey Battalions was the most important.

But the Maps Officer at G.H.Q., although an expert surveyor, was concerned only with the supply and distribution of maps. Survey in the field had hardly even been thought of as a possibility at that time. The Royal Engineers were first brought in contact with the problems of observation when the 1st Ranging Section, R.E., came to France in October 1914. Strictly speaking, the Ranging Section was not engaged in the work of observation at all. Its duty was to fix the position of an aeroplane flying over the enemy lines. The aeroplane was seeking out enemy guns, and when directly over its objective it dropped a smoke bomb and this was supposed to indicate the position of the gun. Of course, the aeroplane observer could fix the position of the gun by reference to his map, but by adopting this method it was hoped to get the information more quickly to our own Gunners. One must recall that at that time there was no wireless, and one had to await the return (perhaps) of the aeroplane for any information that the observer might have gathered on his flight.

From the earliest days Survey men were objects of suspicion. A member of this Section was arrested when carrying a theodolite. The reason given for his arrest was that no one but a German would attempt to make war with such queer instruments! This sounds barely credible, but his C.O. writes: "Oh yes it is. I bailed him out!" And it is certainly true that right up till the end of the war, Survey men were being arrested frequently on much the same grounds.

The 1st Ranging Section, R.E., consisted of one officer and four other ranks, all from the Ordnance Survey at Southampton. They were attached to the 8th Divisional Artillery. Their method of working was to set up two theodolites some distance apart, fix their own positions, and await the aeroplane. When the aeroplane went up, the surveyors kept it in view in their instruments and, at the moment when the aeroplane made its signal, they read the bearings on their instruments. The position was calculated, and the result passed on to the Gunners. The development of wireless soon rendered these experiments superfluous, and they do not seem to have had much direct influence on the subsequent development of Flash Spotting and Sound Ranging.

By the beginning of 1915, the Ranging Section was employed almost entirely on survey duties—much of this being done for the artillery. Consequently, in April 1915, this Section was withdrawn from the 8th Division and attached to the General Staff (Maps, G.H.Q.) for survey in the field with the whole Expeditionary Force. At the same time the name was changed to the 1st Ranging and Survey Section, R.E., and the stage was set for the expansion that was to follow.

37

Flash Spotters & Sound Rangers

Despite the many changes that followed, this control by the General Staff at G.H.Q. continued until the end of the war. Every question of more than local importance was referred to G.H.Q. for a ruling, and it was probably due to this that the Groups and Sections were able to expand so rapidly and with increasing efficiency on sound lines, because without this unified control there is little doubt that some of the Observation Groups, at least, would have been diverted to other jobs. In the early days, when performance was not up to promise, some artillery formations were of the opinion that the Groups and Sections were only duplicating the work of the Gunners and could see no use for either Flash Spotters or Sound Rangers, unless they came under their command.

It was a fortunate circumstance that the C.O. of the 1st Ranging and Survey Section was no stranger to the difficulties that were facing the artillery at this time. As the officer in charge of the trigonometrical work of the Ordnance Survey before the war, it had been his business to study in co-operation with the R.A. many similar problems connected with the coast defences of this country. The R.A. and the R.E. had a joint responsibility for these defences. The Sappers ran the lights and the submarine mining, provided the proper orientation and fixing of the graduated arcs for the heavy guns, the surveys of the gun positions and of the datum points, and the survey of the position and height for the depression range-finders. Except for lights and submarine mining these were some of the tasks that faced the 1st Ranging and Survey Section on its formation. But, of course, the conditions were very different in many ways, and in many cases it was necessary to devise quite new and original methods. Amongst these new methods were those of the Flash Spotters and Sound Rangers, but the reader should remember that Observation Groups and Sound Ranging Sections were formed to deal with only one aspect of a much bigger problem. They could not have functioned properly without the purely Survey Sections, and in the same way the work of the surveyors would have been incomplete without Flash Spotting and Sound Ranging.

The work of the Observation Groups and Sound Ranging Sections was so closely allied to that of the artillery that, to many people, it seemed strange that it was done by the Engineers, and not by the artillery. All the working contacts of the Groups and Sections were with the artillery, and even on the administrative side they never came under the C.E. or C.R.E. But it will have been gathered that the choice of the Engineers for this task was not accidental. Apart from the more formal reasons for this choice, there can be no doubt that the personalities of the two officers who were first called into consultation must have played a large part in the final decision. Between them they had the requisite store of experience, knowledge, tact, and drive, which are all so badly needed when new ideas have to be developed. And when success crowned their efforts, who were better fitted to carry on?

In October 1915, the Third Army organized an Artillery Survey Section. It was technically an R.A. unit, and they supplied the bulk of the personnel and at first administered it. But from the very first it was the O.C. 1st Ranging and Survey Section who organized the work, and the Gunners gave him a free hand in this respect. These conditions only continued for a few weeks when the whole detachment was handed over to the R.E.

But it was not long before this section changed its name

to the Artillery Survey Detachment—and for a very
good reason. In the Army it is customary to refer to units
by the initial letters in their name. If the Artillery Survey
Section had gone on using this name, it would have been
an "ASS!"

At this time the 1st Ranging and Survey Section had
been split into three parts to carry out the survey work
in each Army, and they were re-named the Topographical
Sections, or, as they were always called, Topo. Sections.
In the Third Army the O.C. Topo. Section was put in
charge of the Artillery Survey Section for training and
technical methods, but the administrative and tactical
control remained in the hands of the R.A. This dual
control did not last long, and the detachment was soon
under the command of the O.C. Topo. Section.

When the authorities decided that the Engineers should
undertake the task of locating hostile battery positions,
as well as other survey work, it was decided to use sound
as well as sight for this purpose. It should be realized that
at this time sound ranging was hardly an accomplished
fact. It had only progressed sufficiently far to show that
it was a practical proposition, and that with some
improvement it should prove a valuable aid. The authorities took a good deal of persuading, but eventually
permission was granted for the formation of a few Sections
to try it out. So that the Topo. Sections were formed with
Sound Ranging Sections as well as visual Observation
Sections.

The growth of the Sound Ranging Sections will receive
separate treatment in Chapter 7, so that the rest of this
chapter, and the next two chapters, will be devoted
mostly to the growth of the Observation Groups. But it
should be remembered that the Groups and Sections
grew up side by side, and that they were engaged on the

same task. Almost all the conditions that affected the Flash Spotters affected the Sound Rangers, so that, unless a clear distinction is made, the reader will be safe in assuming that most of what follows applies to both the Observation Groups and the Sound Ranging Sections.

The fact that the Observation Groups in the Third Army were originally R.A. units, and that even when they came under R.E. control most of their personnel were R.A., played a considerable part in the development of Flash Spotting in this area. From the beginning, they had the "ear" of the people whose work they had to supplement—that is, the artillery. Ideas could be discussed without prejudice, and close contact led to a free exchange of opinions.

At this time there existed a somewhat similar Section in the XI Corps in the Second Army, but it was entirely an R.A. concern. In November 1915 it was expanded to an Army organization, but it was not until February 1916 that it came under the control of the R.E.

In the First Army there was no organization in existence and, when it was decided to organize Flash Spotting under the newly formed Topo. Sections, conditions were as different as possible from those in the Third Army. In the first place, the Army decided that no R.A. personnel were to be employed, and as all R.E. officers with survey experience were already fully employed, it meant that officers had to be found from infantry or other units to organize the work. The fact that they were not R.E. officers did not make them any less capable of doing the work than if they had been serving with the Engineers. But it made the task of gaining the confidence of the R.A.—who were often apathetic, to say the least of it—a much more difficult task than it need have been. Kilts, or even a set of bagpipes, might help to strike terror into the heart of the enemy, but they did not help to impress the Gunners with the idea that the owner had anything to contribute to the science of gunnery.

But from the standpoint of the Engineers themselves, the lack of any R.A. officers was a serious drawback. It was difficult to acquire a knowledge of artillery technique and understand the standpoint of the Gunner from casual contacts. This order was rescinded in January 1916, but, although a few Gunners were recruited in the rank and file, there were never any Gunners amongst the officers.

Although these handicaps were overcome, this initial contrast between the First and Third Armies remained very marked right up till the end of the war, when, in many ways, there was considerable uniformity in all the Armies. In the Third Army they could always count on the Artillery providing men and opportunities for experiment, whereas, in the First Army, the Groups usually had to make their own opportunities, and find their own men.

In the other Armies the Groups were formed later with the initial experience of the First, Second, and Third Armies to guide them, so that in these cases they started on a recognized footing, and contact with the R.A. was on a reasonable basis from the beginning.

The Third Army Artillery Survey Section started out with seven Observation Posts (later known as Survey Posts), spaced along the whole Army front. Each post was manned by one officer, with six observers, a telephonist, and a cook. Following artillery tradition, the officers were expected to do a good deal of observation personally. Actually, with so few observers, it was not unusual for the officer to take a definite turn of duty in the Post when men were sick, etc. There was telephonic communication between neighbouring Posts, and also to some artillery formation, but there was no communication through a telephone exchange.

In the First Army a start was made with two Posts at the South of the area and two Posts at the North end, but there was no communication between these two sets of Posts. In such very flat country, these four Posts might have been said to cover the whole front, but not very efficiently. The personnel of the Posts was the same as in the Third Army, but there was only one officer to every two Posts. As in the Third Army, the officers spent much of their time in the Posts actually observing.

In a subsequent chapter the methods of locating hostile artillery will be explained in detail, so it will be sufficient for the present to say that the method employed at this time was very crude, but not wholly ineffective. In fact, the principles underlying the methods used then were proved sound, as subsequent development was more on the lines of development of apparatus and refinement of technique than change of method.

Each Post had a map of its own front mounted on a board, and on this map was marked all the known information about hostile batteries. By means of a thread fixed at the position of the Survey Post, the observer could lay out bearings quickly.

If two or more Posts got bearings to a gun that was firing, they could lay off their bearings and fix its position, and when that was done, pass it on to the artillery. So that it will be seen that the whole of the technical side of the work of the Flash Spotter was carried out at this time in and from the Survey Posts themselves. At the start, the bearings from the Posts were also used to calculate the position of the enemy gun. But this was a very laborious task, and showed no advantage over the graphical method, and it was soon dropped.

In the First Army, the artillery were so distrustful of the capacity of the Flash Spotters to achieve results that they ordered that every "flash" noted, together with its bearing, should be reported to them straight away. This order was never formally rescinded, but it gradually fell into disuse, as the artillery soon got sick of being flooded out with useless messages. But it had two very unfortunate results. Firstly, it interfered greatly with getting accurate results, and secondly, when the Posts were able to get good results, the artillery had become so used to useless messages that much valuable information was overlooked. It took a long time to correct this position.

An example of this may be given. A Group officer happened to be present at the Corps H.A. office when a discussion was in progress as to whether to order retaliation in a certain area. The difficulty arose from a shortage of ammunition and a suspicion that the enemy shelling was not as bad as reported. In other words, it was thought that the troops might be "windy." The Staff were genuinely worried, but ammunition was scarce and had to be husbanded. The Group officer suggested that they should ring up one of the Survey Posts, as they could tell from their log almost every round that had fallen in the previous twenty-four hours. This was done, and the artillery were so satisfied with the result of their inquiries that, from this time on, increasing use was made of the Flash Spotters' reports. But what was not pointed out then was that all the information that they got from the Posts had been telephoned to them previously, but apparently ignored.

Another method used at this time for getting locations was by scrutinizing the logs of the Posts. Each Post had a

44

chronometer (in reality a watch), and the time of each "flash," recorded to the nearest one-fifth second, was entered up in the log. At this time, and for some time afterwards, telephonic communication was very bad at certain Posts, and many possible locations would have been lost if Posts had had to rely on communicating with one another. But when the logs were assembled each day at H.Q., they were scrutinized to find if different Posts had taken any bearings about the same time. If so, the first test applied was to see if these bearings intersected at a point where it would be reasonable to expect to find hostile artillery. Then a closer study had to be made of the times. Few of the pseudo chronometers could be relied upon to keep correct to within a few minutes in twenty-four hours, so a difference in the actual time when the "flashes" were seen from the different Posts was of no great significance. What was most significant was the time interval between the "flashes." If these corresponded closely, there was prima facie evidence that both observers were on the same gun.

There were a number of other difficulties in accepting even this evidence but, despite appearances, this scrutiny yielded remarkably good results at times. The observers, never having to handle the results themselves, had no belief in this method and, perhaps, if they had it might have yielded better results than it did.

These were the conditions existing at the end of 1915. A technique had been evolved that yielded results, but more and better results were required to justify a separate existence for these sections. Sufficient experience had been gained to show that this could be done, so the work was pressed on—and these remarks apply to Sound Ranging as well.

But it was also apparent that the Topo. Sections as a

whole would have to be reconstituted to meet the changing conditions. Observation work and sound ranging were only two of the many tasks relegated to the Topo. Sections. There were other Sections for survey, map drawing and printing, letterpress printing, photography, and map supply. It sounds like an odd job lot, but a little consideration will show that all these different Sections were engaged on work that was fundamentally the same. But these Sections, as well as the Groups and Sections, were increasing in numbers and importance, and it was essential that the Topo. Sections should be reorganized to meet the changing conditions.

It will be remembered that the 1st Ranging Section consisted of 1 officer and 4 other ranks. Their numbers at this time (the end of 1915) can only be a matter of conjecture, as they were being added to day by day, but for survey work alone there were 6 officers and 57 other ranks employed at November 1915.

To meet the changed conditions the Topo. Sections were reconstituted as Field Survey Companies (F.S.C.), and the sections engaged on observation work acquired an identity of their own for the first time. In the new authorized establishment each of the different branches already enumerated had a definite amount of personnel allotted to them, and most of these Sections were in charge of a separate officer. The officers commanding the Field Survey Companies acquired the status of Commanding Officers.

The hostile battery location was to be done by Observation Sections (subsequently renamed Groups) and Sound Ranging Sections, but the authorized establishment for the Observation Sections was rather peculiar. For, whereas it laid down the numbers to be employed in each Survey Post (8 men), it did not define the number of

The Groups and Sections are Formed

Survey Posts to each Observation Section, nor the number of Sections to a Field Survey Company. It was as though the numbers of men in a Platoon were laid down by regulation, but the number of Platoons to a Company and Companies to a Battalion were left to the discretion of the C.O. of the Battalion. What was described rather grandiosely as the H.Q. of the Observation Section was staffed by 1 officer and a batman.

When this new establishment was being drafted, it was thought that direct control of the Observation Sections would remain at Company H.Q. The man in the field was to be relieved of all but the most urgent tasks. All the data collected by the Posts were to go to Company H.Q. to be collated, and from Company H.Q. were to issue orders as to what to do or not to do. To assist the C.O. in this task an officer was appointed at H.Q. who was designated the Compilation Officer.

As things turned out, both Observation Sections and Sound Ranging Sections very soon became almost self-contained. That is to say, instead of Company H.Q. trying to keep all the threads in their own hands, the Sections were encouraged to do everything possible for themselves. As a consequence of this, the Compilation Officer was no longer concerned with the working of the Observation Sections, but as he was still concerned with their results, something must be said about his task, although he belonged to Company H.Q.

When the Artillery Survey Section was formed in the Third Army, it was realized that, however successful this Section might prove, the addition of another source of information, without co-ordination with the existing sources, would only make for confusion. The main sources of information at that time were air photographs, R.F.C. reports, Corps Intelligence reports, and R.A.

47

observation reports. There were at least three lists of locations issued periodically, and, as they differed widely from one another, it is hardly surprising that any and all lists were distrusted.

The work of co-ordination was undertaken by the R.A. and supervised by the O.C. Topo. Section, and in December 1915 a special Section, called the Compilation Section, was formed. This was put in charge of a Survey officer attached to Army H.Q. for air photo work. He had to deal also with other allied problems, but these do not concern us here. But that was the origin of this appointment, and this explanation accounts for the rather curious name attached to his office.

Eventually the duties of this officer developed on very different lines in each Army. In some Armies the Survey Battalions compiled the "authoritative" hostile battery lists; in others this was done by the artillery themselves; but in every Army the Survey list could be relied upon for accuracy. The work of the Compilation Office had a great deal to do with the ultimate appreciation of the work of the Groups and Sections. From the start, accuracy and reliability were the foundations on which the Groups and Sections worked, and this was ensured by passing all their results through the Compilation Office at Battalion H.Q. Results from Groups and Sections were sent, in the first place, direct to the local artillery formations concerned in case immediate action was called for. But no records were prepared or broadcast except from Battalion H.Q., and only after they had been subjected to scrutiny by the Compilation Office.

This scrutiny was no formality. The Compilation Office received copies of every relevant report and the R.F.C. supplied copies of all air photos as soon as printed. Sometimes the Compilation Office had to deal with as many as four hundred photos in one day. The average was about a hundred. When necessary, the R.F.C. would always arrange for photos to be taken of special areas. All these photos were scrutinized as they came in for any traces of gun pits. If there was anything to suggest that something on the photo might represent a gun pit, the information was carefully filed for future use.

In the same way, all the other reports that came in were searched for confirmation of the Survey results, or, what was equally important, for anything that might throw doubt on them. When this happened the matter was immediately taken up with the people concerned to see if it was possible to reconcile the differences.

And so it was that when the reports reached the man at the gun, he knew just exactly those targets which were accurately located and active; those which were active but whose location was doubtful; and those about which doubts of all sorts existed. All the essential information was on the lists and this enabled the artillery staffs to make the most effective dispositions for counter battery work. In this way the Gunner gained confidence in the work of the Flash Spotters and Sound Rangers, and the Flash Spotters and Sound Rangers themselves were never tempted to put "eye wash" before accuracy.

Thus it will be seen that the Flash Spotters were launched on their career of usefulness with a considerable amount of freedom to develop as circumstances demanded and on sound lines. And as things turned out, these Sections developed all the characteristics of independent units. So far as the individual observer was concerned, it was to his Section or Group H.Q. that he turned for everything, and the H.Q. of his unit—the Field Survey Company or Battalion as it afterwards became—was as remote as Brigade or Division to the ordinary soldier.

Despite this they were intensely loyal to their unit, and were ever jealous of its good name. But, although suggestions were made from time to time that the Observation Groups—together with the Sound Ranging Sections —should be separated from the Field Survey Bats. they remained in there units till the end.

2

HOW THE OBSERVATION GROUPS EXPERI-MENTED AND EXPANDED

THE second phase in the development of the Observation Sections covered the whole of 1916 and the first few months of 1917. It was the critical period of development, as any show of apathy or lack of initiative at this time would have led, probably, to the disappearance of these Sections as independent units. But both enthusiasm and determination pervaded all ranks, and 1917 saw the fruition of their efforts in a general recognition of the value of their services.

Although it was the stationary condition of the line that brought these Observation Sections into being, they were constituted as mobile units from the first. Many authorities doubted their value in other than stationary conditions, but the Sections themselves never doubted that they could render good service under any conditions. Every Survey Post was self-contained, and every encouragement was given to them to learn to do as much as possible for themselves. A two-wheeled cart was the only transport provided, and proved rather inadequate in some ways, but it was sufficient to make the Posts independent at a push.

The need to keep the Sections mobile had a considerable influence on their development, both apparatus and methods had to be considered in terms of mobility. This is one of the reasons why the establishment defined neither the number of the Sections nor the number of Posts to each Section. If the Sections were to be ready to cope with any situation that might arise, it was obvious that there had to be some flexibility in the numbers employed.

At the time when this establishment was under consideration the form of organization that was envisaged was one where a number of Posts would be chosen to cover the Army front, and a number of officers would be appointed to supervise their work. The control was to remain at the Field Survey Companies H.Q.

But, even before the authority for this new establishment came through, the Third Army were working on the true Group system—that is, groups of three, four, or five Posts, controlled and supervised from the Observation Section's H.Q., subject, of course, to the orders of the Officer Commanding the Field Survey Company. This change was not so much an experiment as a logical advance. Once the idea of one officer to one Post was abandoned, it became clear that the direct control of the Posts from the Field Survey Companies H.Q.—far in the rear—was too cumbersome to be effective, but this idea made the newly authorized establishment out of date before it came into force.

The Second Army Flash Spotting Sections were taken over from the Corps at this time and embodied in the 2nd Field Survey Company, and they adopted the group system right away. In the First Army, owing to the apathy that existed there, this change was not made until July.

In the spring of 1916 the British Army Front was extending rapidly, and this led to the formation of the Fourth and Fifth Armies with the accompanying Field Survey Companies. New Observation Sections had to be formed for these areas. In the case of the 4th Field Survey Company, they started by taking over some of the existing Groups of the 3rd Field Survey Company, and, in this way, they were enabled to start with a trained nucleus already in position. The 1st and 2nd Field Survey Companies also supplied some men. The 5th Field Survey Company had to form all their own Sections, but the other Armies supplied the nucleus.

In some respects it might be said that the Observation Sections of the 4th and 5th Field Survey Companies were the most "typical" of all, as they were started after the course of development could be foreseen. So that they were started on sound lines without either the special advantages of the 3rd Field Survey Company, or the legacy of ineffectiveness that hampered the work in the First Army.

But throughout the war, even apart from small differences in technique, organization, etc., every Section or Group retained an individuality of its own. This was probably due to the fact that Group Commanders were generally left pretty well alone, so long as they could "deliver the goods." The extreme individualist with a scorn for every and any form of control and the stickler for precedent had equal opportunities for leaving an impress on the men and the work of their Group. It was generally found that a "thruster" had a Group that always seemed to be trying out new stunts and clamouring for more men and material, whereas a Group Commander who was just quietly efficient had a Group which would probably have been described in the same way.

The formation of the first Group came about in this way. One Post up at Bienvilliers was left without an officer. The officer in charge of the adjoining Post at Hebuterne felt that he could get better results if he had complete control over two Posts. So he asked for and got permission to take over this other Post. At that time the method of getting Posts on to a flash was for the man who saw the flash in his director to call out "Flash" to the telephonist in the dug-out below. The telephonist called out "Flash" again, which was heard by the telephonists in the dug-outs at the other Posts, who in their turn called out "Flash," which was heard by their observers, who then looked out for the flash. Obviously this method was too slow, cumbersome, and inaccurate. So the two posts were disconnected from the main line of Posts down the Army front, and two D3 telephones were fitted in the Post itself, and the observer was supplied with an earpiece to fit over his head. This worked much better, so a third Post was connected up. It was then found that by tuning the D3 in each Post to a different note the observer soon recognized which Post was "buzzing," and the men at H.Q. could also distinguish the Posts and tell when two or three Posts were on the same flash.

A feature of this Group control was that the Posts, instead of being in direct communication, were connected to one another by telephone through an exchange at Group H.Q. This, to begin with, made necessary the constant presence of someone at Group H.Q. so that, by degrees, more and more persons were attached to Group H.Q. The officers were increased to two, as it was quite impossible for one officer to carry out all the duties. And it was also found that eight men were quite inadequate to man a Post continuously all round the clock. As one man was an A.S.C. driver, and one other man had to do the cooking, this only left six men available for duty in the Post. Two men were required in the Post all the time and leave, temporary sickness, and other causes, always reduced the personnel available. It would probably be true to say that, taking the Group as a whole, it was unusual for more than 80 per cent of the personnel to be available at any time, and frequently the percentage was less, so that it became necessary to increase these numbers.

54

Experiment and Expansion

There was no uniformity in the way these Posts were manned; so much depended on local circumstances that it was usually left to the N.C.O. in charge to arrange the turns of duty as he thought best. Conditions varied so much. In some cases, the men lived close to the Post in comparative comfort; in others, their billet might be reached only after a couple of hours of trudging over shell-pitted ground. In the first case, it was usual to arrange four-hourly spells of duty, with one long spell from midnight to 8 a.m. In the other case it was usual to have a dug-out built in close proximity to the Post, and for four men to man the Post for twenty-four hours, working in pairs for spells of perhaps two hours at a time. A day on and a day off, as it were. Sometimes they would be up for as long as forty-eight hours at a time.

In most cases it was usual for two men to do a long night spell. Experience showed that most results were obtained between dusk and midnight. From midnight till the "morning hate" began there was usually little doing, and the "morning hate" was generally of short duration, so that by making the night spell a long one, the men got the maximum possible number of nights in bed.

In this connection, it would not be out of place to remark here that the Observation Groups must have been about the only units in the British Army—or any other army—where a humble Sapper could have his breakfast brought to him in bed. This was quite a usual thing. The observers who came off duty at midnight had to get back to the billet before they could turn in, so it was probably long after midnight before they got to bed. To enable them to get a decent "doss," their pals used to "carry up" their breakfast to them. Is it any wonder that one observer, after two years spent with the infantry in the line, described this as "like being in Heaven"?

Flash Spotters & Sound Rangers

The N.C.O. in charge usually did a regular turn of duty in the Post. But he had a good many odd jobs to attend to. A good N.C.O. on this job was a regular "father" to his little bunch. Scrounging a bit here and wheedling a bit there, he could do a lot to make his Post happy and efficient. At all times he had to accept many of the responsibilities that usually fall on an officer. When a squad was billeted in an area where there were civilians, he was generally called upon to exercise a good deal of tact. The treatment that the British soldiers received from the civil population often led to considerable bitterness, although in some areas the greatest good will prevailed between them. There was always a tendency in these villages when things went wrong, or anything went missing, to blame *les soldats Anglais*, and as the Survey men were the "permanent" representatives of the race they were expected to take the blame. But a tactful N.C.O. could generally straighten things out, and the Survey men became *bons camarades* again. One of these N.C.O.s who had been nearly eighteen months in one village used to be addressed by the villagers as *M. le Maire*!

From February 1916 till late in the autumn of the same year experiment, development, and expansion was the common experience of all the Sections. The Fifth Army Observation Sections were barely started when the battle of the Somme began, and they were rather thrown out of their stride. The 4th Field Survey Company, and to some extent the 3rd Field Survey Company, were engaged on this front also, but the advances were, relatively, so short that they only had to move their Posts forward by degrees, and so they had no difficulty in dealing with the situation.

One point emerged very clearly from these operations.

Experiment and Expansion

That was that the Groups would have to make themselves quite independent of outside assistance if they were to become fully efficient. This was particularly the case with regard to the telephone lines. When everybody was on the move, the calls on the Signal service must have been enormous, and it is hardly surprising that the Groups (at least some of them) found themselves almost out of action for days on end owing to the condition of the lines. In one Group at least, over a period of three weeks, there was never more than one Post through to Group H.Q. at any one time, and sometimes none at all. And this despite the fact that the Observers spent nearly all their time on the lines. The trouble lay in the fact that probably 90 per cent of the lines were on Signal routes, and breaks and earths on these lines had to await their turn for attention.

The remedy for this—as for so many other troubles—was more men. By the autumn the Groups had, by constant additions, grown so much beyond their establishment that it was decided to regularize the position, and a new establishment was authorized in December 1916.

When this new establishment was under consideration great hopes were based on the increase in personnel that was expected. But when consultations were started it was found that the question was not "What do you require?" but "What can you do without?" which, in effect, meant fixing the numbers at the existing level. Perhaps this was not a bad thing at this stage, as it made results dependent on efficiency, and discouraged grandiose schemes.

The Observation Sections were officially termed Observation Groups in this new establishment, and a H.Q. staff for the Group was introduced. This allowed for 2 officers and 10 other ranks, which comprised an N.C.O. in charge, telephonists, computers (for the

Plotting Board), clerks, and a cook. There were two A.S.C. drivers (1 M.T. and 1 H.T.) and 2 batmen. The transport consisted of 1 light car, 1 motor-cycle with side-car, and 1 cart. Compared with the 1 officer and batman authorized in February, this showed a remarkable increase, although, even with this additional personnel, there was no surplus to meet shortages due to leave, sickness, etc.

At the Posts the numbers were raised by 4, making 12 other ranks in all as against 8. This was still too low, as apart from the reasons given before for none of the Posts ever being at full strength, there was the clearly realized need for men to work on the telephone lines as well as observers. But although it was admitted that for maximum efficiency the personnel should be greater than that authorized, it was deemed more important to have the existing position regularized than to press for a theoretically perfect establishment. So that the numbers authorized at this time represented, not what was considered needful, but the bare minimum with which the Groups could function. In judging whether these numbers were adequate for manning a Post all round the clock, the reader should bear in mind the difference between the numbers "on the strength" and the numbers "available for duty." Very few men were aware that the nominal roll of their Post showed twelve men on their strength, and most of them when told of this reply, "Well, we never saw them." Eight to ten was the usual number available at any time.

This establishment still contained the flexible provisions of the first one. It laid down the numbers at Group H.Q. and the numbers at each Post, but it did not say how many Groups there were to be in each Field Survey Company, nor did it say how many Posts there were to be to each Group. But, at the same time, there was a "gentleman's" agreement that no imaginary Groups or Posts were to be formed, and that each Field Survey Company could have the personnel of one Post in excess of the number required to man the existing Posts, so that the work should not be crippled by the absence of men on leave, etc.

So far we have considered the growth of the administrative side of the work of the Groups rather than their technical development, but the two things were really very much dependent on one another. Certain things might have been done if the personnel had been available and, on the other hand, certain technical developments demanded a certain minimum personnel, so that at all stages in the growth of the Observation Groups administrative and technical developments went hand in hand.

When the Topo. Sections took over this observation work from the different people who had been experimenting, the first task was to tackle the purely Survey questions. So far, the experiments had proved inconclusive, largely because the Survey problems underlying the task were not properly realized. This, of course, presented no special difficulties to the Topo. Sections, as they were specialists in Survey work.

The next thing was to arrange for the proper co-ordination or synchronization of bearings from different Survey Posts. When bearings had been taken from two or more Posts to a gun flash, some means had to be devised for determining whether the different Posts had been observing on the same gun flash. The method first adopted was to record the time of every observation or bearing, and this method, with its advantages and disadvantages, was described in the last chapter.

A further improvement was effected when the Posts

were linked up with neighbouring Posts by telephone. The observer who first noticed the gun firing could call out each time that it fired, and his neighbour was then in a position to judge whether he was observing on the same gun or not. This direct communication between Posts was of greatest assistance in guiding the observers in the other Posts on to a gun that had been spotted by one of them, and so in increasing the numbers of locations obtained. But although this was an advance on timing alone, it depended too much on the human element to give entirely reliable results. The tendency for any observer—no matter how skilful or highly trained he may be—is for him to see what he wants to see, and it was clear that on the elimination of this "human element" the success of Flash Spotting would depend.

It was the introduction of the Group system that solved this difficulty. The Posts, instead of being connected directly on D3 telephones, were given ringing phones which were connected through a small telephone exchange at Group H.Q. and so could be connected or disconnected at will by whoever was in charge at Group H.Q. This telephone exchange was replaced later by what was known as the Flash and Buzzer (F. & B.) Board, and this proved a nearly perfect solution of this problem. But as the method of working with the Flash and Buzzer Board will be explained in some detail later there is no need to describe it here.

The Flash and Buzzer Board might never have come into use if it had not been for the vagaries of the little call shutters on the standard telephone exchange. It was by watching the fall of these shutters that the observations were synchronized, but if there was the slightest fault on the line, no reliance could be placed on these shutters falling as required. But it is, perhaps, as well that these exchanges had this weakness, as it is probable that the Flash and Buzzer Board would never have been introduced if they had worked smoothly, and this would have been a real loss.

The Flash and Buzzer Board was tried out first in May 1916, but it was November of that year before it was on issue to all the Groups but, once all the Groups were supplied, it might be said that the period of experiment was over and the technique of the job was settled. Many more months were to pass before the Groups had sufficient experience to make the best use of this technique, but December 1916 does seem to be the date when the Observation Groups established themselves as indispensable.

Much thought was given to the provision of suitable instruments for use in the Survey Posts. Theodolites were used at first but were soon displaced by the Artillery Director, but more will be said of this later. Meanwhile it is sufficient to remark that a completely satisfactory instrument had not been devised up till the end of the war.

One instrument that was tried in these days was intended to help the observer to pick up the direction of a gun by sound. It was in the form of a tube some six feet long, and at each end was a small horn to collect the sound. In the middle of the tube were two earpieces which the observer wore. The idea was that when the tube was placed at right-angles to the path of the sound, the sound would be heard at the same intensity in both ears. If not so placed, it was expected that the sound would be louder in one ear than in the other. It was known as the Claude Orthophone and had been designed as a Sound Ranging device. It is unfortunate that it did not work, as nothing was so exasperating as to hear a gun firing time after time, and not to be able to make out the direction from which the sound came.

On the other hand some of the Observers became remarkably acute at judging the direction from which a gun report was coming. There are at least two cases on record of an intersection between a proper bearing to a gun and a bearing from the sound giving a position that was subsequently confirmed. This, of course, was not a normal method of working, but it shows how, when a "good" result was not obtainable, no evidence was ruled out.

Once the Group system became universal, it became pretty clear that the normal Group should consist of four Posts and cover, approximately, a Corps front. This corresponded to the actual conditions nearly everywhere. The only real exception was the "Forest Group" in the 1st Field Survey Company. This Group was the first one formed in the First Army, and consisted of seven Posts and covered two Corps fronts. When it was formed in July 1916, the reasoning that led to this grouping was quite logical. For one thing, it was proposed that this Group should be controlled from one of the Posts, instead of from Group H.Q. As the Post chosen for this purpose had a clear view over the area of both Corps, it seemed to be illogical to make an artificial boundary between certain Posts.

The control was not carried out from the Survey Post itself. The Survey Post was right at the top of a church steeple, and a room was built just below the church bells. Mercifully, they were never rung. But the idea in this was that the officer on duty should spend most of his time in the Post looking for "flashes." When he spotted one, he was expected to rush down the ladder and direct the other Posts to the spot, or, alternatively, if another Post spotted the "flash" in the first instance, he could dash up to the Post and satisfy himself that the "flash" was really where they said it was.

Perhaps this puts the idea in rather a crude form but, in essentials, it does illustrate it. Unfortunately, it was found that, if the front was quiet, it was no more possible for an officer than for any other rank to see non-existent "flashes" and, if it was active, there was no advantage in turning out an experienced observer to make way for someone with less experience. In any case, if "flashes" were coming through there was usually plenty of work for the officer on the Plotting Board.

Another of the advantages expected from this double Group was, that with four, instead of two, officers it would be possible to have one officer on duty at all times—day and night. But it was found that no particular advantages accrued from this, and after a trial of about two months, control was shifted to Group H.Q. as in other Groups. It still continued to function with the seven Posts and, on the technical side, there was no reason why it should not have gone on in the same way, but what made a change inevitable were administrative difficulties. With three junior officers it was difficult to apportion the work in such a way that each took a share of the responsibilities without making a lot of unnecessary work, and although different arrangements were tried, they never worked smoothly. In the autumn the Group was split into two, but both H.Q.s remained under the one roof. But this arrangement was rather artificial and, in the spring of 1917, they were finally constituted as separate Groups.

It was in the spring of 1917 that it was decided to standardize the nomenclature of the Groups. Each Field Survey Company had named or numbered their Groups to suit themselves, which made no difference as long as the Groups remained in their own Army. But the British Army front was always increasing, and Army fronts were changing, and a Group might be transferred overnight from one Field Survey Company to another, although it still remained in the same area and worked with the same formations. If the name of the Group had to be changed to suit the nomenclature adopted by the Field Survey Company to which it had been transferred, there was considerable risk of confusion. In addition, it was liable to lose its identity, which was undesirable.

In most Field Survey Companies, the Groups were known by numbers and the Posts by names. In one Field Survey Company both the Posts and the Groups were known by names. These names were not chosen haphazard, but served a useful purpose. The Posts were named after shrubs or trees, and the name of the shrub or tree was chosen to suggest the name of the place where the Post was situated, Laventie was called Lavender; Fosse 3 was called Fir-tree; Lorette was called Laurel; and so on. The first Group formed was named Forest, because the branches (telephone lines) from the trees were grouped there. The next Group was called Jungle—on the principle of going one better. Prairie Group was situated in country that was as bare as the prairie, and the name given to Heather Group was a concession to the nationality of its C.O.

One Group took the names of London Theatres as names for their Posts, and so that there could be no mistake about it, they got out posters from home and posted them along the trenches leading to the Observation Posts. At the entrance to "The Criterion" was an enormous poster of Miss Doris Keene in "Romance"—a truly romantic setting for the lady.

Drawn by P. S. Willats, 1918

FLASH SPOTTER ON DUTY IN THE POST

Experiment and Expansion

In another Group the Posts were known by letters—
A, B, C, D. In signal language these letters are known as
"ack," "beer," "cee," "don," and thereby hangs a tale.
A certain Christmas night was quiet as the grave, and
misty. The boys in the billet who had been having a
Yuletide jollification did not forget their two comrades
who were carrying on in the Post, for at midnight they
sent them up a bottle of champagne. All went well until
about 2 a.m. when Group H.Q. put through the routine
call.

"Hullo, beer?"

Faint noises heard on the 'phone.

"Hullo, beer? Is that beer speaking?"

"No," came a drowsy voice, "this is champagne—
hic—speaking!"

When it was decided to standardize the Groups, the
existing Groups in the line were numbered from the north
downwards, and Groups that were formed subsequently
were given a number there and then, so that the number
by which a Group came to be known was no guide as to the
period of its formation.

3

HOW THE OBSERVATION GROUPS FULFILLED
THEIR PURPOSE AND WERE DISBANDED

By 1917 the Groups had passed from a period of experiment to a period of expansion and development. They had got over most of their "teething" troubles by then. New Groups were being formed continuously, and they were universally accepted as useful and permanent additions to the fighting strength of the Army. The Sound Ranging Sections had also found their feet, so that the road was now open for advances to be made on other than technical lines.

The Compilation Offices had, from the first, ensured the co-ordination of the results of the Groups and Sections, and conferences of Group Commanders and Sound Ranging officers at Company H.Q. had advanced co-operation between the Groups and Sections as well as advancing the technique. But co-operation with other units was a plant of slower growth. Until the autumn of 1916, the task of watering this plant was left almost entirely to the Survey men. Many weary and fruitless hours were spent trying to make contact with different units and formations that were supposed to be particularly interested in Flash Spotting and Sound Ranging. Even when cordial personal relations were established, and even when people were prepared to accept all the arguments put forward by the Survey men, it was very difficult to overcome the "departmental" spirit. "Quite so, old man. But that would mean taking a man off some other job, and the General might not like it." This was a typical form of reply when some scheme for co-operation was put forward. But what the speaker really meant was "Quite so, old man. But we are quite capable of running our own show in our own way, thank you." There were exceptions, of course, but, on the whole, this is fairly representative of the attitude of most people to the Groups and Sections at this time—1915 and early 1916.

The Kite Balloons were amongst the first to co-operate actively with the Flash Spotters, but, despite this, the "departmental" attitude was always very strong here. Most Group officers had the feeling that the Kite Balloon people were under the impression that the Flash Spotters were trying to "steal their thunder." There was an amusing incident that seems to bear this out.

An O.C. Balloon came to the conclusion that it was a waste of time and energy to put his balloon in the air when conditions were poor for observation. By putting through a line to the Flash Spotting Group, he could find out at any time whether, if the balloon went up, they should be able to see anything at all. So a line was laid from the Group to the Balloon, and the O.C. Balloon reported to his Wing Commander his bright idea. He was promptly told that he could co-operate as much as he pleased with the Group, but that he had to take up his balloon and see for himself what things were like, no matter what the Survey men might say. But "balloon-atics" are accustomed to ups and downs, and this bold man obeyed orders by getting into the car of his balloon, and rising ten feet or so off the ground. He then rang up the Survey Post and gathered all the latest news. Armed with this first-hand information, he rang up his Wing and made his report on the front, after which he got permission to descend. Needless to remark, this little game did not last very long.

Flash Spotters & Sound Rangers

Still, "balloonatics" were always cheery souls, and they had an engaging habit of playing gramophone records on the ground to cheer up the observers in the balloon. If flashes were few and far between, the Survey men used often to get through to the balloon and "listen in."

There was not much direct contact between the Groups and the R.F.C. except when wireless sets were installed, but that was a subsequent development. On the other hand the R.F.C. were amongst the first to recognize the value of their work. One direct service that the Flash Spotters could render to the R.F.C. was in sending particulars when a machine came down on our own side of the line. When the R.F.C. got early information of this sort they were often able to send out and salve the machine. But this was only a side-line.

An interesting case of co-operation leading to valuable results happened on the Somme. For a period of three weeks all the Groups had been taken off every other job at noon each day to fix the position of the enemy Kite Balloons. This was a very tricky and unsatisfactory sort of job. The balloons never came up at the same place two days running, and, as they never stayed steady in the air, two posts could never be sure that they were observing the same balloon. In any event what was required was the ground position. Every day at 1 p.m. a special "priority" call went through to the Field Survey Companies H.Q., but as the Groups never heard what these messages were required for they began to get rather weary of the job. But at last they realized what they had been working for. One day, about half an hour after the "priority" call had gone through, a squadron of our own planes were seen heading across the enemy lines. Shortly afterwards one Post after another was ringing up H.Q. with the message "Enemy balloon descending in flames."

68

Fulfilment

Altogether, nine enemy balloons were brought down in this attack, and it received special mention in one of Field-Marshal Sir Douglas Haig's despatches.

Events on the Somme in 1916 led to the appointment of Counter Battery Staff Officers (C.B.S.O.), known to the vulgar as "Counter Blasters." German artillery tactics were changing from day to day, and it was obvious that complete co-ordination and co-operation was needed amongst all the agencies gathering information about the enemy artillery. The most accurate or comprehensive information was useless if it took several days to filter through to where it was required. The C.B.S.O. devoted himself to this task—using every source of information, and getting it quickly to where it was required.

The first "Counter Blasters" made such a good impression that it was not long before there was one with every Corps. The institution of this officer was a great help to the Groups and Sections. No longer had they to run about the battle area looking for someone to take an interest. Now they need deal with one officer only. It cannot be said truthfully that all the "Counter Blasters" immediately took the Survey men to their hearts. There were still too many prejudices and rivalries to be overcome. But in the course of time the reliability and consistency of the Groups and Sections came to be realized, and early in 1917 they had the satisfaction of feeling that their work was being appreciated.

Co-operation developed on different lines in different Armies, but the system in force in the First Army illustrates, as well as any, the principles involved. A Report Centre was established at each Group H.Q. It consisted mainly of a telephone exchange connected to the nearest Observation Groups, Sound Ranging Sections, Kite Balloons, Artillery H.Q., and Corps H.Q. There was also

69

a wireless receiving set. Information of any kind affecting location units was sent to the Report Centre in the first place, and the Report Centre was responsible for seeing that it was passed on as rapidly as possible to everyone concerned. Aeroplane calls were passed on in the same way. There is no doubt that this arrangement materially increased the number of locations obtained, and many doubtful results were turned into certainties. The Report Centres were not Field Survey Sections. They were supervised by the Group officers, but this was merely a matter of convenience.

The need of experienced men to form a nucleus for the new Groups led to a good deal of heartburning. The men who had been together since 1915 and 1916 in little Groups at each Post had formed very close ties of friendship and rather resented the breaking up of the happy home. The Group officers, also, felt that it was rather hard that, just as they were getting into the swing, they should have to part with so many experienced men and N.C.O.s and start all over again with new and untried personnel. But the time had gone past when it was possible to put an untried Group into the line and leave it to seek its own salvation. So the changes had to be made, but although the men that were transferred benefited by accelerated promotion, etc., most of them had a hankering after their old Group. There seemed to have been something of the pioneering spirit in the older Groups that was lacking in the newer ones.

Up till now each Field Survey Company had got its personnel where it could, and had trained them when it could. But these new Groups were urgently required and, in addition, they were expected to deliver "the goods" as soon as they were in the line. Instead of having to convince other people that their work was of some value, they had to live up to a reputation that was already accepted.

The other sections of the Field Survey Companies were likewise expanding rapidly at this time and, to meet this situation, the Depot Field Survey Company was formed at G.H.Q. in April 1917. They undertook the recruitment of the new personnel for all the Survey Companies, and they also undertook their training. For this purpose they formed a School for Observers. The personnel of this School consisted of one Captain and ten other ranks, of whom six were instructors. This School was not an entirely new idea as the 3rd Field Survey Company had had a school of their own since March 1916, and it was this School that was transferred to G.H.Q. The 2nd Field Survey Company and the 4th Field Survey Company had run courses of instruction for observers, but they did not have anything in the nature of schools.

There were four different courses provided. (1) Preliminary Course; (2) Advanced Course; (3) Computers' Course; (4) Signallers' Course. Courses 1 and 2 lasted for three weeks, and Course 3 for two weeks, whilst Course 4 lasted for four weeks. The instruction was both theoretical and practical, and the same for both officers and men, except that officers were expected to reach a much higher standard at the examinations that concluded the courses.

A list of some of the subjects taught is of interest as it gives some idea of what was required from even a sapper. Of course, many of the men had only a superficial knowledge of some of the subjects, but N.C.O.s had to be well grounded in them all. Some of the subjects included in these courses were:

Flash Spotters & Sound Rangers

The School had an elaborate Dummy Range in which gun flashes were simulated by electric lights and gun smoke by smoke puffs from "bee puffers." A complete Group was installed, with H.Q. and four Posts, and all instruction was carried out under conditions that simulated, as closely as possible, those met with in the line. Later on the School had the use of a "real" gun (a six-pounder), which was used when practising observation for ranging.

The formation of the Depot Field Survey Company was of great advantage all round. The Survey Companies H.Q. and also the Groups themselves were relieved of much detailed administrative work, and the Group officers were thereby enabled to devote much more of their time to the tasks of observation.

With the problem of fixing hostile batteries by cross-observation pretty well solved, much more attention was given to ranging our own guns on the enemy. Although the primary object of the Groups (the location of hostile artillery) always received the most attention, the greater time devoted to ranging yielded increasingly good results from now on.

Another thing to receive a good deal of attention from this time on was the question of mobility. As pointed out before, the Groups had always been organized as mobile units, but until the methods of work and the true functions of the Groups were clearly determined, it was not possible to work out any form of procedure or drill, one might say, on a detailed basis. But by 1917 the Groups knew pretty well how they stood, and they framed their plans accordingly.

This was one of the directions where the Depot School was of the greatest use. Because, although the Groups in the line could draw up their plans, they had no opportunities of trying them out and, certainly, no chance of rehearsing their personnel in their duties.

To attain a high degree of mobility, two things were needed. Firstly, it was necessary that the Group should be independent of even their own Battalion H.Q. on the technical side. Up till now many technical services were performed for the Groups by other Sections of the Field Survey Companies. For example, the Survey Section surveyed their Posts and prepared their Map Boards. Many stores were held at Battalion H.Q. and only issued as required. In most Groups there was someone who was capable of carrying out these duties for the Group without outside help, but a certain amount of training was necessary, in most cases, to ensure that the work was done in the most efficient way.

The second question was how to get in and out of action quickly, so that the Group could move from one position to another without being out of action too long. This was very much bound up with the question of reeling in the telephone lines and reeling them out again at the new position. As long as the line was fairly stable, the Signal Corps supplied and maintained long lengths of telephone line. But it was obvious that in the event of anything in the nature of a general advance of the line, the Groups could go forward and take up a new position long before Signals could find time to attend to their needs. As the Groups had always had to erect and maintain a certain portion of their own lines they had a fair working knowledge of what was required. But here again, to get the best results, some training was needed, and this was supplied by the Course for Signallers at the Depot Field Survey Company.

Plans had also to be made to meet the particular circumstances that might arise on the immediate front of each Group. No general principles could be laid down here and each Group had to work out its own salvation.

The operations of 1917 did not give the Groups much experience of mobile operations. Advances were small, and, as a rule, the position was best met by pushing forward one Post at a time.

In November 1917, a new Field Survey Company was formed for service on the Italian front. This was the 6th Field Survey Company and two Groups were formed to go there. No. 26 Group arrived there on December 28th, and No. 25 Group on January 9, 1918. These Groups were formed at the Depot with a nucleus of experienced men, and were put through the usual course of training there. Except for a period of about one month, there were never more than two Groups with the 6th Field Survey Company. No. 26 Group was sent on to Salonika in April 1918, but another Group (No. 29) had been formed in Italy itself in March without the assistance of any personnel from the Depot. Twenty per cent of the personnel were supplied by Nos. 25 and 26 Groups, and the remainder by the artillery and other units.

The formation of this Group is rather interesting as it shows the change that had come over the scene since 1916. It was the artillery who called for the formation of this new Group and, rather than do without it, they supplied much of the personnel, whereas in 1916 the artillery were withdrawing their men from the Observation Groups just at the time when they might have been of the greatest use.

It would also seem as if the artillery Survey work of the Field Survey Battalions was more fully appreciated in Italy than elsewhere.

In the Earl of Cavan's despatches on the operations that led to the final defeat of the Austrian armies, there is this paragraph, which is worth quoting as it illustrates the peculiar value of the work of the Field Survey Battalions.

The extract is as follows: "(13) At 11.30 p.m. on the night of 26th Oct., the bombardment of the hostile positions opened along the whole front. The fact that no single British gun had opened previous to this hour deserves special mention. Both Heavy and Field Artillery were registered by the 6th Field Survey Coy., R.E., and the fact that the bombardment and the subsequent barrage were excellent in every way reflects the greatest credit on all ranks of this company."

So that by the beginning of 1918 the Observation Groups had reached maturity, and the whole of the Western and Italian Fronts were under observation. Another Group was being formed to go to Egypt, and the 26th Group was sent to Salonika, so there was no front, or section of the front, that was not covered.

Meanwhile the whole question of the establishments of

the Field Survey Companies was again under consideration, and a revised establishment was issued early in
1918. The Field Survey Companies became Field Survey
Battalions, and the Commanding Officers became Lieu-
tenant-Colonels.

So far as the Observation Groups were concerned, the
only change made was the provision of one more officer
in each Group. There is no doubt that an increase in the
personnel at the Posts would have been made if possible.
But at this time there was no question of how many men
were needed, if the existing numbers could be expected
to carry on at all, so that, no matter how desirable an
increase of numbers at the Posts might have been, no
change was made.

Nevertheless, the demands on the services of the
Groups were constantly increasing. In particular, the
calls on the Groups for Ranging and Calibration work
were threatening to interfere with their hostile battery
location. To meet this situation the 3rd Field Survey
Company duplicated three Posts in each Group, and the
artillery supplied detachments to man these. These
detachments consisted of 2 officers and 12 other
ranks. They were known as Ranging Sections, and were
administered and controlled by the Observation Groups,
but of course they did not form a part of the Field Survey
Battalions. It was almost a reversion to the position in
1915. These Sections remained with the 3rd Field Survey
Battalion until the close of hostilities.

In the 1st and the 5th Field Survey Battalions similar
Sections were formed, but never achieved the same
success. For one thing, they were not formed until the
operations of 1918 were in full swing, and the difficulties
of personnel, equipment, transport, etc., were more
accentuated than ever, and it was clear that an increase

in the personnel of the Groups was required if they were to be able to carry out all the calls on them for ranging. But the circumstances of the time forbade this change.

Every Observation Group on the Western front was involved (with one exception) in the German offensive in the spring of 1918. The Group that had this distinction was No. 10 in the 1st Field Survey Battalion. Nos. 9 and 11, which lay just north and south of No. 10, were only affected at one Post, but still they did have to make a move.

The experiences of the different Groups at this time were many and various, but in every case they managed to get away without sustaining any serious losses in men or material. But the lack of adequate transport was acutely felt by them all. With only a two-wheeled cart at each Post, many valuable stores had to be left behind, together with much less essential equipment. What was even more trying to the individual observer was the ruthless scrapping of "souvenirs" that took place. As things were, this loss of stores did not prevent them getting into action again quickly, as the advance continued sufficiently long to give Battalion H.Q. time to re-equip them in essentials. But it might not have been so easy to re-equip these Groups if it had not been for the fact that most of the Battalion Quartermasters had a hidden "cache" of surplus equipment on which they were able to draw. Very improper, of course, but very useful help in time of trouble. With only horse transport at their disposal, there was no alternative for a Post, once the line was broken, but to get out as quickly as possible. It sounds very ungallant, but their instruments and equipment were to the Flash Spotters what guns were to artillerymen. Without these they were useless and, as they were not easily replaced and likely to be of much

77

interest to the enemy if captured, it was essential to take
no risks.

During the retreat artillery work was generally on
visible targets or cross-roads, so that there was not much
need for the special services of the Groups. In the south,
all the Groups of the 4th and 5th Field Survey Battalions
were reassembled in the rear and were used to form a
part of "Carey's Force" for the defence of Amiens, where
they suffered severe casualties.

On the Third Army front the retreat was more
methodical, and the Groups were kept in action all the
time, shifting bases every day and keeping in touch with
a heavy battery or brigade. On the Lys front much the
same thing happened, but in this case it was difficult
to find sites for the Posts. The country was dead flat,
heavily timbered, and closely intersected by hedges—a
condition of affairs that made a rapid choice of points for
Observation Posts out of the question.

On the First Army front—the sector north of the La
Bassée Canal—the German advance was both rapid and
deep, but at the end of three days the Group that had to
retire got into action again. But until the line was more
or less settled, it had to make constant moves, and it is
doubtful if it served any real purpose until then. There
were plenty of visible targets for the artillery, and it was
difficult to get results through to them in any case.

When the new establishment was brought in, one of
the changes that was made at Battalion H.Q. was the
provision of two officers with the rank of Major to relieve
the C.O. of much of the routine work connected with
the Groups and Sections.

One thing that made the appointment of these officers
essential was that, except under trench warfare conditions,
it was physically impossible for the C.O. of the Battalion

to keep in touch with the Groups and Sections. The tactical control of the Groups and Sections was largely in the hands of the artillery, and it was generally exercised from Army H.Q. As far as the officers in the Groups and Sections were concerned, it was a case of "theirs but to do and die." In fact it probably would be correct to say that most of these officers were so engrossed with getting results and the technicalities of their job, that they hardly realized that "tactics" had anything to do with them at all.

But one example might be given to show the serious consequences that resulted when the Groups and Sections were improperly used. At Passchendaele, our artillery commanders, without much experience of the technique of Flash Spotting or Sound Ranging, insisted on these Sections being pushed up close to the line. The result was that neither the Groups nor the Sections could keep their telephone lines working and so they were not able to "deliver the goods." The Counter Battery Office had to fall back on information obtained solely from the air, with the result that the German artillery was largely unmolested, and the feature of this battle was the damage done by the enemy gun fire.

The provision of these officers went some way to improve control. Their business was to keep in close touch with the artillery at Army and other H.Q., and try and foresee their requirements and keep the Groups and Sections informed. Actually, their duties were never very clearly defined, and the question of control was never really satisfactorily settled even by the end of the war. In addition, these officers were never provided with any form of transport and they had to beg, borrow, or steal when they wanted to set off on their rounds. This was a handicap in more ways than one, for nothing caused

79

more friction and unsettlement in the Survey than applications for the "loan" of a car.

The reader may think that to dismiss the events of the spring and autumn of 1918 in a few paragraphs is to give very short measure. In every branch of the Services these critical days were full of incident and of abiding memories, and the Observation Groups were no exception to this rule. But at present we are only concerned with events or circumstances that influenced the development of the Groups, so we must leave these exciting incidents for a later chapter. Because although the Groups found themselves working under an entirely new set of conditions, no changes in either their form of organization or their methods of working became necessary as a result of their experiences then. That is not to say that they learnt nothing from experience, but such changes as were made were of minor importance.

But there is one circumstance connected with the retreat that is worthy of mention here, because it illustrates so clearly the very unusual form of organization of these Observation Groups. The N.C.O.s and men at the Posts had been accustomed almost from the beginning to work without any direct supervision from the Group officers. That is to say, that all the details of the daily round were arranged by the N.C.O. in charge of the Post, and he had to rely on himself to see them carried out. The time that even the most conscientious Group officer could devote to visiting the Posts and billets was strictly limited, and the times of these visits were, naturally, erratic, but even so, with direct telephonic communication to Group H.Q. he could always get advice from his C.O. or, in an emergency, get his C.O. to visit the Post on short notice.

But, when these attacks developed in 1918, in nearly every case the Posts found their communication with

Fulfilment

Group H.Q. cut off before anyone knew what was happening, so that not only the N.C.O.s, but such men as happened to be on duty in the Posts at the time, had to take full responsibility for making very serious decisions. It was not just a question of whether to retreat or stand fast—serious enough as such a decision must be—but also such questions as to what to salve, what to abandon, and what to destroy. When it came to the question of destroying valuable instruments, the responsibility was no light one.

It is, of course, true that N.C.O.s and men in other units had to make similar decisions, but in their case it was generally due to exceptional or accidental circumstances. In the case of the N.C.O.s and men of the Observation Groups, it was a general experience and one that was foreseen.

By 1918 most of the Group H.Q. were located under the same roof as that of a Sound Ranging Section. This had always been considered desirable, as Flash Spotting and Sound Ranging were essentially complementary means of fixing gun positions, and, except in the sporting sense, their work was not competitive. But in 1916 neither the Groups nor the Sound Ranging Sections were entirely sure of themselves, and, in consequence, they each preferred to "gang their ain gait." Complete co-operation between the Groups and Sections had been tried in the Third Army at that time, but the time was hardly ripe for that experiment and the results were not of much account.

But an examination of a captured position in September 1917 yielded strong evidence that the enemy had been successful in deceiving the Groups with "dummy flashes." This discovery gave considerable impetus towards bringing the Groups and Sections together. Actually, what gave the greatest impetus to this movement was the purely human desire for companionship. There were only two officers at a Group and three at a S.R.S. and the advantages of joining forces were, from a social point of view, many.

But, although there may have been ulterior motives at work, when the Groups and Sections came together they soon found that their work was improved and simplified by the change. It was always a matter of great difficulty to decide what information to pass on when it had to be telephoned. The "book of words" will tell one that all information is valuable, which is perfectly true, but nothing annoys a person so much as being called to the telephone at regular intervals to listen to news that appears to be pointless. The only result, in such cases, is to reduce all information to a common level of insignificance. An example of this has been given already.

When, however, the Groups and Sections found themselves working in the same or adjacent rooms, the exchange of information and news of all sorts was easy and natural, and as they each got an intimate knowledge of the other man's job, they got to know the exact value to place on any piece of information. Whatever difficulties had arisen in bringing the Groups and Sections together, no one was ever heard to complain that the change was not of mutual benefit.

By June all the Groups had been re-established in the line, and were working normally again. From then until the whole line moved forward, much of the time of the Groups was taken up with ranging and calibration. By this time relations with the artillery were cordial everywhere and the feeling that not only was the job worth doing but that it was appreciated gave an added zest to the work. So that, when the advance started on August

8th it found the Groups "on their toes" and ready for any eventuality.

The Field Survey Battalions seemed to be something like the universe as pictured by the modern physicist. Something that expanded infinitely. Because, once again, their establishment came under review. They were "wisibly swelling" but the powers that be, whilst agreeing that everything that the Field Survey Battalions were doing was necessary, put their metaphorical feet down and said that the work would have to be adjusted to the men available as they were unable to find men to keep pace with the work.

Indeed, they went further than that. As will have been gathered, in most cases it had been usual for more men to be employed than the numbers actually authorized by the establishment. This custom had always been recognized, as the business of getting sanction for a new establishment was necessarily a slow one. However, the man-power situation was by now very difficult and the Field Survey Battalions were told that they must conform to regulations in the future.

The Observation Groups were not much affected by this order. At this time any extra personnel at the Groups were "attached," as a rule, and so unaffected. But in considering the new establishment for the Groups it was decided that the flexible conditions had to go. That meant to say that the new establishment would provide for so many officers and men with so much transport for each Group, and whether the Group had to man five Posts or three, these numbers would not be varied. The previous arrangement was certainly more advantageous from the point of view of the Groups, but one had to admit that, from the standpoint of the Adjutant-General's Department, it was unsatisfactory, as they had no means of checking the strength of the Groups or of estimating the possible demand for reinforcements.

But it was March 1919 before this establishment was authorized, so that it never became effective during hostilities. It allowed for 3 officers and 79 other ranks and assumed a distribution of four Posts to every Group. The 79 other ranks included one C.Q.M.S., 53 Survey post observers, 12 linemen, and 1 carpenter. A 30-cwt. lorry was added to the transport at Group H.Q. At the time of the Armistice there must have been about 2,800 officers and men serving with the Observation Groups.

When the Army advanced into Germany after the Armistice the Groups that went forward were brought up to this strength from the Groups that were left behind. This was officially termed the "Higher Establishment" and was well named, as it was higher than anything that existed whilst hostilities were in progress.

When the advance started on August 8th, the Groups were well prepared to meet the new situation. No attempt was made to follow up with every Group, as experience had shown that to get the Groups in and out of action quickly called for more men than were available for all the Groups, so that some of the Groups went out of action altogether and their personnel was used to reinforce those Groups that were following up.

The experience of the Groups during the advance varied a good deal. In some cases the enemy retreat was so precipitate, and the roads so bad and crowded, that the Groups could not keep up. In other cases, where the retirement was more orderly, they were more successful. Once they knew where they were to go into action, they took from three to five hours to get going. They occupied a much shorter base than was usual under more settled conditions but, once they had got accustomed to the task, they averaged as many locations as under the more usual conditions.

After the Armistice the Groups were assembled at the H.Q. of their Battalions, and, except for those Groups that accompanied the Army of Occupation, they ended their days as the Observation Groups of the Field Survey Battalions whilst there. In the re-modelling of the Army after the war their duties were taken over by the artillery, as was to be expected, but some of the personnel was transferred at the same time, so that continuity in the task was retained, and it is satisfactory to note that the contacts set up then between the Royal Artillery and the Royal Engineers in this work are still retained.

4

SURVEY POSTS AND THEIR EQUIPMENT

THERE were more than a hundred Survey Posts stretched along the line of the Western front, and in these Survey Posts more than two hundred pairs of eyes kept ceaseless watch on the enemy country day and night, winter and summer, year in and year out.

What were they looking for?

Anything at all, but particularly for enemy guns. Soldiers have always been trained in the art of concealment, but in the last war concealment was brought to a greater pitch of perfection than ever before. When a man or a gun showed up it was only for a moment, and it was this momentary exposure that made it so difficult to fix the position of anything by the usual methods. And so it became necessary to adopt new methods to meet the difficulty.

The term Survey Post used to describe these Observation Posts was an official term to distinguish their function from that of other Observation Posts. Structurally, they differed little from the usual Post, except that, probably, they were a little more solid and permanent, but among the men themselves they were always referred to as "O.P.s" and the term Survey Post was confined to official documents or, perhaps, to those occasions when inquisitive strangers had to be "shooed off."

This "shooing off" business was always a worry. These Observation Posts were all carefully selected, and often the position chosen was the only suitable spot for hundreds of yards around. It was of the utmost importance that nothing should be done to draw the attention of the

86

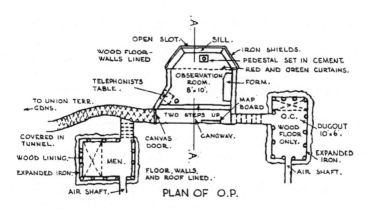

OPEN SLOT. SILL. IRON SHIELDS.

WOOD FLOOR-WALLS LINED

PEDESTAL SET IN CEMENT.
RED AND GREEN CURTAINS.

TELEPHONISTS TABLE.

OBSERVATION ROOM. 8'×10'.

FORM.

TO UNION TERR.
←GDNS.

MAP BOARD

O.C.

TWO STEPS UP.

DUGOUT 10'×6'.

WOOD FLOOR ONLY.

COVERED IN TUNNEL.

CANVAS DOOR.

GANGWAY.

WOOD LINING.

MEN.

EXPANDED IRON.

EXPANDED IRON.

FLOOR, WALLS, AND ROOF LINED.

AIR SHAFT.

AIR SHAFT.

PLAN OF O.P.

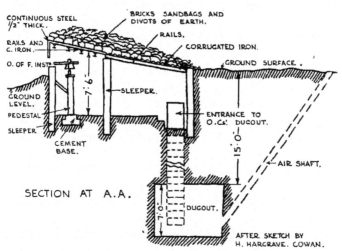

CONTINUOUS STEEL 1/2" THICK.

BRICKS SANDBAGS AND DIVOTS OF EARTH.

RAILS.

RAILS AND C. IRON.

CORRUGATED IRON.

O. OF F. INST.

GROUND SURFACE.

7'-6"

GROUND LEVEL.

SLEEPER.

PEDESTAL

ENTRANCE TO O.Cs. DUGOUT.

SLEEPER

15'-0"

CEMENT BASE.

SECTION AT A.A.

AIR SHAFT.

DUGOUT.

AFTER SKETCH BY
H. HARGRAVE. COWAN.

SKETCH OF SURVEY POST WITH LIVING ACCOMMODATION ATTACHED

This post was on the Somme, and the sketch shows the very primitive conditions under which many Survey men lived for months on end

enemy to that particular spot. But, despite this, all sorts of
people used to stroll up casually in full daylight. The
mildly curious could generally be induced to make
themselves inconspicuous and scarce: but others with an
inflated sense of self-importance used to make things very
difficult for the observers, particularly if they happened
to be senior officers accustomed to getting their own way.
But in these encounters the men could always be sure of
backing in the highest quarters—"no pass, no admittance."

How important it was that nothing should be done to
draw attention to these spots can be illustrated by what
happened to an Observation Post on the Somme. This
Observation Post was built in the ground at the foot of a
tree. A General had a temporary Observation Post
somewhere behind from which he intended watching the
attack on July 1st. As he found that the tree beside the
Survey Observation Post obstructed some of his view, he
gave orders for it to be cut down. This was done despite
the protests of the Survey men, with the result that,
within a very short time, the Observation Post was
rendered useless. Another example—in this case due to
thoughtlessness—was when some sappers started, in full
daylight, to revet a sap leading to an Observation Post
hidden under an old haystack. The result of this careless-
ness was that the haystack was shelled for forty-eight
hours, and an Observation Post that had done yeoman
service for nearly two years was completely obliterated.

The Posts were spaced at convenient distances from
one another. Two to three miles was about the usual
spacing, but the principal consideration was that every
part of the enemy front as far as was practicable should
be covered by at least three Posts. These conditions were
not difficult to arrange in the flat country north of Lens,
but further south, in the rolling country, it was more

difficult to ensure this arrangement. On the Italian front, amongst the hills, it was impossible. Where they scored on that front was in getting plenty of height for their Posts.

Height was always a most desirable feature. It not only meant a wider angle of view, but it simplified the observers' task. If the Survey Post was well above the target to be observed, it was often possible to pick out the approximate position of the target on the map straight away. This not only saved time in getting a true bearing on the gun, but also helped the observer in directing other Posts. Even at night, when only a flash was to be seen, it helped to be high up, because generally a flash was much better defined when seen from above than from ground-level.

It should be realized that, as a rule, all that could be seen of a gun was the muzzle flash when it was fired. Under the most favourable conditions this appeared in the instrument as a bright red spot. Most usually it was a reddish glow with a red heart in the middle. At other times all that could be seen was the glow, but even under the last conditions an experienced observer could centre his instrument on it with surprising accuracy. This glow effect, of course, could only be seen at night. By day there was only the flash or a smoke puff to be seen.

A glow in the sky might be due to causes other than a gun flash, and even experienced observers were misled at times in consequence. On one occasion, an observation reported by a Post, and actually confirmed by another, gave the surprising result that both bearings were the same although the Posts were five miles apart. The intersection was at "infinity," and the object observed turned out to be a star rising in a mist. In similar conditions, the rising moon was more than once reported as either a flash from a big gun, or a "fire behind the enemy lines, sir."

When ranging for the artillery, the observer had to pick up the flash of the burst. Although the burst usually sent up a shower of bricks or earth that was of little use, as only the flash showed where the shell had struck. But to pick up the flash of the burst was much easier than picking up the muzzle flash, because the observer knew, approximately, where to expect the burst and had his instrument trained on that spot. Nevertheless, it called for quick wits because the flash only lasted a moment, and he had to get his bearing in that moment or lose it altogether. This probably gave more anxiety than anything when ranging was first tried. The men had had no experience of picking up the ground flash and if many rounds had been missed, the confidence of the Gunners would have been lost.

The distance of the Posts from the line varied from a hundred yards to two or three miles as a rule. But there were two Posts that must have been from seven to eight miles behind the line. One was at La Gorge, and the other at Notre Dame de Lorette. But no effort was made to push Posts forward. The distance from the line was determined—when the Flash Spotters were free to make the choice—almost entirely by the necessity for getting certain parts of the enemy area into the field of view. If there was a choice of positions, the choice usually fell on the position where it would be easiest to keep up the telephone lines. But a choice was seldom offered. Circumstances, or the lie of the land, usually decided the question.

In Flanders there were several Posts in the steeples of churches. Some of these were in ruins, but in others daily services were held, and the observers used to come and go at all hours of the day and night. This led to a rather amusing mistake on the part of a Roman Catholic padre.

This padre had seen the same men coming and going from the church at all hours and he was a little puzzled why such devout worshippers were personally unknown to him. One day he approached two of the observers as they were leaving the church after coming off duty.

"Are you R.C.s.?" inquired the padre.

"No, sir," replied one observer. "We are F.S.C.s."

The Post that was situated within a few yards of the front line was at Hill 70. This space of a hundred yards used to shrink to a minus quantity at times, as the troops were sometimes brought back to the support line behind the Post during the day, leaving the Survey men to hold the fort, as it were. To keep up their spirits they were given revolvers and a good supply of bombs. But lest the reader should imagine that these two observers contemplated holding up an enemy advance all on their ownsome, it should be explained that the bombs were meant for the rapid destruction of the Post and its fittings in the event of the enemy coming over.

This Post was interesting in another way, as all the observing was done by means of a periscope. The very limited field of view (about two minutes) made observation very difficult until the observers got accustomed to it. It was about three weeks before they got a "flash" at all, but after that they soon acquired the knack of it and got some useful results. The close proximity of their targets compensated, to some extent, for the limited field of view.

There was never any advantage to be gained by pushing Posts very far forward. The nearer one got to the line the more difficult it became to keep telephone lines in working order, and, as will be learnt, good lines were essential for results. Also, a Post that was likely to be shelled or sniped at all regularly was always a weakness in a Group. Even if looked at in the most callous way, the Observation Groups could not afford many casualties. Trained men were too scarce. So that, except for special reasons, the personnel were always withdrawn from a Post if it was likely to get hit.

Although it was never mentioned at the time, there is no doubt that everyone realized that good work could not be expected from a man when under considerable mental strain. This remark, of course, does not apply to those situations where it was *essential* that the observer should stick to his task. When this occurred it seemed as if the feeling that if anything happened it was unavoidable keyed a man up and enabled him to give of his best.

The Flash Spotters never used dummy trees or any of these fancy arrangements if they could help it. For one thing, there had to be room for at least two men and their instruments, etc., and for another these were usually too frail and unsteady for instrumental work. But they were always on the look out for anything that would suit their purposes, and anything that seemed as if it would answer was given a trial. One of these samples was used on the Lys sector in 1918. Dismantled, it was a lorry load of tubes, each about four feet long, with longer bracing rods. Being assembled and erected, it was a hollow triangular tower, very frail in appearance, rising dizzily to a height of 120 feet where it poked its head out of a wood of giant trees. On the very top was rigged up a triangular-shaped box with plank floor and canvas sides. Observers were supposed to nip up the iron stays like monkeys, but this was a bit too much of a good thing, and so vertical ladders were lashed up the side.

But there was one interesting example of what might

be termed natural camouflage at Laventie. Here the church had been reduced almost to a heap of ruins, and of what had once been a fine square brick steeple only two walls remained in a very precarious condition. Obviously, it might fall at any moment, so it could not house an Observation Post. But inside the angle of the two walls the engineers built a wooden lattice tower which was independent of the brick walls, and on top of this, and just below the top of the wall, was built the Observation Post. A view over the enemy lines was obtained by removing a few of the bricks from the wall. It is doubtful if the enemy ever realized that this steeple was being used for observation purposes, as it was only fired at intermittently. Actually the observers were more afraid of high winds than the shelling. In a high wind the whole contraption, framework and steeple, used to rock about and make the observers sick.

Lacouture church steeple was intact, but the church itself was badly knocked about and, doubtless, the masonry was none too strong. It received periodical attention from the enemy artillery but, although the church was reduced to ruins, and the surrounding graveyard was all churned up, the steeple was never hit. This was all the more curious because, after the Post had to be evacuated in 1918, the men who had manned it for so long had the strange experience of ranging on it for one of our own batteries. Fifty rounds were fired, but still it stood intact.

It must have been the rather gruesome surroundings of this Survey Post that led the observers to use a purple velvet coffin pall as a curtain to keep out the draughts. Certainly it was not with the idea of keeping one handy, because, if Jerry became too assertive, they did not wait to climb down the ladder provided, but slid down the bell rope. Those who remember Bairnsfather's *Curfew shall not ring to-night* will be able to visualize the scene.

At different times, the Groups had to make use of chimneys. These were never popular, although they generally gave a good field of view. The difficulty about these was that if they received a direct hit, it was almost certain to bring down the whole show—a most unpleasant prospect for the observers. In the case of a steeple there was usually a sporting chance that one hit would leave the steeple still standing, and give the observers a chance to get out. But in the case of a chimney, it was almost certain that one hit would be sufficient to carry away the ladder at the very least. In one case when the Survey were occupying one of a pair of chimneys in a factory, the observers had to sit and watch the other chimney being shot at until, eventually, it was brought down. They were not long in finding "alternative accommodation!"

Fosse 9 at Annequin was, in many ways, an almost ideal Survey Post under the conditions that existed on that front (La Bassée) in 1916 and 1917. The Post was built inside a colliery rubbish tip. The tip was almost a perfect cone, and was very similar to the rubbish heaps that one sees at the china clay pits in Cornwall. Access to the Post was through a tunnel driven from the back of the heap. It stood a little more than a mile back from the line and good billets were near at hand. At least that was so until a battery chose the back garden for their guns. Only the aperture showed from the front and, unless one knew that it was there, even this was not seen from ground-level. When the Fosse was shelled the shells exploded harmlessly in the coal-dust. Only a direct hit on the aperture could do any harm, and if things got too hot, the observers had only to stroll out to their back door to be in complete safety.

To build a Post such as this was unusual. Fosse 3 was on a similar colliery tip, but the Post was just a hut on the top, and this received a direct hit in 1917. But in the case of Fosse 9, when the Observation Group wanted to establish a Post there the artillery were already in possession of the top. They refused to let another hut be built, as they said that it was asking for trouble and the position was too valuable to risk its destruction. Nevertheless, it was the artillery themselves who nearly brought about this disaster. Late in 1917 someone upset a lamp in their Observation Post, and not only was the hut destroyed but the Fosse itself took fire. This had its compensations, because on cold winter nights, when men were freezing in other Posts, the men on Fosse 9 were working in their shirt sleeves. At one time it seemed as if the Survey Post would have to be abandoned also, but, luckily, this disaster was avoided. It is pleasant to record that the artillery were able to carry on by using the Survey Post until their own little spot cooled down.

This Survey Post and the tunnel were built by French miners in 1915, and the job lasted, with very few repairs, until it was evacuated in 1918.

The most usual type of Survey Post was the conventional dugout type, with a shell or splinter-proof covering. These were built on the crest of any ridge that offered a decent field of view over the enemy lines. As these Posts were often only a few hundred yards from the line, anything in the nature of a tower or raised structure was out of the question. As a rule the Post was connected by a trench to a deep dugout, which, in addition to providing a funk-hole, often served as a temporary billet for men off duty.

Flash Spotters & Sound Rangers

It would be a mistake to assume that the ground Observation Posts were necessarily inferior to the raised Observation Posts such as church steeples. It was a common experience that the most promising sites often gave the most disappointing results when occupied, whereas sometimes places that had been occupied as a temporary expedient until something better could be found proved so useful that no change had to be made.

During the advance, less elaborate posts had to serve. If a suitable spot could be found, shelter from the weather and observation was all that could be attempted, but it was generally possible to fix on some spot that was not too far from an abandoned German dugout or "pill-box," which served to give some sort of protection from gun fire. "Some sort" is used advisedly, because, although the British Tommy always had the greatest admiration for the German dugouts and other forms of shelter, when he came to use them the entrances were all facing towards, instead of away from, the enemy. Consequently, although the enemy might pound away at the roof and do no harm, one round landed at the front door might, in a manner of speaking, come right down to the kitchen and spoil the broth.

Much the same considerations applied when attempts were made to use abandoned German Observation Posts. The aperture always faced the wrong way, and when a new aperture was made on the other side an icy draught made the place almost uninhabitable, no matter how carefully all the chinks were stopped up. During the advance tree Observation Posts were frequently manned but were quite useless for Flash Spotting purposes.

On the Italian front there was never any difficulty in finding sites for Observation Posts. On the Montello front they were all situated on a mountain range rising to about 700 to 800 feet, and about seven to eight miles long. When the British front moved to the Assiago Plateau the Observation Posts were all on mountain tops 5,000 feet up. Even on the Montello front none of these Posts were easy to get at. This account of a visit to the Observation Post on Monte Salder will be of especial interest to those who were more used to crawling on their bellies through mud to get to their Observation Posts.

"A visit to this Observation Post was a terrifying experience, as there was an aerial cable way running to the top, and, although it was expressly stated that it was only to be used for sending up ammunition, or bringing down wounded, the Field Survey Company with their bland indifference to 'rules' made regular use of it. One sat in a sort of tray (about 5 feet by 2 feet with sides about 1 foot high) which dangled from two wheels on the cable way and was hauled up by an endless wire. For some distance one was in view of the Austrian lines, and when they felt 'sporty' they would loose off a few rounds, which might have blown the support sky high or the car off the wire. On these occasions the car appeared to travel at a snail's pace, and it was not at all comforting to look over the side and see the ground some hundreds of feet below littered with broken cars. The regular inhabitants of this Post, being used to this mode of travel, used to have the unpleasant habit, when taking up a trusting visitor, of rocking the car sideways."

And this brings us to consideration of Group H.Q. Group H.Q. was rather more than a place from which to carry on administration and issue orders on tactical matters. H.Q. was an integral part of the mechanism of observation. They did not and could not observe from Group H.Q., but, nevertheless, they controlled the actual observers when looking for guns. Any Post that was disconnected from Group H.Q. was, to all intents and purposes, out of action as long as this disconnection lasted. In the same way when it was necessary for the Posts to move, it was not possible to concentrate on moving the Posts, leaving H.Q. to follow when convenient. The whole Group—Posts and H.Q.—had to move as one body.

As a rule, both billets and officers were under one roof at Group H.Q. Apart from the more obvious conveniences of this arrangement, it was essential for officers and N.C.O.s to be on the spot, as they were too few in numbers to provide for one of each being on duty throughout the twenty-four hours. Group H.Q. might be anything from a château to a series of dugouts, and in some cases tents were used, but that was usually a temporary expedient.

What determined the location of Group H.Q. was the need for a more or less central position, to make it as easy as possible to get to and from the Posts. Also, as there were so many telephone lines coming into the Group, it was essential that the H.Q. should be near a permanent route of Signals. Later on, it was usual to try and get both the Groups and Sections under one roof. In areas where there were many houses standing, it was not easy to get the desired accommodation, as there were sure to be many civilians still in residence, but when the villagers got to know that there were considerable financial advantages to be had from housing the "Survey," satisfactory accommodation was usually forthcoming.

At Vielle Chapelle Group H.Q. was housed in an estaminet which continued to carry on business in one large ground-floor room, whilst, immediately across the passage in the corresponding room on the other side, all the work of Group H.Q. was carried on; one side of the passage dealing out rest and refreshment, the other side death and destruction. In the devastated areas convenience had to give way to the necessity of finding any sort of shelter convenient to a Signal route.

The essential equipment for Flash Spotting control at the Group H.Q. was the Flash and Buzzer Board and the Plotting Board. In addition there was an ordinary telephone switchboard with six or eight lines, but this was required for communicating with outsiders, and played no part in the actual Flash Spotting. The Flash and Buzzer Board was used for synchronizing the observations. The idea originated in the French Army, but it was modified and improved by an officer of the 3rd Field Survey Company, and it was this improved design that was adopted in the British Army. It is generally acknowledged that the invention of the Flash and Buzzer Board did more than anything else to enable the Flash Spotters to get quick and accurate results, and so put Flash Spotting "on the map."

The Flash and Buzzer Board was a special type of telephone switchboard by which H.Q. could speak to Posts singly, or to two, three, or four Posts at a time, as circumstances dictated. The same connections were available for the Posts. In addition similar connections could be made to neighbouring Groups and the Posts in these Groups so that, at one and the same time, three Posts in one Group might be working together, whilst the fourth Post was working with Posts in the neighbouring Group.

But the special features of this switchboard was the addition of a little light and a buzzer on each line. By depressing the key in the Post the observer lit up the little light on the board and at the same time he sounded the buzzer. Now the operator at Group H.Q. could arrange whether the pressing of the key would light the lamp and start the buzzer or only light the lamp. By this means it was possible for all the Posts to press their keys at once and show their lights, but only one need actuate the buzzer, although all the Posts were through to one another. This was the distinctive feature of the British design, and, as will be learnt, the feature that made the Flash and Buzzer Board so useful.

With this board in use, whoever was in charge at Group H.Q. was in a position to keep the Posts in close touch with one another, or in isolation, and at the same time keep himself informed of all that was going on.

In this way all the Posts could be kept in touch with the Post that had first picked up the "flash," but if the observer at another Post thought that he had picked up the same "flash," that Post could be cut off from the others, although still able to light up the lamp at Group H.Q. In this way the operator at Group H.Q. was able to see whether both Posts were observing on the same "flash", without any chance of one Post being influenced by anything that was going on in the other.

It was this that supplied a check on all results that was independent of the frailties of human nature. Either the lamps lit up at the same time, or they did not. In this way one could say definitely whether the observers had a "good" intersection or a "wash-out." Meanwhile there was no interruption of the contact between the "leading" Post and the other Posts which were still searching.

The Plotting Board was a large scale map (1/10,000) mounted on a board and covering an area that embraced the Survey Posts themselves and those portions of the enemy lines that were under observation. Each Post was carefully marked on the map, and a little hole was made at that point. Through this hole passed a strand of catgut. Towards the opposite side of the board an arc was drawn from each Post and graduated in degrees and minutes. By pulling out the thread and placing it on the appropriate reading on the arc, one could see on the map where this particular bearing lay. This saved having to draw the bearing out on the Board with the aid of a protractor, and when no longer required the thread was drawn by a weight down through the board, leaving it free of all encumbrances.

The position of all known batteries and any other useful positions were marked on the board, but beyond these no other markings were made.

A supply of drawing instruments, tables of logarithms, and some special charts for ranging completed the technical equipment of Group H.Q .The ranging charts were of various types and were used to save time when preparing for a "shoot." In some cases a mechanical device was used instead of these charts, but these were all "home-made" and were not on issue. Nearly every Group had a pet idea of their own for this purpose.

A supply of the most up-to-date information from every source about hostile battery locations was always at hand. This was supplied daily and was in constant use.

The essential equipment of a Survey Post consisted of an instrument with which to take bearings, a telephone, a chronometer, a stop watch, and a press key. The complete equipment comprised many other articles, such as binoculars, maps, etc., and such sundries as electric torches, note-books, and similar odds and ends, but the first four articles mentioned were the essentials. A book in which to enter the log was a *sine qua non.*

For observation purposes the ordinary surveyor's theodolite was used up till the summer of 1916, but it was unsuitable in many ways. Everything was seen in it upside down, and the field of view was narrow. This was a serious defect, as the most difficult job in getting a bearing was to get the object observed into the field of view. Another defect was that it was difficult to handle in the confined space in an Observation Post.

Fortunately, someone recalled that there was in store at home a supply of artillery directors that had been designed for use in similar conditions to those under which the Observation Groups were working. These instruments (Directors, Observation of Fire, Mk. V) belonged to the Siege Batteries R.A., but were deemed too heavy for work in the field. But in semi-permanent posts, such as the Observation Groups used, this was not a very marked disadvantage, and the installation of these instruments gave considerable impulse to the work of the Posts. They were only graduated to minutes, as against seconds on the theodolites, but the image showed the right way up. They could not read vertical angles, but at this time this was no drawback. On the whole they served their purpose well enough until a supply of specially designed instruments came along in 1917.

The first of these specially designed instruments to become available was one designed by the Service Géographique of the French Army for their own Flash Spotters. It was called the *longue-vue monoculaire à prisme*, and was made by a French firm. In the opinion of many of the observers this was the finest instrument, optically, that they had. It was provided with a revolving eyepiece which gave three different magnifications, and this was a convenience. The principal defect was that the mounting was too light to stand up to hard wear, and a shaky instrument was always a nuisance.

In this respect the Watkins instrument was much

superior, and by some considered the better instrument
of the two. Many changes in design were suggested and
tried out, but it could not be said that the perfect instrument was ever forthcoming. Weight was always a limiting
factor, and it is always a task to reconcile rigidity and
light weight.

In the French instrument the graticules were particularly clear, and as they played an important part in
fixing a bearing, an explanation of what a graticule is
may not be out of place. There must be some means of
telling when the object to which a bearing is to be taken
is in the centre of the lens of the telescope. For this
purpose a fine hair (actually a piece of spider's web) is
fixed inside the tube, and appears as a very fine line which
does not interfere with the view. This is called a graticule,
but, in addition to this central graticule, there were a
number of other hairs arranged on either side of the
central one. These were fixed in position to indicate an
angle of so many minutes from the central line, so that,
provided the observer could get the object within the field
of view, he could get a bearing with considerable accuracy,
even although he had not a chance to get it on the centre
line. In the ordinary way he did, of course, get the flash
on the centre line. Once he had the flash in the field of
view of the instrument, he read off, say, ten minutes right
by the graticules, and altered the setting of his instrument
accordingly. The next time he saw the flash it naturally
came very close to the centre, and with the graticules to
guide him, he was not likely to move his instrument too
far between flashes. Without this guide, it must have
taken him much longer to work his instrument into the
right position to get the flash centred.

The stop watches supplied had no unusual feature, but
they served their purpose, and that is all that one can

require of anything. But some comment must be made on the chronometers.

To the lay mind a chronometer is a timepiece that performs prodigious feats in the way of time-keeping, but it was not at all clear what the Ordnance Department considered the function of a chronometer. To the observers, the "chronometers" as issued did not appear to be superior in any way to ordinary watches, and their time-keeping properties were none too brilliant, but there were exceptions.

In the early days of Flash Spotting, when results depended on accurate time-keeping, the Posts were supplied with chronometers that had been borrowed from private sources. An interesting watch of this description was one that belonged to Sir Douglas Haig, who later on became the famous Field-Marshal. It was a beautiful piece of mechanism in a gold case, and was a presentation of some sort. Every observer who handled this watch coveted it, and there is little doubt that if the Post had been hit it would have been "destroyed by enemy fire." That, at least, was the standing joke amongst the men themselves, but it had a tragic sequel, as the Post received a direct hit one day and the two men on duty were blown to bits. For some reason or other, this watch was not in the Post at the time it was hit, and when the so-called "chronometers" came on issue, it had to be returned, and the observers felt quite a sense of relief that such a source of temptation had been removed.

But all the watches lent in this way were not of this high standard. It may have been patriotism that induced the owners to hand them over to the Government, but there was a grave suspicion in some cases that the owners had been taking advantage of the opportunity to get rid of "white elephants."

Posts and Equipment

Mention must be made of the Giffard Telescopes that were used in many of the Posts. They were very fine telescopes, but the interesting thing about them was that Col. Giffard, who was an optical designer of some note, had designed and constructed these from his own glass and at his own expense for the use of the troops at the front. How many he provided altogether is not known, but the Observation Sections got about fifteen of them.

The only remaining object that was essential to the working of the Post was a press key of some sort. This was sometimes an ordinary press key such as telegraphists use, but in the Survey Post it was not used for sending messages but to actuate the Flash and Buzzer Board at Group H.Q. Sometimes an ordinary bell-push was used.

The telephone system was an essential part of the system for getting results, quite apart from its use and convenience for other purposes. Every Post was linked to every other through the Group exchange and the Group exchanges were linked to one another. These were all private lines, or, perhaps, exclusive might be a better word, because the greatest length of these lines was constructed and maintained by Signals. The usual arrangement was for Signals to allocate lines on their "permanent" routes which they maintained, and the Groups laid, or at least maintained, the lines from there to the Post or Group H.Q. During the advance in 1918 many of the Groups laid and maintained all their lines themselves.

The length of these lines varied according to circumstances, but there must have been about twenty-five miles of lines, on an average, to each Group, or a hundred miles in each Army area. The proportion of these kept up by the Groups themselves was probably less than five miles per Group. But the portion that they had to maintain themselves was just that part where trouble was most usual. It was the end of 1917 before any special personnel was allocated for this task, and until then the observers had to be their own linesmen. In heavily shelled areas this threw a great strain on the observers because, in addition to performing their usual spell of duty in the Survey Post, they had to turn out to attend to the lines. This duty was probably responsible for more casualties in the Groups than any other, but it showed the rank and file at their best. Without orders from anyone, these men used to sally forth from the comparative security of their Posts or dugouts and try to keep the lines working at any cost. Many gallant actions must have gone unrecorded, but some did come under notice and receive an honourable award.

Originally, the Posts were supplied with Buzzer (D3) phones. It was thought that when the lines were bad the Posts could carry on by "buzzing" their messages, but this proved useless, and in any event, the introduction of Group control necessitated the use of the ordinary ringing phone. Signal lamps were also supplied but seldom used, and soon discarded.

All these special instruments were supplied through different sources. Some came through Ordnance and some through Signals. Others were "lent" by the artillery, and still others came through the General Staff at G.H.Q. This was not a very satisfactory arrangement, as distribution was often erratic and uncertain, so that, when the Depot Field Survey Company was formed, they took over the supply of all these specialities to the Groups, except for Signal stores.

5

HOW AN OBSERVATION GROUP WORKED

If you had entered a Survey Post on a clear afternoon, you would have seen two figures seated in front of an aperture which might, possibly, have been about 4 feet long and about 1 foot high. Above the aperture there would have been a bit of sacking rolled up. This, you would have learnt, was to hang over the aperture when the observers wanted to use a light at night. This was not due to any sense of modesty, but to show a light anywhere near the line at night was to ask for trouble.

Across the entrance you would probably have found a whole series of screens, sacks, etc. Nearly all Survey Posts were draughty, and no amount of ingenuity seemed to be able to rectify this trouble. This was particularly true of Posts in steeples and chimneys.

One observer would have been seated in front of the instrument which would have been fastened to a stout beam or similar support. Close to his hand would have been the press key, and—if it was in order—he would have been wearing headphones with a breastplate transmitter. In front of the other observer would have been the telephone and a pair of binoculars. A stop watch and a log book would have lain on a little shelf close to hand.

If there had been no unusual activity, the observers would have been chatting quietly together, whilst their eyes ranged slowly over the front. From time to time they would have used the instrument or the binoculars if their trained eyes fell on anything unusual, and although probably you would not have realized it, their ears were also on the alert.

One of the observers would have risen to let you take his place at the aperture, but it might have been that one of them would have had to leave the Post to let you in. Some of the Posts, particularly in church steeples, were a pretty tight fit for two.

If you had been a newcomer to the battle area, the scene that lay before you would have occasioned a good deal of surprise. From even the poorest Survey Post the view extended for many miles, but, except when an attack was impending or taking place, you would have noticed no signs of life or of movement anywhere. On the Somme all you would have seen were miles and miles of bare soil. Never a man, a beast, or a tree. Even the trenches and the barbed wire were inconspicuous to the untrained eye. Further north, where less material damage had been done, the outlook from a Post was not so desolate. In these parts, without the aid of glasses, you would not have realized that nearly every building within sight had been rendered uninhabitable in some way, and at a distance shattered trees would not have caught the eye.

"But," you would have queried, "where are the trenches?"

You would have seen the map and you would have known that below and in front of you lay a network of trenches—British and German. The observer would have trained his instrument on to a certain spot and you would have been invited to have a look. You might have seen a heap of soil or chalk, which the observer would have told you was the famous Hohenzollern Redoubt. From his description, you might or might not have been able to follow along the front and, perhaps, get a glimpse of the wire, but never a man or a beast would have been seen.

"Is it always as quiet as this?" you might well have asked. "Why is there no firing going on?"

The observer would have told you that it would have been very surprising if something had not been going on within his range of view. The stillness would have been deceptive, but the difficulty would have been to pick up anything in the instrument. If the wind had been in another direction you might have heard the rattle of machine-guns every now and then, but, as things were, all was silence.

The observer might have called your attention to something happening away over to the right.

"Do you see what appear to be little tufts of cotton-wool every now and then? These tufts of wool are trench-mortar shells bursting, and you may be sure that no one within a quarter of a mile of that spot thinks that the front is quiet."

As for the bigger stuff, unless there had been something in the nature of a bombardment on, a good deal would have depended on luck whether it was possible to pick it up or not. Single rounds might have been coming over at intervals of fifteen minutes or half an hour, but if a good breeze had been blowing, the smoke and dust would have disappeared quickly, and, unless we had heard the bursts, they might well have passed unobserved.

You would have been rather thrilled if you could have caught a sight of the enemy. If the front had been fairly quiet the observer might have been able to oblige you, but it would only have been an odd man or so, and he would not have appeared sufficiently large in the glasses to have enabled you to see his face. The thrill would have been a very mild one.

But if, by chance, the observer had spotted a body of men you would have seen him call up another Post to try and fix their position. Then, after a report to Group H.Q., you would have seen a number of shells burst close by, and you would have seen the party scuttle for shelter. One hardly dare admit it in this year of grace 1935, but in 1917 this probably did give you a thrill.

A question that you might have asked if you had been visiting in northern France, was whether the Germans were working any of the pits that could be seen nearly everywhere.

The observer would not have been able to give you a straight answer, but he would have called your attention to a pithead just below the Post. It would have appeared deserted, but in the sidings lay trucks fully laden with coal waiting to be taken away. No smoke came from the chimney-stack and it seemed that, if the pit was worked at all, it must work only at night, but, if you had watched carefully, you would have seen a thin wisp of steam coming from a pipe on the engine house, and you would also have seen that the pithead pulley was turning, but so slowly and steadily that it was barely noticeable. Soon the cage would have been up and the pulley would have ceased to turn. Some miners would have stepped out of the cage, and would have disappeared quickly behind some of the mine buildings. And so it would have gone on, slowly, gently, but unceasingly. Thus it was evident that if the pits on the other side of the line were being worked, there was no doubt that they would have used the same precautions.

Even if you had served in the line, the view from one of these Posts would have given an entirely new impression of the battle front. Things that would only have been glimpsed or seen in part would stand out in their entirety, and perhaps an "objective" that had for long been nothing but a mark on a map would now be seen for the first time.

Having got to know something about what could be seen from a Survey Post, and something about the instruments that the observer used, you would have been taken back to Group H.Q. It might have meant a long trudge on your own feet, but most probably a car would have picked you up and taken you some of the way.

On arrival at Group H.Q. you would have been shown into a room, or perhaps a hut or a dugout, and looking round what would have appeared to be the most conspicuous object would have been a table, but this, as you would have guessed from the threads dangling below, was the Plotting Board. In one corner a telephonist would have been seated in front of a small exchange and the Flash and Buzzer Board. In another would have been a trestle table covered with all the paraphernalia of an Army office, and seated beside it would have been a worried C.Q.M.S. busy with indents, returns, etc., etc. Some odd boots, tunics, etc., in the corner would have shown that one room served for all the activities of the Group.

If you had been a very distinguished visitor, the person at the Plotting Board would have been, most probably, an officer. But although it was generally possible to arrange for an officer to be present to greet "distinguished" visitors, it was not possible to arrange for "flashes" to come through in order to demonstrate how enemy guns were located. So if it had been a sapper (known officially as a Computer S.P.) who had greeted you, you would have had no reason to be disappointed. He, or a companion, was always on duty at the board, and he knew as much about getting intersections as any of the officers.

If you had been very undistinguished, he would have told you that he knew a blank sight more.

You might just have had time to take all this in when a buzzer sounded, and you would have noticed a little light glow on the Flash and Buzzer Board. You had been supplied with a pair of headphones so that you could listen-in to all that passed. Without further orders the telephonist would have switched this call through to the phone lying beside the computer. He would have taken up the instrument and have listened.

"Fir-tree speaking."

"H.Q. speaking."

"There is a gun firing on the R.E. dump at Noyelles. We can't pick it up, but it seems to be coming from somewhere south of La Bassée."

"Are they sending over much stuff?"

"No, just about one round every twenty minutes."

"All right. I'll put the other Posts on. [To the telephonist] Tell the other Posts that Fir-tree reports a gun firing on Noyelles from somewhere south of La Bassée."

The telephonist would have called up the other Posts and would have delivered his message simultaneously in this fashion.

"Hello, Birch."

"Birch speaking."

"Fir-tree reports a gun firing on Noyelles from somewhere south of La Bassée. Keep a look out, will you?"

"Right oh! Have they got a bearing yet?"

"Not yet. Hello, Forget-me-not?"

"Forget-me-not speaking."

"Did you get that?"

"Yes, that's O.K."

"Hello, Sycamore."

"Sycamore speaking."

A Group at Work

"Are you on to it?"

"That's O.K., Jimmie. We're looking out for him."

(To prevent misunderstandings, it should be explained that the telephonist was not calling up and conversing with Fairyland. The flowers and trees mentioned were the code names for the Survey Posts. Nor was "Jimmie" the code word for Group H.Q. That is just put in to indicate that, at times, even Survey Post observers could unbend.)

If you had been watching the computer you would have seen that he had glanced at his watch (a so-called chronometer), and that he had made an entry in the log book which lay on the board close to hand. He would have turned then to the hostile battery lists, which, likewise, lay on the Plotting Board. These lists gave all the latest information about the enemy gun positions, where they were located, when they were located, what they were firing at, calibres, etc., etc. From a study of these, and from his own experience, the computer would have made up his mind as to the most likely places to seek for this gun. Pulling out the threads from each Post, he would have laid them through the suspected position. He would have read off the bearings from each Post to the area it was proposed to search, and he would have instructed each Post in turn to observe on a certain bearing. After giving these instructions, he would have added, "Fir-tree, leading."

He might have asked, and probably did ask, for more information before he made up his mind as to where to tell the Posts to look, but you would have noticed that once the computer had made up his mind as to the most likely spot for the search, the initiative had passed from the Post to Group H.Q. Another thing that you would have noticed was that as all the Posts and Group H.Q.

were linked on one line, there was no need to repeat a message several times over. If H.Q. spoke to one of the Posts, or one of the Posts to H.Q., all could hear what was said, so that, if any Post had an additional bit of information to impart, all knew that it had been transmitted, and there was no confusion from different Posts calling H.Q. to give the same piece of information.

After the computer had issued his instructions to the Posts, there would have been a pause. The men in the Posts would have been heard chatting to one another, passing information, or making surmises. There would have been a certain amount of general gossip and local scandal interspersed amongst the technicalities. The prospects of leave, or how Phil May lost "beaucoup" francs at poker last night, but underlying it all there would have been a certain air of restrained excitement. But if the rounds had been coming over thick and fast instead of at long intervals, as in this case, there would have been no "back chat." There would have been a tense silence, only broken when information was being passed on.

"Hello, Fir-tree?"

"Fir-tree speaking."

"Forget-me-not speaking. Did he fire again just now?"

"Yes. Another round has just come over."

"Ah! I think I saw him. Hello, H.Q? I think I got the flash just now."

"Can you give me a bearing?"

"Hold on a minute."

In a few moments Forget-me-not would have given a bearing to where he thought he had seen the flash. The computer would have laid off this bearing on the Plotting Board and reconsidered the position in the light of this more definite knowledge. If the bearing had passed within reasonable distance of any known gun position, there was presumptive evidence that it might have been one of these, but if there were no known positions near to this bearing, it might have been that (1) the bearing was very far out, (2) what the observer had seen was not a gun flash at all, or (3) they were on to a position that had not been located before.

In this case number (1) could have been ruled out. It was daylight, and the observer was an experienced man who could be trusted to get pretty close with the help of landmarks. Number (2) might have been quite possible— the glint from a piece of glass or some polished metal could easily be mistaken for a gun flash in bright sunshine, but no great harm would have resulted if it had turned out to be so. Number (3) represented what would have been the most likely state of affairs, and the computer would probably have acted on this assumption.

The computer would have explained to you that under these circumstances there was not much that he could do, until he got a better bearing from the Post, but the Posts were still busy exchanging information.

"Hello, Fir-tree? Birch speaking. Do you think that we can see it from here?"

"I think so. Do you see that farmhouse just by the cross-roads?"

"No. It is behind a little ridge."

"Well, further down the road there are two trees. Can you see these?"

"Yes. I can see those all right."

"Well, from here, the gun seems to be about two hundred yards to the left of these and a good way in front. There is something that looks like a pole sticking up not far away."

And so on.

You might have been getting a little bored by now.

Nothing much seemed to be happening, and it looked as if it might take all day to get even one position. And it might have been so. The time that it took to get a location varied from a few minutes to several hours, but once a flash was picked up it was never abandoned as long as the gun went on firing.

"Buz-z-z-z-z-z!"

"Did you get it that time, Fir-tree?"

"Yes, the bearing is so and so, but I have not got it right yet."

"All right. Hello, Forget-me-not? Look on bearing so and so. Hello, Birch? No need to change your bearing. Hello, Sycamore? Can you see anything?"

"No. We cannot see anything in that area for the Fosse."

"All right. Break off." (To the telephonist) "Cut off Sycamore."

The next time the buzzer sounded, Fir-tree would have sent through a true bearing, and the computer would have written out a message for the telephonist to transmit to the artillery and anyone else concerned.

Flash from Fir-tree so many degrees and so many minutes AAA Firing on L.11.c.8.5.

"What," you might have asked, "happened if none of the other Posts got on to the flash? Was it of any use by itself?"

If the Post had heard the gun firing, they could have timed the interval between the time when they saw the flash and the time when they heard the report. With this information, the distance of the gun from the Post could have been calculated with approximate accuracy. It might have been several yards out, but if the same gun had started to fire again—say at night—this approximate position (possibly within 100 yards) would have made it much easier to direct the other Posts where to look. Also, it might have been that the Sound Rangers had located this gun, and, if this single bearing had passed through the position of their location, it would have been valuable confirmation. There were many other conditions where a single bearing might have been of the greatest value, so everything was carefully recorded and classified for future use.

From time to time Fir-tree had buzzed, indicating in this way that the gun had fired again. At last, as the buzzer sounded, two lights glowed on the board. This showed that Forget-me-not had picked up the flash, and the chances of getting a good location were bright. Another round or so had to be fired before Forget-me-not could give a true bearing, but when that had been obtained it was laid off on the Plotting Board. The computer read the map co-ordinates at the point where the two threads crossed, and that established the position of the gun.

Until this position had been checked no message would have been sent off. This check, you would have learnt, was the most important part of the routine. It was essential, particularly at night, to make sure that both the Posts were observing on the same flash. The "leading" Post had been sounding the buzzer every time the gun had fired, and the other Posts had heard this "buzz." If, at the moment the buzzer sounded, another Post had seen a flash in the direction expected, there was reasonable grounds for presuming that both Posts had seen the same flash.

But it would have been quite unsafe to act on this assumption. You might have thought that it was a rare coincidence for two batteries to fire at almost the same moment, but it was by no means rare. Also at night it was unusual to see the flash itself. What the observer usually saw was a reddish glare. This might have been quite small, or it might have lit up the whole lens of the instrument. All the time there was a constant display of Very lights, shell bursts, etc., etc., so that when the observer heard the leading Post buzz, he could quite easily imagine that he had got the flash.

By daylight, the chances of deception of this sort were not so likely to occur, but, under the stimulus of the buzzer, a man's eyes could play some funny tricks.

So that, when a second Post declared that they had picked up the flash, the computer would have ordered the telephonist to cut it off from the leading Post. When next the leading Post buzzed the second Post would not have heard the "buzz," although all the others would, but if this second Post had really got on to the same flash as the leading Post, both lights on the Flash and Buzzer Board would glow simultaneously when the gun fired. If it had been something else that they had picked up, the two lights would not have shown on the board simultaneously, or, if their eyes had been playing them tricks, one light would not have shown at all.

So you would have kept your eyes fixed on the board. By this time it is quite possible that you would have been infected by the air of excitement that worked up when an intersection was imminent, and when the two lights glowed out together, you would have exclaimed "Good," or perhaps "Bon." A true location!

The computer would now check his bearings on the Plotting Board and send a message to everyone concerned.

Intersection from Forget-me-not and Fir-tree on gun at B.13.a.4.6 AAA Firing on L.11.c.8.5 AAA."

Unless there was something else awaiting their attention,

the Posts would have continued observing on this flash in the hope that Birch might pick up the flash, because, if three Posts could have got bearings at one and the same time, the location was one that for all practical purposes could be reckoned dead true. But even an intersection— that is a location from two Posts—was quite accurate, provided the angle of intersection of the two bearings was not too narrow.

Locations were classified for accuracy as P, Q, or R. P meant that the error of the location might be taken to be not greater than fifty yards, and Q not more than a hundred yards, and R not more than a hundred and fifty yards. If you were unfamiliar with work of this nature, you might have thought that even the best results were not very accurate. But these letters did not necessarily represent that there was any error at all and, in any case, not many guns could shoot with greater accuracy than Class P results, so that no purpose would have been served by striving for greater accuracy.

But no result was accepted unconditionally until it had been confirmed from some other source. There was no means whereby an observer could distinguish between a "dummy" flash and a real one. Some observers did claim that they could tell a "dummy" when they saw it, but that was a very doubtful claim.

There was one question that must have been at the back of your mind all the time you were watching and listening. "How many locations does a Group get in the course of a day?"

The figures varied considerably, but the experience of most Groups was that there were periods when the flashes came thick and fast, and then would come a spell, lasting for some weeks, when locations were few and difficult to get. An analysis of the results from six of the

Flash Spotters & Sound Rangers

Groups over the period from December 1917 to September 1918, under what were judged to be average conditions, showed that 7,540 locations were obtained. This in round numbers represents four locations a day per Group. On the whole it would have been fair to say that five or six locations a day represented a pretty good bag, but that a complete blank would not have been unusual or even disappointing.

You would have been interested in comparing these figures with comparable figures from the Sound Ranging Sections. They had 11,315 results in the same time, which means that they got about three locations to every two from the Flash Spotters, but the two systems were complementary rather than competitive, so one would not have drawn any conclusion as to whether one system was better than another.

But your chat might have been interrupted by a telephone call.

"Corps Heavy artillery on the line."

The computer speaks.

"Hello, Corps? Forest speaking."

"Counter Battery officer speaking. We are going to engage that gun that you have just reported. Can you range for us?"

"That's all right, sir. Who is going to shoot?"

"X Battery, but they will not be ready for a few minutes."

"Very good, sir. Put them through when ready." (To the telephonist) "Warn Fir-tree and Forget-me-not."

The computer would have set about measuring the distance from each Post and from the battery to the target. When he had this information, he would have selected three different coloured charts which he would have taken from a drawer. He would have placed these, the one over the other, on a sheet of glass which was lit up by a light placed below it. He would have adjusted these sheets so that the straight lines on the charts would have corresponded to the angles of intersection of the bearings from the Posts and battery at the target.

On looking at the result of this you would have seen three sets of parallel lines all crossing; the centre lines all crossed at one point which corresponded to the target. The distance between the lines on each chart was different, although it represented the same amount when measured in angles. But the battery and the Posts were all at different distances from the target so that the distances covered by a certain angle were bound to be different in each case.

This operation would have taken from two to three minutes to perform, and it is probable that there would have been time for some simple explanations before the battery came through.

First of all, you would have wanted probably to know whether every gun was engaged immediately it was fixed as in this case. The answer would have been no. Unless there was some very special reason, no immediate action would have been taken. The locations made by the Groups were to provide targets, for counter battery work, which was carried out to plan and to a time-table.

One thing must have occurred to you. "Why, if one can plot the position of a gun accurately by the method described, is it necessary to have all this paraphernalia to fix the position of a burst?"

The difficulties in using the same methods for ranging as for locating were mostly practical ones. When locating a gun, the object for which the observer was seeking was stationary, and there was no need to read angles until such time as the observer was satisfied that he had his instrument truly directed. But when ranging each burst occurred in a different place, and as the observer had to get a bearing to every burst, he had no chance to swing his instrument round on to the bearing. Instead, he fixed his instrument on a known bearing (the bearing to the target) and read off the bearings of the bursts on the graticules as so many minutes right or left of the centre line. Of course, these readings might have been converted into true bearings by simple addition or subtraction, but calculations of any kind, especially when working against time, were best avoided.

Another reason for not using the Plotting Board for ranging was that the Gunners were accustomed to receiving reports from their own observers as so many minutes right or left, and so many yards over or short. They needed this information for the laying of their guns. If the Plotting Board had been used it would have been necessary to plot a new arc for every battery that the Group had to range, so that if a certain amount of drawing had to be done, it was just as well to draw out something that was better suited to the particular job on hand.

When ranging was first tried all these charts were drawn out by hand—a different one each time. But the principal reason for using prepared charts was the necessity of saving time.

The battery would have been ready by now, and this is the sort of conversation that might have ensued.

"Hello, Forest. Are you ready?"

"All ready now."

"What are conditions like?"

"Not too bad, but I will put you through to the Posts. They can tell you better."

"Which Posts are ranging?"

A Group at Work

"Fir-tree and Forget-me-not. Hello, Forget-me-not? Will you speak to the battery?"

"Hello, X? Forget-me-not speaking."

"X speaking. What is visibility like?"

"Not too bad, sir, but it is getting a little misty."

"Let me know if it gets too thick. We do not want to waste ammunition."

"Very good, sir."

"Hello, Fir-tree. How is it with you?"

It should be remembered that the battery, the two Posts, and Group H.Q. were all on the same line and everything could be heard by any one of them.

"Not too bad, sir, I don't think it will get any worse."

"All right. Wait for the 'stand-by.' The time of flight is nineteen seconds."

"Very good, sir."

Pause.

"All ready?"

"Yes sir."

"Stand by! FIRE!"

Twenty seconds elapse. The computer speaks.

"Give me your bearing, Forget-me-not."

"Ten minutes left."

He places the point of a pencil on the appropriate line on his chart.

"And you, Fir-tree."

"Fifteen minutes right."

The computer places another pencil on another line, he runs up both lines until he reaches the point where they intersect, then he reads off:

"Hello, X? Seventy-five yards over, and five minutes right."

"Hum! All right."

Another pause.

"Stand by! Fire!"

And so the job goes on.

You would have realized that this was an extremely accurate and rapid method of ascertaining the fall of the rounds, and you would have been told that it was just this reliability and accuracy that made the Gunners suspicious of the method when it was first tried. The man behind the gun always liked to think that he was knocking spots off whatever he was shooting at, and if an F.O.O. got a burst right in the centre of his director he felt justified in sending back an "O.K." just to keep things cheery. But the Survey observers had no proprietary interest in the guns—they ranged for anyone that needed their services—and in any event they were not asked to say where the rounds fell. That was the job of Group H.Q., so that their results were based on cold hard scientific facts and gave no scope either to the optimist or the pessimist.

If the round had fallen on the target both Posts would report zero bearings or "O.K.s," but it was rare to get the O.K. from both Posts, and this seemed to damp the spirits of the Gunners at first. There was no doubt that this system of ranging appeared to make their shooting worse instead of better, and so was suspect. One officer, who seemed to be impressed by the potentialities of the system, candidly confessed that he could not afford to use it. He claimed that the battery had a good record but that if he had to report, day after day, that he had fired so many rounds and never an O.K.—well.

One development of this system of ranging was of particular interest—that was the use of this method for gun calibration. It should be explained that much of the shooting done during the war was by the map. That is to say, that the gun layer knew his own position on the map and also the map position of his target, but he could not see his target from his gun. Under these conditions he had to lay his gun by making a series of weird and wonderful calculations based on the known trajectory of his gun. But after the gun had been in use for some time, it got worn and the trajectory altered. The amount of this change could only be ascertained by actual measurement of the fall of the rounds at certain settings of the gun dials. This meant hauling out the guns and taking them back to an artillery range somewhere far behind, an inconvenient and time-wasting affair; but when it was found that the Observation Groups could report the fall of the rounds with sufficient accuracy this was no longer necessary, as the guns could carry out a calibration shoot when in position. This was a service that was utilized more and more frequently as the war progressed.

There was another system of ranging that you might or might not have learnt about. That was ranging on the air burst. This was a method of ranging on targets that were not in sight from the Observation Posts, but whose position was known. The theory of ranging on the air burst is simple. Instead of letting the shell strike the ground (where it would not have been seen) it was fitted with a time fuse which was set to explode the shell somewhere over the target where it could be seen from the Observation Posts. The observer would fix these bursts in the air, and when the bursts were taking place exactly over the target, the gun layer had only to depress his gun by a known amount to hit the target or, at least, to be sure that he was getting very close.

You would have realized that this system proved extremely useful in many circumstances, but although the theory was so simple, in practice there were many complications to be overcome. But although the Survey

Bats. were anxious to use the method, it was only found possible to install the necessary apparatus and train the personnel in one or two of the Groups, so that it was very unlikely that you would have seen it demonstrated on a casual visit.

By this time you possibly had had enough of explanations and demonstrations, so that when the next call was put through, you wondered what was coming. But this is what you would have heard, most likely.

"That you, Jones?"

"Yes. Jones speaking."

"Tea's ready."

"Right oh! Tell Benyon to bring in another cup. I am bringing along an officer."

"Right."

And so—as Mr. Pepys might have said—to tea.

6

HOW SOUND RANGING WAS DONE IN THEORY AND PRACTICE

IT is not very difficult to understand the principles on which Sound Ranging is based, if one does not approach the task with the idea that there is something "mysterious" or "magical" about it. Many people, after a visit to a Section, professed themselves more "mystified" than ever, but that was only because they failed to distinguish between the simplicity of the principle and the complexity of its application. In this chapter the two things are kept quite distinct, and the reader who is interested should have no difficulty in understanding how the Sound Rangers located the position of enemy guns from the sound of the report.

(1) THE ADVANTAGES AND DISADVANTAGES OF SOUND RANGING AS A METHOD OF GUN LOCATION

In sound-ranging, a gun is located by means of measurements made upon the sound wave spreading from the gun, and a Sound Ranging Section can only work if this sound reaches its recording stations. The great foe to sound ranging is an adverse wind. If the wind is blowing from the recording station towards the gun which is being recorded, the gun report which is thus coming up-wind is deflected upwards owing to the wind being stronger in the upper air than it is near the ground. Hence the report as received by a ground-station is faint or inaudible, not because the sound has further to go in struggling against the wind, but because it is thrown upwards and passes overhead. On the other hand, when the wind is blowing from the gun towards the observer, conditions are ideal. The sound is deflected downwards, and the sound wave running over the ground has a sharp crest, as it were, on which measurements are easily made. This effect of wind is far more important than the effect of intervening hills or other obstacles (except in mountainous country), and hence the recording microphones of a Sound Ranging Section could be placed almost anywhere, an elevated situation being unnecessary. The sound curved down over the hills or buildings. Owing to the working of a well-know nprinciple which our French *confrères* called *Principe de l'embêtement maximum*, or "Principle of maximum cussedness," the wind on the Western front in the war was generally blowing from our lines towards the enemy lines. A long spell of westerly weather put all the Sound Ranging Sections completely out of action. In this we were more unfortunate than our Flash-Spotting colleagues. If the weather was misty, it was clear that no zeal could enable them to get locations, but if the wind was westerly our plight was not so easy to explain, and we had to accept the well-remembered "gingering up" with what equanimity we could.

The other great disadvantage of Sound Ranging methods is the complexity of the wiring system. The Sections had double wires running from H.Q. to six microphone stations and two forward Observation Posts. It was reckoned that the whole totalled about forty miles of wire, and it had to be good wire with a low resistance and freedom from earths and other faults, a much higher standard than that demanded of telephone cable. This meant the need for some time in getting the Section into action, a lot of upkeep, and a big risk of interference by cutting of the wires.

On the other hand, there are compensating advantages.

A. Record of a German Howitzer

This shows how the pressure wave created when the gun was fired makes a "break" at the instant at which it reaches the corresponding microphone. Vertical divisions correspond to 1/10 sec., and these are sub-divided to read to 1/100 sec. It also shows how the regular spacing of the microphones cause the breaks to form a regular pattern

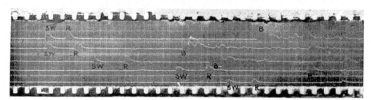

B. Record of a 77 mm. Field Gun

This shows the (SW) shell wave, (R) report, and (B) burst. Much information can be gathered from a film such as this by inspection only. We can see that the gun must be nearly opposite the two microphones on one flank as the report arrives at these almost simultaneously. It is a long way back because the breaks made by the report form a convex pattern. The bursting shell must be opposite microphones 2 and 3, and nearest 3, and somewhere near the base as these breaks form a very deep curve. We know that it is a gun and not a howitzer that is firing from the presence of breaks caused by the shell-wave. Something might be learned of the calibre of the gun from the characteristics of the gun report break. Compare these with those shown on record A

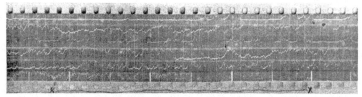

C. Record of a High Velocity Gun

This is the record of a gun firing made in the Ypres Salient on July 24, 1917, just prior to the Third Battle of Ypres. From this record the computer was able to locate a gun, and it is reproduced here to enable the reader to see why skill and experience were needed to read these films when the front was active

SOUND RANGING RECORDS (Recorded by R Section)
(See "Sound Ranging in Theory and Practice")

Sound Ranging in Theory and Practice

Mist or fog is no obstacle to sound. In fact, conditions are ideal in misty weather both because the wind is generally light and the temperature of the air is very uniform. Since other methods of location are difficult or impossible under such conditions, Sound Ranging may be of great value. It has a further great advantage in that it gives so much information about a battery which is being located. It is possible to record the positions both of the gun which is firing and the burst of its shells. Hence the target on which the battery is firing or registering is accurately known. The calibre of the gun can be gauged by a simple calculation which gives the time of flight of the shell, and if any doubt still exists the target can be visited (after the lapse of a discreet time interval) and a fuse or two dug up. Local information on this point is also useful, if one remembers to divide by two the estimate of the calibre formed by those on the spot. Under good conditions the accuracy of location is adequate. An accuracy of 100 yards or so is attained, and this is sufficient to identify the battery position on a photograph from the air. A report from a Sound Ranging station thus gives time, position of battery firing, number of guns, calibre, and target. Such information is of much more value than the knowledge that a gun of unknown type is firing from a certain point, as will be clear to anyone acquainted with counter battery work.

(2) PRINCIPLES

The principle of the method is very simple (Fig. 1). Sound travels with a velocity of about 1,100 feet per second. When it reaches the observing stations, it is in the form of the arc of a circle with the gun at its centre. We measure the time-intervals between its arrival at certain stations, shown as M_1, M_2, M_3 in the figure which we will suppose

I   129

to be plotted on a map. The sound reaches M1 first, for example. One second later it reaches M2, and two seconds later M3. We draw around M2 a small circle of 1,100 feet radius (the distance travelled by sound in one second) and around M3 a circle twice as large. A large

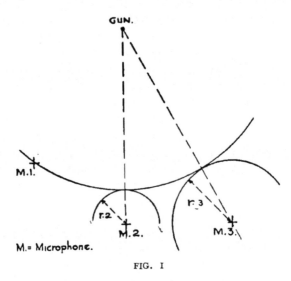

FIG. I

arc, which goes through M1 and touches the other two circles, will then have the gun at its centre. In practice, another method of plotting the gun position was used. Strings were fastened to the mid-points of M1M2, M2M3, etc., and scales were marked out on the edge of the Plotting Board by previous calculation. When a time-interval of a given amount was registered between M1 and M2, the string was laid on the corresponding scale division. The intersection of the strings on the Plotting Board gave the gun position. The method of plotting, however, is of minor importance; if the arrival of the sound at three or more places is recorded, it is always possible to find the origin of the sound.

(3) THE APPARATUS

The apparatus used in the British Army was designed by M. Bull of the Institut Marey in Paris, and was originally one of several types with which the French Army was experimenting. The sound was recorded by microphones of a special type, which will be described below. When the sound arrived at the microphone, an electrical impulse was sent along the cable to the recording station. This impulse caused a wire in a "string" galvanometer to give a kick. The galvanometer contained six "strings" (i.e. fine wires), each connected to its own microphone. In this type of galvanometer, a "string" or fine metal wire is stretched from supports along a narrow gap between the poles of a powerful electromagnet. As the "string" thus lies in a very strong magnetic field, when a current passes through it, it is dragged sideways. In this way, it is possible to detect very minute currents. It was fascinating to watch the strings kick one after the other when a gun was firing, and then a few seconds later to hear the gun itself at H.Q. The shadows of the strings were thrown by a lamp upon a slit behind which a cinematograph film was in motion while recording was under way. When the film was developed, the shadows appeared as white lines running along the film, and, if the "string" had got a kick, it appeared as a break in this line. At the same time the light was interrupted a hundred times a second by a toothed wheel, so that "time markings" were automatically ruled on the film as it ran. (See the illustration facing page 128.) This illustration shows how the differences in time of arrival can be read to 1/200 second. The apparatus sounds complicated, but in practice it is reasonably fool-proof. We owe this to the mechanical ingenuity of M. Bull, who made the first models.

(4) THE LAY-OUT

It was our practice to use six microphones at recording

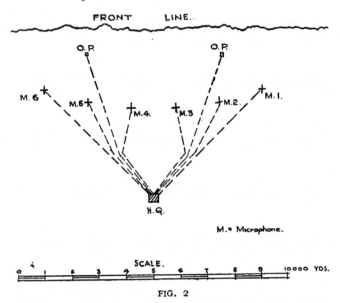

FIG. 2

stations. These were spread out along a "base" about nine thousand yards long and four thousand yards behind the front line. It will be realized that these are round figures, and that daring spirits often managed to push their bases closer to the front. (See Fig. 2.)

H.Q. was at any convenient point behind the base. Well in front of the base were one, or more often two, posts for "forward observers." The forward observer had a telephone, and a key which when depressed set all the recording mechanism in motion. Since he was in front of the base, he heard the sound first and thus had a few seconds' grace in which to start up the machinery at H.Q. before the sound got to the microphones. The whole recording machinery sprang into action in less than a second.

The forward observer was a most important unit. He had to recognize what was "worth taking." He recognized the sound of an enemy gun, and was able to estimate roughly its direction and target, phoning his report to H.Q. The difference between good and bad observers was colossal, and in fact the Section depended entirely upon their judgment for its material.

When a record had been taken the film was cut off, developed and fixed (we got the time for this down to a few seconds), and handed over to the computer, who read off the time-intervals and plotted the gun position. The computer was also a "key" unit. A good man would get an accurate location from a record which a poor computer would entirely misread. It requires a knack which is only attained by practice and experience of physical measurements.

(5) THE NATURE OF THE SOUND-WAVE

Why all this elaborate apparatus? Why not have a short base, and men with tapping keys recording the arrival of the sound, as indeed was tried in the early days of Sound Ranging? To see why the elaborations are necessary, we must consider the nature of the sound-wave. Sound travels 1,100 feet per second. Therefore, if we make a mistake of 1/100 second in measuring the time interval between arrival at M_1 and M_2 (see Fig. 1), we are ten feet wrong in the radius r_2, and so the sound-wave arc will be placed wrongly. Since the gun is very much farther from M_1 and M_2 than they are from each other, this error is very much magnified when we plot the gun position, becoming perhaps 100 feet. It is still further magnified when we take into account the fact that the intersections from different bases cut at rather a fine angle. It is easy to see, in fact, that we must not make errors of more than 1/100 second if the location is to be worth anything. Hence the elaborate microphones and recording apparatus, for a man with a tapping key cannot be relied upon to work closer than 1/10 second, and has to be good to do that.

It will further be clear why the base has to be so long. The intersections must not be too fine, just as in flash-spotting. Further, the sound-wave is not perfect. Local irregularities of wind and temperature cockle its surface (like light coming through a cheap window-pane). If we imagine trying to survey a distant object through two theodolites a short distance apart and looking through irregular window-panes, we can picture the impossibility of using a short base. Various "short base" enthusiasts have arisen from time to time, encouraged by good results achieved in perfect conditions, but most were convinced of the sad necessity for a long base in actual practice.

The lay-out and apparatus were thus determined by the nature of the sound-wave itself.

(6) Shell-wave and Gun-wave

The great bugbear of the early days of Sound Ranging was the shell-wave. A high-velocity gun fires a shell which travels faster than sound. Such a projectile makes an infernal loud crack, much louder than the gun report, and this arrives a few seconds before the gun report, which it often completely drowns. Anyone who has had a h.v. gun firing over his head knows the effect. Our first microphones naturally registered the "shell-wave," which was useless for purposes of location, and not the true gun report.

Various tales hang round the solution of this difficulty. We early realized what we had to do. The shell-wave is very noisy, but high-pitched. The gun-wave is a low "boom," not easy to hear, but which has a much bigger pressure behind it and rattles windows, etc. This pressure was brought home to us in an interesting way. The first Sound Ranging Section had a billet at La Clytte, where the farmhouse had the usual primitive sanitary retreat, cosily situated as an annex leading out of the kitchen. When one sat down, one closed the only aperture between the hermetically sealed farmhouse and the outer world. A six-inch gun fired over from an emplacement about a quarter of a mile behind. The rending shell-wave only affected the ear, but the pressure of the scarcely audible gun-wave behind it caused one to rise slightly but perceptibly. Obviously there was a good deal of energy in the pressure-wave, and if only we could use it our difficulty was solved. The next step was made by Tucker, of Tucker microphone fame. Just beside his camp-bed were two small holes (mice?), and he noticed that the pressure caused a freezing jet of air to play on his face whenever the report arrived. He had been making experiments on the cooling of a hot thin wire by an air jet, and he had the inspiration to make a microphone which embodied this principle. A thin wire was stretched over a small hole in a container (empty rum jars were very convenient and easily obtainable) and heated electrically. The gun-wave cooled it as explained above, and so lessened its electrical resistance, and the galvanometer recorded the effect. Directly we had got the right wire from England we rigged up a rough apparatus to try out the idea at Kemmel in 1916. I will never forget the thrill of seeing the first record, in which the shell-wave hardly made the galvanometer string quiver, while the gun-wave gave an enormous kick. The real success of our Sound Ranging dated from that day, because not only shell-waves but other unwanted sounds of high pitch, such as rifle fire, traffic, and bad language in the neighbourhood of the microphone, were equally well eliminated. A curious difficulty with the first microphones was that small insects so enjoyed the warmth of the hot wire that they used to creep into the holes and break the wires. We made an issue of small grids to the Sections to stop this, and "Protectors, Earwig, Mark I" duly appeared in the Army List of stores.

(7) Corrections for Wind and Temperature

These corrections had an important effect on accuracy, and were difficult to estimate. Temperature and wind at ground-level could easily be measured, but, as explained above, the sound from the gun arrives after pursuing a path high in the air and curving down again to the microphone. We got an excellent supply of meteorological reports, but the best information was supplied by our own "wind sections." Two of these, located well behind the front, exploded charges at known points at intervals of a few hours, and sound-ranged them as if they had been guns. They thus found the effective wind and temperature for Sound Ranging purposes by noting the error of their locations, and their data were sent out to all Sections.

(8) Advantages of Regular Base

One of the most ingenious devices which was of essential importance was the use of a regular base. Lloyd-Owen and Gray were the first to see the advantage of this, which at first sight appears a rather fussy and artificial ideal. By a regular base is meant a spacing of the microphones at absolutely equal distances on the arc of a great circle facing the enemy line. The advantage of the regular base is that the "breaks," or kicks of the six galvanometer strings registering the arrival of the sound at the microphones, form a regular pattern on the ciné film. This will be noticed on the films reproduced. The regularity made it possible to work even when a lot of guns were firing. A trained eye can very quickly get so accustomed to the appearance on the film of the regular series of breaks which belong to one sound, that they can be picked out from amongst a number of other noises, so that guns could be recorded even when a moderate "strafe" was going on. In the last two years, regular bases were always used. It took a little adjustment of the base upon the terrain to find six places which were on a regular arc and also suitable for the microphones, but it could in practice be always done. The surveyors of the Field Survey Companies were most sporting assistants in fixing the sites for this rather novel problem.

(9) Conclusion

In conclusion, I cannot refrain from quoting the translation of an extract from a German order. This extract was circulated by Colonel Jack to "All Field Survey Companies" on June 23, 1917.

Group Order.—"In consequence of the excellent Sound Ranging of the English, I forbid any battery to fire when the whole sector is quiet, especially in east wind. Should there be occasion to fire, the adjoining battery must always be called on, either directly, or through the Group, to fire a few rounds."

The joke was that the Tucker microphone at that time

made it possible to disentangle the records of half a dozen batteries firing at once, let alone two, and locate them all. One must give full marks, however, for that bit about the east wind—they realized what was our worst adversary.

W. L. BRAGG

7

FIRST EXPERIMENTS IN SOUND RANGING AND SUBSEQUENT EXPANSION

SOUND Ranging was unknown in August 1914. It is believed that the matter was discussed in the Austrian Army sometime prior to the war, but nothing seems to have come of these discussions, and it may be said that Sound Ranging was something entirely new in 1914.

The first experimenter to receive official support was a professor from the observatory at Paris, who was serving at the front. In September 1914 he received permission to return to Paris and carry on his experiments there. On his arrival in Paris he called into consultation a scientific confrère from the Institut Marey, and it is interesting to note that this collaborator was the son of an Irishman, although resident in Paris.

Anyhow, these two men put their heads together and experiments were started on three independent but allied lines of attack. The first was to use men with tapping keys which registered the time of arrival of the sound of the gun at the observer on a smoked cylinder. The second was to use carbon microphones registering in the same way. The third was to use carbon microphones registering by means of a very sensitive galvanometer.

The first and third methods gave most promise of ultimate success, and they were the first to be submitted to a proper test. The first experimental Section was laid out at the Institut Marey, and full-scale tests were carried out on both these systems. The first official test was held on November 17th and was carried out in the presence of three French Generals. Two guns were fired at a point about 4,000 metres away, and each gun fired three rounds. These guns were located to 20 metres for line and 40 metres for range. This seemed to satisfy the authorities, as Sections were formed to test out these two methods in the line.

Other experimenters were hard at work, and even as early as January 1915 the French had two Sections in the line working with stop watches. One was installed on the Arras front, and the other just on the left of the British front north of Ypres. These Sections came to nothing, but the French Army never limited themselves to one system, and there were at least two other systems developed and taken into limited use. Altogether, about this time—1914–15—the French Army seems to have given every encouragement to experimenters to show what they could do.

Of the three systems tried out at the Institut Marey the first was eventually abandoned. The second system was slow in developing, but eventually this formed the basis of the "T.M." method which was adopted officially by the French Army. The third system (which came to be known as the Bull system) was adopted later and developed by the British Army. When the American Army came in they adopted the British system. So that it may be said that all the systems in use in 1918 developed from the experiments at the Institut Marey.

In the British Army several investigators took up this problem independently and proposed schemes for dealing with it, but none of these reached the practical stage. Some of the senior officers of the R.A. also interested themselves in the matter in 1914, but things never seem to have been carried very far. It may, of course, be that the ease with which the French scientist could travel between his laboratory in Paris and the front line had something to do with the way in which Sound Ranging developed in the French Army, whilst it remained neglected in the British Army. The Frenchman could always fix up something in his laboratory, and if he could interest any of the authorities in his experiments they could roll up and see for themselves what he was doing. Nevertheless, there does seem to have been a lack of imagination amongst those who might have been expected to help things on at this period, because it will be noted that of the three schemes tried out by the French at this time the only one that embodied anything in the nature of a novel idea was the Bull system. And M. Lucien Bull was half Irish, half French, so that it was not the superior inventiveness of the Frenchman that gave them this lead.

Still, it was the French who first took it up; and it was the French who first tried it out, and, if in the end the British system proved itself superior to the French system, much of the credit for this must go to the French for their pioneer work and for the ready assistance they rendered when the British Army first took the job in hand.

The French Section using the Bull apparatus arrived at the front at Tracy le Mont, near Compiègne, on January 6, 1915. The expedition only remained at the front for a week, but this was long enough for the experimenters to find out some of the defects of their apparatus. In one respect this expedition was very unfortunate, as the wind would persist in blowing from the wrong direction. (Even in 1918 it was sometimes difficult to get people to realize that, if the sound of the gun did not reach the microphones, that was not the fault of the Sound Ranger or his apparatus.) So they were unable to locate any enemy guns, although they did locate the position of their own batteries and of shell bursts with great success. The disappointing nature of this trial was attributed to a lack of sensitivity in the microphones, which was certainly true, but later on it was discovered that the real reason was that, at that time, they were ignorant of the *onde de choc* or shell-wave.

This Section returned to Paris to carry out some obvious improvements in the apparatus, and by the spring of 1915 the French were sufficiently convinced of the practicability of Sound Ranging to order three complete sets of this apparatus.

In March 1915 an Engineer officer in the British Army wrote a report on Sound Ranging as he had seen it in Paris, but nothing came of this. In the following month another R.E. officer (in this case from the War Office) was so impressed by what he saw and heard whilst in Paris that he set out straight away for G.H.Q. Arriving there, he did not make the mistake of writing a report. He went straight to a number of senior officers, and, apparently, what he told them was sufficient to make them realize that something was going on that they could not afford to neglect, because the upshot of these interviews was the appointment of a committee of three to go to Paris and investigate.

This committee consisted of three experts—one on survey, one on electricity, and one on artillery. The artillery expert soon returned to G.H.Q., but the Engineer officers stayed on and in due course reported (one under protest) that (1) in their opinion Sound Ranging was a practicable proposition and (2) that the Bull system was the best.

Still the authorities seemed to be dubious, and the committee were sent off again. This time they went to visit a Sound Ranging Section in the line. On their return they reported as before—that Sound Ranging was a practicable proposition.

The matter now came before the Experiments Committee at G.H.Q. and they decided against ordering any apparatus on the ground that the method had not yet reached a sufficiently practicable stage! To the onlooker this committee seems to have been provided with a very inept name!

Still, there were others more experimentally and imaginatively minded who were not prepared to see the matter shelved in this way and, thanks to their persistence, the Experiments Committee authorized the purchase of one experimental set. The order for this set was given in June 1915. It was made by Mr. Bull in Paris and delivered in October 1915.

Meanwhile the services of a young scientist with a considerable reputation had been secured to take charge of the proposed Section. He had some knowledge of gunnery, but no experience in the line. He had as an assistant an expert mathematician, and there were two men for sundry duties—an electrician and an instrument maker.

This party arrived in France in August 1915, and the two officers visited a Bull Section in the line to find out something of the task facing them. Returning to Paris, they picked up their apparatus, which had all been installed in a sort of motor caravan, and the first British Sound Ranging Section arrived at the front on October 18, 1915. The place chosen for this experiment was the front between Dickebusch and Mont Kemmel.

In addition to the caravan with the apparatus, this Section was equipped with two Singer light cars, and when we read of the personnel allotted at this time it would almost appear that the Sound Rangers should claim to have been the "Fathers" of the mechanized Army, because the establishment was now 2 officers, 2 other ranks, and 4 M.T. drivers. Two of the drivers were for the lorry—a lorry had to have 2 drivers—but, as this particular lorry never moved unless the line moved, even one might have been reckoned a luxury at that time. Still, in the Survey, no one paid much attention to how a man was labelled. There were always plenty of jobs for everyone, and most men knew better than to stand on their dignity.

This party was soon reinforced by another officer who was serving with a battery in the line and who was an electrical engineer in civil life. At the same time a lineman was lent by a neighbouring unit.

The numbers allotted to this first Section must seem almost farcical to anyone acquainted with the multiplicity of duties that had to be attended to by all ranks before there was any time to attend to the job itself. But it must be remembered that a Sound Ranging Section was something quite new which did not fit neatly into the existing Army organization. What was contemplated at that time was that the Signal Corps would do all the outside work for the Section, both for installation and upkeep, and that officers and men would only have to get results and keep the apparatus in order. Neighbouring units would ration and probably cook for such a small body.

The upkeep of lines by Signals was soon found to be impracticable. Delays and uncertainties were inevitable, and the inconvenience of having to rely on others for one's daily bread was soon apparent. But none of these things was apparent until they were tried, and this accounts for the very small personnel allotted to this first Section.

Sound Ranging from 1914 to 1918

This Section located its first gun on November 2nd, and by December they were getting results that were sufficiently good to show that there was "something in it," and orders were given for more Sections to be formed.

It should be realized that this Section, quite apart from the inadequate personnel provided, had, in the words of one report, to meet "every kind of difficulty." To begin with, Sound Ranging was admittedly in an experimental stage in 1915, but as there had been so much difficulty in getting even this one set of apparatus, it was evident that results were the only thing which would fetch any sort of approval from the authorities. So that many handicaps were endured, and makeshifts accepted until that happy day arrived.

For example, it was originally intended that the Section should have a 5,500 yards base. But the Signals, who, of course, had only a certain amount of personnel of their own available for the job, foresaw the difficulty of keeping up lines of this length, and so the base had to be cut down to 3,000 yards, which meant a considerable sacrifice of accuracy. That was the type of difficulty that might have been avoided, but there were others that were not so easily overcome. The microphone itself was the real culprit. It was extremely sensitive to everything that was not wanted, and relatively insensitive to the gun report which was wanted, so that it was only under very favourable conditions that a really satisfactory location could be claimed, and these locations were nearly all confined to howitzers. To locate a gun it was necessary to use "caustics"—but that is something that is beyond most of us, so no attempt will be made to explain. The result of all these difficulties was that, at this time, no attempt was made to locate closer than the sub-square of the map (an area 500 yards by 500 yards), but as this provided badly needed information it was considered sufficiently good to justify the existence of this Section and the provision of three new ones.

It will be remembered that at this time there was a Topo. Section in each Army, and two of these newly created Sound Ranging Sections were allocated to each. When the Topo. Sections became Field Survey Companies in February 1916, the establishment for the Field Survey Companies made provision for the inclusion of Sound Ranging Sections and the personnel was based to a certain extent on the experiences of the experimental Section on Kemmel and designed to make them more self-supporting. They were allotted 3 officers and 18 other ranks, including 1 sergeant, 1 instrument repairer, 1 photographer, 3 linemen, 2 telephonists, 3 forward observers, 3 batmen, and 4 M.T. drivers. Transport consisted of 1 30-cwt. lorry for the apparatus, 1 15-cwt. box-car, and 1 light car. The box-car was provided with a C.A.V. dynamo, and the intention was that the charging of accumulators for lighting the lorry and apparatus should be done from this car. About a year later the Sections were supplied with 3-kW Austin lighting sets for this purpose.

Sound Ranging Sections were now designated by the letters of the alphabet, beginning at the end. The original Section, which for some time remained an experimental Section, was called "W" Section. This form of designation was very useful in preserving secrecy, as it gave no clue of any kind as to the work of the Section, and only the very curious were stimulated by this complete lack of information. The postal address of the officers and men of the Sound Ranging Sections must have been about the simplest on record. E.g. "W Section, B.E.F., France."

The officers for these new Sections were all sent to

W Section for a week's training. As the apparatus was completed the Section officers took it over in Paris and drove up with the caravan to the site that had been chosen for the particular Section. When they got to the site the first job was to survey the base. This was done by the Topo. Section of the Field Survey Company concerned, and, as they were one of the family, so to speak, no great difficulties arose. The wiring of the base was done by Signals, but things were not so easy here. A good deal depended on the technical capacity of the Signals officer engaged on the job whether it was done properly or not. Sometimes it was not easy to get them to understand that "comic airline" was not good enough, but it was still more difficult to get them to give their undivided attention to the job. Wiring up these Sections was something outside the ordinary scope of their work, and (always a great difficulty in the Army) it was being done for a unit outside their own formation. Naturally they tended to neglect the Section if their ordinary duties were pressing. And it was this same difficulty—getting authority for this, that, and the other thing, and then finding someone to recognize this authority—that made progress so slow at first.

At that time it took about three or four weeks on the average before a Section was getting results. In some cases it took nearly two to three months, but by 1918, when the difficulties of ground and shell fire were infinitely worse, Sections could get into action in from two to three days. By 1918, also, the Sections had a good deal more in the way of equipment and they worked on much longer bases, so that it can be realized how much had to be learnt in 1916 about organization and kindred matters as well as about more technical matters.

Some attempt was made in the Third Army to form

Sections to work with stop-watch methods. The French Sections using this method had got some surprisingly good results, and it was thought that some Sections working on these lines would help to fill the gaps in the line between the Sections using the Bull apparatus, but nothing came of these attempts. It was soon found that the period of training necessary for the personnel to acquire the requisite skill was too long. Nevertheless, the sheer simplicity of the stop-watch method always seemed to attract people, as schemes were constantly being put forward for its use.

The "Claude Orthophone," which has already been described in the chapters on Flash Spotting, was tried out for Sound Ranging at this time but quickly discarded. The Germans used a similar device right up till the end of the war, but as their system of Sound Ranging never advanced much beyond the stop-watch method, a sound bearing of this sort would be relatively important.

June 1916 marks the date when Sound Ranging became an accomplished fact. The invention of the Tucker microphone at this time made it possible under favourable conditions to locate any sort of gun with a high degree of accuracy. All that remained to be done was to devise means of getting the same degree of accuracy from records taken when conditions were not too favourable. But after all the Sections had been supplied with these microphones, there was no need for them to apologize for their existence. Not that any Sound Ranger ever did, but even as late as 1918 there were always some people who were incredulous, and prior to the invention of this microphone the Sound Ranger had always to go warily and not make any greater claims than those that could be substantiated to the full. What he hoped to achieve left the sceptics cold.

By August 1916 the Sections had established themselves

as a necessary part of the equipment of the Army, and it was decided to provide one Section for every Corps. In this way it was hoped that every part of the front would be covered. Increasing success meant increased work, and the personnel had to be increased to 36 officers and men—3 officers, 1 instrument repairer, 2 photographers, 5 linemen, 3 telephonists, 2 computers, 1 carpenter, 1 cook, 10 forward observers; batmen, drivers, and transport remained as before.

But the lorry was no longer used to house the apparatus. In many cases it had been found essential to take the apparatus from the lorry and house it in a dugout. Even when this was not essential for safety, it was found very inconvenient to work in the cramped surroundings of the caravan. Even later on, when the Sections were making many and rapid moves, nobody ever suggested that the apparatus should be put back. It was not installing the apparatus that took up the time, but getting the base wired up, and for this job one could not have too much transport, so that it was a distinct advantage when this vehicle was freed for other purposes.

But, unfortunately, the Sound Rangers were not the only people to realize the usefulness of these lorries, and many a Sound Ranger wondered where the advantage was when Survey H.Q. "borrowed" their lorry for an indefinite period, or when they were ordered to "lend" it to a neighbouring Group for "about" a week. Still they dare not protest too much because it was well known that the A.S.C. authorities were of the opinion that these Sections were doing themselves rather well with M.T. Besides that, the more dependent H.Q. was on the Sections for transport, the more eager they would be to fight their battles with those who cast greedy eyes on their lorries!

The winter of 1916–17 found twenty Sections in being

and the whole front covered with the exception of some parts of the Somme area and the Ypres salient, in which areas there were considerable difficulties in working.

In November 1916 an officer from W Section was sent to England to start an experimental Section on Salisbury Plain. There were two very good reasons for starting this new Section. The first was the very obvious difficulties of carrying out research so near the front, and in a Section that was also engaged in "getting on with the war." The other reason was that the artillery were forming an Overseas Artillery School on Salisbury Plain and it was considered very desirable that there should be a Sound Ranging Section there to familiarize the Gunners with the new science and convince them of its efficiency. This Section had the usual "teething" troubles, but very soon justified its existence.

W Section still carried on as an experimental and training Section, but the front was becoming much more active, and so it was decided to start a separate experimental Section at G.H.Q., and 2 officers and 5 other ranks were sent there to form the nucleus. By this time these officers and men were thoroughly acquainted with conditions in the line, both physical and acoustical, so there was no need for their actual presence there. Many ideas could be worked out just as well at G.H.Q. as in the line, and there were now plenty of Sections with experienced officers to give ideas a try out under working conditions. In the same way it was not necessary for either officers or men to receive their first training in the battle area. Many of the officers and men who had been trained by W Section had to establish new Sections in the line with only their own wits to guide them, but by 1917 the officers and men undergoing instruction were going to serve as juniors in established Sections, or, if in new

Sections, they would be serving under experienced officers. Under these circumstances, it was a distinct advantage for both officers and men to receive their preliminary training under the more peaceful conditions at G.H.Q.

This new Section had three different functions: (1) experiments on apparatus and methods, (2) upkeep of existing apparatus and construction of new, (3) instruction. The School of Instruction, although remaining a part of the Experimental Section in theory, was almost a Section on its own. The Experimental Section became a part of the Depot Field Survey Company when it was formed in the spring of 1917, and it was allotted an establishment of 4 officers and 24 other ranks.

The Experimental Section workshop was in charge of an officer with a permanent staff of sixteen to which could be added, at most times, half a dozen reinforcements undergoing instruction as instrument repairers or waiting to be posted to a Section. The equipment consisted of two screw-cutting lathes, five small bench lathes, one milling and one drilling machine. The whole plant was driven by an oil engine, which also worked a lighting plant which supplied light for the Depot and charged up the accumulators required for the instruments. There was a large test-room where ten Sound Ranging instruments could be set up together for testing. The routine work was mainly as follows:

(1) The testing of new apparatus and carrying out necessary alterations. (The first twenty sets were made in Paris. The rest by the Cambridge Scientific Instrument Company in England.)
(2) Repairs and renewals.
(3) Bringing the older instruments up to date.
(4) Construction of a large number of accessories.

(5) Construction of Plotting Boards.
(6) Providing similar services for the Flash Spotting instruments and apparatus, and, in fact, for all branches of Field Survey activity.

This workshop was of the very greatest value. Quite apart from its usefulness in developing experimental apparatus, it must have saved a tremendous amount of material. Things had never to be discarded for want of a spare part. "Send it to the Depot," and it came back as new. Another good influence that it had was in restraining the enthusiastic but incompetent amateur mechanic from "messing about with the apparatus."

The school at its busiest had a staff of 3 officers and 4 N.C.O.s, and usually had 10 to 12 officers and 40 other ranks under training. There were four principal courses. The officers' course lasted seventeen days; the computers' course fourteen days; and the course for forward observers a week. Instrument repairers underwent training in the workshop.

The following abstract of the course for officers gives a good idea of the theoretical and practical work of a Section. It should be understood that all officers taken for training had to possess a fair knowledge of both mathematics and electricity.

ABSTRACT OF SYLLABUS

Object of Sound Ranging, history, etc.
Method of working.
Corrections required (asymptote, wind, temperature).
Calculation of formulae for corrections.
Times of flight.
Film reading.
Shell-wave, Bertrand's Graph, etc.
Types of break on film.
Accuracy of location.

Sound Ranging from 1914 to 1918

Ranging.
German artillery and shells.
Details of apparatus, microphones, etc.
Maps, system of grids, etc.
Preparation of Plotting Board.
Organization and work of Section in action.
Upkeep of lines.
Hostile battery maps.

The mornings were given up to lectures and class work and the afternoons to practical work. Despite this distinction, no more theory was taught than was necessary for a proper understanding of the job.

The computers' course covered much the same ground, but it was treated in a much more elementary fashion. Much of their time was devoted to acquiring speed on the Plotting Board.

Let us return to the Sections in the line. By 1917 twenty Sections were at work and rapidly gaining experience and confidence. In January of this year the first of the conferences that were to do so much to increase the efficiency of the Sections was held at Armentières. Not only were these conferences valuable for disseminating new ideas, but they helped to stimulate competition. But most Sound Rangers will remember these conferences for the chance they gave for making social contacts, and they helped to develop a sense of camaraderie amongst Sound Rangers that was hard to match. If all stories be true, they generally found time to discuss something more bracing than caustics and cosines!

Ranging for our own guns was taken up at this time. As in the case of visual observation, a great part of the problem was to get the results out quickly. To meet this difficulty, various forms of graphs were used. As a rule, Sound Ranging Sections did most of their ranging when circumstances made it difficult to use other methods.

Two examples might be given of the peculiar value of ranging by sound under unusual conditions.

The famous German gun known as the Courrieres Gun was about eleven miles behind the line. There was no guarantee that if a plane went over to range it would be left unmolested to send back the fall of the rounds, so the Sound Rangers were asked to show what they could do. As a rule, a Sound Ranging Section (for technical reasons) cannot locate bursts at more than half that distance, but it can give the line to a very much greater distance. So it was decided to employ three Sound Ranging Sections at the same time to range for the gun selected to try and silence this nuisance. Accordingly, when the gun was fired each Section gave the line to the burst, and from the intersection of these three lines it was possible to locate the fall of the rounds. This unique shoot was eminently successful.

The most useful way to employ sound for ranging was to engage a hostile gun as it was firing. In this way great accuracy could be secured. On one occasion, opposite Bethune, a German 8-inch howitzer had been brought close up to the line in a dense fog. Obviously it was up to mischief and obviously the gun crew must have felt quite safe, but they got the fright of their lives. After firing two rounds, the Sound Rangers spotted them and the Gunners got on to the gun right away and made things so hot for them that they had to clear out. It must have puzzled them considerably as to what had happened.

Sound Ranging was also used for calibrating our guns, but this was not developed as it was not particularly suited to the purpose.

Two other auxiliary services that were developed in 1917–18 were the Wind Sections and Calibration Sections. The Wind Sections grew out of the needs of the Sound

Rangers themselves. Wind and temperature affect the rate of expansion of the sound-wave and its shape. This made it necessary to compensate the observed time intervals on the films by accurately noting the conditions in the atmosphere in respect of wind and temperature, and deriving the necessary velocity corrections. The Army Meteorological Sections (Meteor) provided some of this information, but this proved to be too general for Sound Ranging purposes. Experiments were carried out by the Experimental Section on Salisbury Plain as to the best way of getting this essential data, and in consequence of these experiments it was decided to establish "Wind" Sections along the front. These Sections were not in the line but close behind, and they worked by exploding a bomb in the centre of a series of concentric circles of microphones. As the point where the explosion occurred was known, the difference between the time when the sound should have reached the microphone and the time when it actually did so gave the exact measure of the corrections that were necessary for wind and temperature at that time.

These Sections did much to improve Sound Ranging, but when movement began in 1918 they were too slow and costly to install to justify their continuance. But by this time rules had been established for estimating the effective wind and temperature from data supplied by Meteor. So in lieu of Sections, an officer and 6 men were attached to Meteor in each Army, and these men worked out and supplied the necessary corrections for the Sections.

Little need be said about the Calibration Sections, as screen calibration was not properly a function of the Survey Battalions. It was only because Sound Ranging apparatus was used, and that officers and men trained in

Sound Ranging computation were required to use it that it was found most convenient to place them under the administrative control of the Field Survey Battalions. In other respects the Field Survey Battalions had nothing to do with their working, although it was always of technical interest to Sound Rangers, as it was the Experimental Section on Salisbury Plain which had developed the system, and all the resources of the Experimental Section at G.H.Q. were at their disposal.

The Battle of Cambrai finally disposed of the idea that Sound Ranging was in the nature of a scientific toy. Apart from the services rendered prior to the attack, H Section got into action fifty-six hours after zero in country that had previously been in enemy hands, and showed that Sections given adequate support could get forward and into action just as fast as the heavy artillery. Unfortunately, it was not long before they had the experience of having to get back nearly as quickly, but even this experience was of value, as it was accomplished without any loss of secret or valuable material. This experience showed that Sound Ranging had definitely become an essential part of the equipment of an army. It could no longer be classed as a weapon for trench warfare only, and in consequence in the months that followed much time was devoted to studying the best methods of getting in and out of action.

About this time the War Office ordered the formation of twelve new Sections over and above those required in France. Consequently thirty-four in all were formed, of which two went to Salonika, two to Egypt, and one to Italy. This left twenty-nine Sections in France during the winter of 1917–18, and this was the greatest number in existence on the Western front at any time. All these Sections were not in the line at the same time, as, with these numbers, it was possible to bring some of them out for a badly needed rest. It should be remembered that some of these officers and men had been working continuously in the battle area since early in 1916, so that the provision of some form of relief came none too soon.

A new establishment for the Sound Ranging Sections was authorized early in 1918, when the Field Survey Companies became Battalions. The strength now authorized for a Section was 4 officers and 39 other ranks—the tradesmen being 2 instrument repairers, 3 photographers, 5 linemen, 3 telephonists, 6 computers, 1 carpenter, and 10 forward observers. This brought up the total strength to 43 compared with the original number of 6. But the numbers were still inadequate if the Sections were to be utilized to the full, and they only represented what was necessary to carry on, not what was desirable.

As in the case of the Observation Groups, a "Higher Establishment" was approved when the advance into Germany was begun. This gave 4 officers and 63 other ranks and represented—approximately—what was considered necessary for efficiency. Of the 63 other ranks, 52 were tradesmen: 6 computers, 8 Sound Ranging operators (a new term for instrument repairers), 12 forward observers, 25 linemen, and 1 carpenter. The increase in linemen will be noticed, and it will give the reader some conception of the difficulties that the Sections faced in keeping in action when in the line.

The German attacks in 1918 raised anew the questions of mobility. The experiences of the Sections varied a good deal, but even when the Sections had no time to do anything but "hop it," no important instruments or documents were lost, although many treasured souvenirs and gadgets had to be abandoned. The Sound Rangers in the Fifth Army joined their comrades from other branches of the Survey to form a goodly part of Carey's Force, and they played a worthy part in holding up the advance and also paid the cost in casualties. This will be told more fully elsewhere, but when they had done their part here they were reassembled and re-equipped, and as the line settled down they went back into action.

In some other parts of the line the Sections had much the same experience without having to take a hand in the actual fighting. But at other places they managed to fall back—what shall we say—"ranging." One Section distinguished itself on the Ypres salient by retiring 7,000 yards and only being out of action for five hours. This, of course, was only achieved by having another base already wired to fall back upon; nevertheless, it was a very noteworthy achievement.

When the advance began, the Sections all knew what would be expected of them, and by then most of them had had some experience of moving warfare to guide them. In addition the school had worked out something in the nature of a "drill" which most Sections had practised. Consequently, they all made as good a showing as circumstances allowed. These circumstances were that those who were responsible for tactical control had different and sometimes divergent views as to what Sound Rangers could do and as to how they should do it. One school of thought was all for "parking" them until the advance was stopped, but another—more adventurous, perhaps—left it to the O.C. the Field Survey Battalion to show what he could do. When this was the case the Sections played a real and important rôle in the advance.

In 1914 Sound Ranging was unknown. In August 1918 the Battle of Amiens was fought and then, and in the days that followed, Sound Ranging proved its worth. What happened then may be best described in the words of an official report. "German batteries had been moved back some eight days before owing to a minor Australian attack. The weather in the interval was misty, but favourable for Sound Ranging, and the Sections obtained a number of locations unconfirmed by any other source of information. These were engaged by our batteries on the day of the attack, and an examination of the ground afterwards showed how effective in every case the counter battery work had been. Sections were all established on a new line two days after the attack. As we pushed forward still further, they were brought up again and were in action in a third position five days after the first attack."

"This was the first time anything like this had been done on a large scale, and it was repeated many times in the ensuing months. It was found that in this kind of warfare, where the enemy put up a fight in one line after another, Sections could always be got into action in less time than it took to bring up heavy batteries and sufficient ammunition to make the next attack, and the number of results obtained amply repaid the work involved."

8

A SOUND RANGING SECTION IN THE LINE

THE Section whose experiences have provided the material for this chapter can claim a special qualification to represent Sound Ranging Sections as a whole, because it was formed in those early days when only one Section was allotted to each Army. Its birthplace was Courcelles au Bois and its first microphone base—4 kilometres long—lay south of Hebuterne and opposite Serre of ill fame in the German lines. The Section came into action early in 1916 with Driancourt microphones, which were carbon microphones, essentially, with diaphragm of wood about a foot in diameter. Each morning they required to be stimulated by smart taps with a mallet on their protective boxes. The shell-wave of a gun disturbed them for such a long time that the gun report was not distinguishable. The Driancourt was replaced after a few months and the base was extended to 7 kilometres.

The Section's H.Q. was first established in a farm-house in the centre of Courcelles au Bois, but the enemy soon put incendiary shells into it and burnt it down. This necessitated a move to a more open position at the north edge of the village. The computing hut, the officers' tents, and the men's huts were set up in an orchard with a 6-inch howitzer battery as a close and noisy neighbour. A similar road ran along the north side of the orchard, and by digging into the bank and building up cover with tree trunks, expanded metal, sandbags, and earth, a splinter-proof shelter of unusual proportions was built to house a clumsy lorry in which all the precious Sound

Drawn by P. S. Willats, October 1918

TINA O.P.

This shows the entrance to a typical ground O.P. It was originally a German
gun pit

Ranging apparatus was arranged. In the cramped interior of the lorry an instrument man attended to the recording apparatus and a photographer developed the celluloid film by hand. The French origin of the apparatus was evident in many particulars of design, but in none was it so exhausting of British patience as in the finicky little terminal screws of the six-string Einthoven galvanometer.

In keeping with the permanence of the great "dugout" was the air line which diverged in two pole routes known as the "right and left six-ways." From the terminal poles low-resistance cable lines radiated to the microphones, taking whatever cover was available. Most line troubles occurred in the cable, as a high insulation resistance had to be maintained.

It was at Hebuterne that the Section tried the experiment of burying armoured cable deep in the ground in the hope of eliminating line troubles once and for all. It was forlorn hope. One of the lines was dug in by a Battalion of infantry in a single night. The cable was laid and the trench filled in before dawn, but on being tested there was no circuit. It was assumed that the cable had been cut by a spade, but it was never proved, for the cable probably still lies deep in the ground.

The armoured cable lines which survived the burying were still cut by shells. The job of repairing them was long and heart-rending, particularly in a lively locality in the cold days which were experienced in the winter of 1916–17.

Line troubles were not all due to enemy action. In this area communication trenches became a hopeless tangle of wire, and, in the confusion, licence was given to Signals and artillery linemen to cut out line on which they could get no reply when they tapped it with a D3 telephone. Some linemen took liberties. For example, a line was to be laid to Colincamps windmill, which was a special Observation Post. The route, starting from one of the air-line poles, was short and crossed open ground covered with long brown grass. The linemen quickly reeled out the cable, and having reached the mill tested it at once. To their surprise the line was dead. Not two hundred yards from the mill they found the line cut by pliers, and yet nobody had been seen. Nobody was in sight now, neither could any trace of the wire be found. They searched the ground back to the air-line pole and there found another clear cut by pliers. As they were returning to H.Q., they noticed a new air-line supported on bean sticks. Part of their new cable had been used as guys for the sticks!

The microphone lines ended in a rough box-like structure made of sticks and wire netting threaded with hessian strips. This was the approved form of wind-screening for the hot-wire microphone. It was as simple and homely as the microphone itself. The screen served the additional purpose of concealing the microphone, although failure in this respect was recorded of the very workmanlike screens put up by a neighbouring Section at Ovillers la Boisselle. Australian troops occupied this front and they were inquisitive. They carried away the wire-netting and the oil drum used for the microphone. In self-defence the O.C. Section indented on "Maps" for six notices, to announce at each microphone—"Danger 3,000 volts."

The Sections' first Observation Post lay under a hedge corner just south of Ligny Farm, facing Serre. It satisfied the first requirement of Sound Ranging Observation Posts in being so far forward that the sound of any enemy gun in the sector reached it a few seconds before the nearest microphone. It was not well placed, however, for seeing the burst of shells other than those in a limited area of the forward trench system. The Observation Post was approached over a crest from Colincamps by way of a communication trench which, in the winter of 1916, was often nearly knee deep in water. It was a perilous matter to leave the trench, for the slope was frequently swept with premature shrapnel from our own field guns, whose shells just cleared the crest with an excruciating din.

Under the splinter-proof head cover of the Post the observer looked out through a long horizontal opening at ground-level. There was a view down a slope to the front lines, which were marked by groups of blasted tree stumps graced with the names of Matthew, Mark, Luke, and John copses. On the opposite hill stood other stumps showing where Serre once stood.

In addition to the field telephone and the switch for starting the apparatus in the distant H.Q. lorry the Observation Post had an outline map with reference grid, on which was superimposed a series of radiating lines. These marked out the enemy gun field into five zones of 20° arc, and the observer was expected to distinguish the direction of a gun well enough to place it in one of the zones. A code was also in use for the rapid and secret communication of all the observations.

A dozen or more earth steps led from the Post down to the dugout. The walls of the staircase and dugout were supported by sheets of expanded metal, and a spare sheet nailed to a wooden frame formed a bed. A second staircase leading into a trench served both as an emergency exit and a ventilation shaft. The Section had not long been in action when the complement of forward observers was increased, and it became possible to establish alternative Observation Posts at Hebuterne and Auchonvillers. It had been recognized that one Observation Post, which, of necessity, had to be on or below ground, was not capable of providing complete information over the whole front covered by the microphone base. It had been found, too, that whilst the Section was not seriously disabled by losing one or two of the six microphone lines, it was put out of action by the loss of the single Observation Post line.

Disaster sometimes came to the Sound Ranging line system, particularly at the opening of an offensive, and to meet such an emergency the whole section was organized to form line-repairing parties. Whilst duty of this kind came only in arduous bursts, the forward observers were required to be continuously watchful and alert. The computers worked in spasms according to the amount of enemy artillery activity and the atmospheric conditions. Westerly winds, as a rule, lifted the sound of the guns into the air away from the microphones and nothing could be recorded. In such periods of inactivity the Section's Computing Officer found solace, between frequent reviving sips of his national spirits, in making working heliographs, cameras, and similar apparatus with bits of wire and cigarette tins. The Forward Observing Officer found time, also, in the intervals between his wanderings on the front to examine his collection of shell fragments and make up his book of "identifications." This was a subsidiary line of activity which began with a course on German Artillery at G.H.Q. and an invitation to officers, so well placed for correlating information as the Sound Ranging Forward Observing Officers, to collect dud shells or fragments for the purpose of identifying or confirming the calibre and type of enemy ordnance.

When the weather became favourable the observers saw to it that not a gun was missed, and the computers were then so hard pressed that the O.C. and the Forward

Observing Officer had to assist them. The computing was then organized in watches throughout the day and night, and the responsibility for assessing the value of a location and for reporting locations to Counter Battery rested with an officer in each watch.

Often at the end of a busy day artillery activity would die down, leaving the Computing Officer still eager, but lacking new film to work on. Some computers would firmly burn the string of old records hanging dry from the "clothes line" over the stove. Others felt the lure of looking back on the day's score and turning over the records again in the hope of increasing it. "Beach-combing" accused many an innocent enemy battery whose only misfortune was that its position was already known.

In the early months of 1917 the Section located a number of explosions in the villages far behind the German lines. They were reported as heavy howitzers, but as being doubtful identifications, because no shell was associated with them. It was not suspected at the time the secrets that would have been revealed if these observations could have been thoroughly investigated, for the cleverly arranged withdrawal of the enemy from a front which appeared immovable was at hand.

One evening the Computing Officer put aside a special film.

"Here," he said, drawing attention to it, "is a clear record of a gun and a shell burst—nothing else on the film."

Moving over to the Plotting Board he continued, "Now, just to check my work, will somebody else read the time intervals on the film?"

As the figures were read out he laid the weighted strings, running through the holes in the board, on the scales at the edge. When all the strings were laid, they intersected neatly at a point.

"K.18 and—let me see—why, that's well inside the German lines. He is firing on his own positions!"

"Exactly!" said the Computing Officer.

The enemy activity had died down that evening, and at a late hour the officer on watch was startled by a telephone call.

"Is that the Gun Sound Rangers?"

"Yes."

"Hang on, General —— wants to speak to you."

There was a long pause, then came the General.

"Have you noticed anything out of the ordinary in your sound locations?" he asked after a few preliminaries.

"No, nothing very extraordinary, sir—oh, one thing, perhaps, we located a gun this evening that put a shell into Louviere Farm, well inside its own lines."

The General apparently had other information of an unusual sort. He decided that the enemy had begun to withdraw, and he decided also to harass him. He attacked next day at Bucquoy, and, though the enemy successfully resisted his harassing, the great withdrawal had begun and the Section had reached a turning-point in its career.

Faced with the necessity for moving forward into action rapidly, the Section ruefully regarded the firmness of its roots after its long undisturbed growth. Its younger sister Section had hardly established itself by then, and it was decided to pool the resources of both Sections to push the new one forward quickly. The first estimate of the depth of the withdrawal was very modest, for the position for the new H.Q. was chosen in a very deep dugout which formed only part of an elaborate system of shafts and galleries in the one-time village of Beaucourt, only a mile on the German side of the old front. It was a nightmare position. It was approached over shell-torn ground, powdered and holed by explosion, and drenched in chemicals. Old shells and masses of rusty barbed wire littered the way. Corpses, withering inside complete uniform and equipment, remained where they fell, and the blackening remains of a German lay at the very mouth of the dugout amongst the blackened and splintered tree stumps. The Sound Ranging instruments had been brought into place in the dugout when the enemy withdrawal continued and rendered Beaucourt useless as a H.Q.

The systematic and complete wreckage of all buildings, the destruction of trees, and the obstructions on the roads in the evacuated territory produced only minor discomforts in comparison with the desolation and pollution of the battle areas, and the Sections advanced with great relief over green, firm, clean ground to Ervillers. Here they established an H.Q. under the lee of the stump of a house wall near an enormous pile of masonry which once stood in orderly shape as a church.

There had now been time for the old Section to uproot itself and prepare to advance, and the new Section was soon left at Ervillers to its own devices. The old Section chose Velu to the south as a new H.Q.; the microphone base covered the section of the Hindenburg line between Havrincourt and Mœuvres.

For the first time in Sound Ranging history the problems of moving quickly into action were to be faced. Rapid methods of line installation were discussed and tried out. Air line was abandoned and line parties assisted by G.S. waggons ran out cables, several at a time, with great speed to roughly located microphone positions. Both the Survey and the cable routes were made good later. No time was wasted in preparing special Posts at the Observa-

tion Posts. Existing holes covered with a piece of corrugated iron served well enough in this new country where
the war had lost its old intensity.

The bold wooded hill called Bourlon Wood dominated
the view over the enemy lines, and on a clear day Cambrai's
chimneys and spires could be seen to the right of the hill.
At Velu the station buildings remained intact, although
all rails and sleepers had been removed by the enemy
before retiring. The station was already occupied when
the Section officers came to look for a suitable H.Q., and
the O.C. refused even a rough earthwork inside the
château gates on the ground that anything undamaged
was a potential booby-trap. He was right as regards the
station, for one day it went sky-high, taking its Australian
occupants with it. H.Q. came to be housed finally at the
corner of Velu Wood in Armstrong huts of framed
canvas. The instrument lorry had been abandoned for
ever.

The Section associated Velu with summer days and
warm nights, improvised hammocks amongst the trees,
occasional hates by the enemy artillery, and daily drumfire
at Bullecourt to the north.

It was at Velu that a 6o-pounder Battery Commander
enlisted the services of the Section to calibrate his guns,
despite the warning he was given as to the standard of
accuracy to be expected. The usual wire screens were
made and erected on rising ground in front of the guns,
and lines were run out to them from the Sound Ranging
recording apparatus, which was arranged to run at high
speed. Only two or three shells had been fired on the day
appointed for the measurement when a German 8-inch
howitzer began retaliation with deadly accuracy, but
with such steady regularity that it was possible to complete the calibration programme by dodging in and out

of cover and returning round for round. The satisfaction was the less on our side, because the German was only receiving "duds"—the safety pins having been left in the fuses to avoid the risk of bursting at the screens.

A few weeks after the Section had established itself at Velu a 12-inch howitzer battery was brought into the wood and rumours spread that this front was to be the scene of a big attack. If the battery came into action at all, it could not have been for more than a day or two and then it disappeared. Soon after there came the news that the Third Army was extending southwards, and the Section after handing over its base and H.Q. to new Sound Rangers travelled by train behind the line to the north, arriving at the new Fifth Army H.Q. at the Château of Proven, not far from Poperinghe.

The Section proceeded to the front charged with the task of bridging the Ypres salient with a microphone line for the first time. The salient had been widened by this time by the capture of the Messines ridge. The microphones followed the line of the canal and the new H.Q. was shared with a Second Army Section, whose base covered the southern flank of the salient, at a farm which came to be known as Tank Farm as it was chosen as a rendezvous for the Tanks which opened the impending Third Battle of Ypres. The apparatus was housed in strong concrete shelters built behind the walls of a barn. Once more the Section faced the difficulties of Sound Ranging on a battle front where the now usual sledge-hammer methods of preparation were in progress. Never had the maintenance of line, particularly Observation Post lines, appeared so hopeless. The north Observations Post was at La Brigue, in the ruin of a small house which had been fortified inside with thick walls and a roof of concrete. An attempt was made at this Post to use short-wave wireless in order to overcome the difficulty of maintaining a line. The apparatus, which was designed for trench use, clipped on to a bayonet stuck in the ground, and the aerial consisted of a loop of four light tubes. The south Observation Post was settled at Hellfire Corner, where the Menin Road crossed the railway cutting south-east of Ypres. The Germans used to fire straight down the cutting, but it was judged that the stout masonry of the bridge where it sprang from the south embankment would make good shelter. The bridge was assailed, however, by large calibre, high-velocity shells, which rocked the Observation Post as if it were floating on a rough sea, and the observers preferred to move a few hundred yards to a flank, although in that position they had only a sheet of corrugated iron to be under.

The time chosen for relief was in the half-light before the dawn, which in those summer days was only a few hours after midnight. At that time the enemy activity was at its ebb, and the observers, following the road to Shrapnel Corner—of ill fame—then ploughed a way across shell-churned country, past a great earthwork in the embankment of Zillebeke Lake, housing a dressing station outside which bodies lay ready for removal. At the top of the ridge they settled down with telephone and switch in a forlorn hope of doing something useful under the bombardment which would surely follow as the day wore on and the gas which would come with the night.

In the stress of these conditions a new idea in Observation Posts was evolved, and it brought a return of activity to the Section robot at a critical time. The new Observation Post was established on top of a big gun pit quite near to H.Q. and well *behind* the line of microphones. The equipment was similar to that used in the forward Observation Post, and there was an additional switch which operated a vane on the apparatus capable of throwing a distinguishing mark on the film. The observer's plan of action was to wait until he heard regular firing, then, judging the interval between rounds, he pressed his switch at a suitable moment. When he had started the apparatus, he pressed the second switch on hearing the gun, so marking the film and giving the computer the same help in identifying the position of the gun "breaks" as when working in a forward Observation Post.

In the first twenty days in which the new Observation Post was used, a hundred and eighty different guns were located, including over a score on each of four favourable days.

It appeared, indeed, to show advantages over the forward Observation Post, for, not only was there greater freedom of observation over the greater part of the shelled areas and no trouble with lines, but high-velocity guns shooting on the "backblocks" were more readily recognized. Unfortunately, the wireless experiment at La Brique came to naught, and the novel arrangement of a forward Observation Post to deal with shooting on trench areas together with a back Observation Post to deal with other shelling was not tried out.

The opening of the Third Battle of Ypres on July 31, 1917, was a fresh milestone in the Section's career. The line system was so mutilated that the whole Section was organized into line-repairing parties. A photographer was killed and an officer wounded on the lines. With renewed attacks, ground was gained slowly from the enemy at appalling cost and the Section followed up, first to a H.Q. in the wall of Ypres and then into the mud on the Pilken ridge.

When the tremendous offensive had spent itself at Passchendaele, with little of its objective achieved, the

Sound Ranging in the Line

Section again moved south with the Fifth Army to St. Quentin and took over a long irregular base from a French Section de Reperage, samples of whose smoke trace records were accepted as the most convenient form of souvenir.

A peculiar combination of circumstances now contributed to make the next few months a period of very interesting and varied experiences. In the first place, Sound Rangers were now being valued by the artillery and the staff at something approaching their real value, and an increased establishment had been allowed. Then the enemy was quietly staging at this very point his first and biggest and most successful offensive, and his artillery activity was very conservative. Finally, the weather was favourable, and the French Section had left an earth-return line system covering an unusually large area.

All this encouraged new Sound Ranging exploits. An opportunity occurred at the outset to try to use earthed lines with the hot-wire microphone. The records were not so free from disturbance as those obtained with the usual metallic circuits, but they were useful enough to produce good locations and to make it unnecessary to go to the trouble of putting down a new line system.

The Section had until now found the difficulties of maintaining itself and carrying on the work of location such that it had not been able to deal with more than occasional calls for ranging. Now, the Counter Battery demand for ranging was insistent.

The first shoot had a sad sequel The efficiency of the enemy anti-aircraft guns on the front at St. Quentin was obvious, and a Sound Ranging location of one of these guns on the southern outskirts of the town was followed immediately by a call for a shoot, which was duly arranged.

The first round fell so far to the right as to be beyond the compass of the ranging curves, and after suggestions—made as tactfully as the circumstances would allow—the Battery Commander swung his gun over in good round measure. The second round fell now, indeterminately, far to the left, and the Battery Commander thereupon severed relations with the Sound Rangers.

A report on the situation to the Counter Battery Staff Officer put him in a state of alarm. The very unity of the Allies was at stake, he said, by our putting so much as a single round into St. Quentin. The French had forbidden it. This incident brought a G.O.C. Heavy Artillery in a critical and unfriendly mood to see the new authority which challenged the accuracy of shooting of his batteries and a G.O.C. Royal Artillery of greater understanding who came with praises and good humour.

By way of harassing the enemy without actually wrecking St. Quentin, our artillery kept up a fire on the approaches. The Section was notified one dark night of an impending shoot on a bridge on the far side of the town. The Battery Commander declined assistance on the ground that he had several hundred rounds to put over in a given time, which was all too short, and he could not begin making corrections! The Sound Rangers' records showed plainly that the rounds were all falling several hundred yards short of the bridge. "All right, thank you very much," said the Battery Commander, and did nothing about it, as the next series of locations showed. Once more the results were passed through to the battery, and then, as the shoot had gone well as to time, the Battery Commander offered to put over his last two rounds to the directions of the Sound Rangers. They reported "target" and next day an air photo was taken. It showed a beautiful cluster of shell holes at a mean position several hundred yards short of the bridge, and one hole at the end of the bridge!

The forward observers, weary of fruitless waiting and stirred by chance aeroplane bombs which fell near them one night out of our own aircraft, began to offer bombs for location. A computer equally weary of waiting plotted them. They were included for general information in the usual reports, and were received coldly and without interest.

It was on this front that the Section had a Flying Corps wireless operator attached for duty. He was equipped with an experimental direction-finding aerial. There had been co-operation with wireless intercepting stations a year earlier at Courcelles, when the Germans first succeeded in establishing wireless communication from the ground to an aircraft as well as from the aircraft to the ground. This development required the enemy to set up ground stations which were connected by land line to a group of batteries, and through these stations messages passed both ways. The primary object of the co-operation of Sound Rangers with direction-finding wireless Posts was the location of these important ground stations and the batteries working through them. Counter Battery also had an interest in identifying the battery call signal with a particular battery for the purpose of retaliation.

Opposite St. Quentin the Section had the idea of making its own uses of the wireless co-operation. A switch for starting the Sound Ranging apparatus was fitted in the wireless cabin. One of the characteristics by which artillery messages were recognized was the concluding signal for the battery to fire. If the messages were picked up on bearings covered by the Sound Ranging base, the wireless operator started the apparatus a little time after the "fire" signal had been received. On one memorable occasion a series of sound records were obtained in this way, and before the enemy battery had concluded its shoot Counter Battery had engaged it. It was a particularly gratifying thought, as the heavies boomed out, that the German observer had unwittingly served a British Sound Ranging Section so well!

Whilst adding to its technical experience, the Section was busily preparing for the threatened German attack, which is described in other chapters of this book. A few days before the attack opened, one of those Sound Ranging functions, called Conferences, was held at Hautecloque, near St. Pol. Few, if any, of the conferring officers up to this time held even field rank. These conferences of junior officers from all parts of the front must be unique in the history of the Army. Papers were discussed in full session, but the comparison of experiences in personal conversation was perhaps of equal value in stimulating the growth of Sound Ranging efficiency.

Three days only remained before the tide of war again began its sweep right up to the old lines, which seemed to have been deserted for ever. Before the tide was stemmed the Section had lost 30 per cent of its numbers as casualties.

Months passed before the Fifth Army remnants came into action again in a new Army. The old section reassembled, not only in name, but with the one remaining officer and the survivors of the retreat. It advanced upon the retiring enemy and received its most cruel blow near the Mormal Forest, where a shell killed six of the men who had served the Section from its earliest days. Its glorious career ended in Germany when the war was done and Sound Ranging was used no more.

P. ROTHWELL

BOOK II

". . . in war, as Napoleon said and Foch endorsed,
'It is the man, not men, who counts.'"

LIDDELL HART

9

AT WORK AND AT PLAY

ANYONE who attempts to write about life in the Groups and Sections will find that two things stand out clearly. One is that there is very little that could be called "typical" except their extreme individuality. The other is that the nature of the country in which the different Groups worked varied so greatly that it is not possible to recreate any setting that would be familiar to all.

Taking the second point first, one found that on the Ypres front conditions were as unsuited for Flash Spotting as could be. There is no need to describe this country in detail. It is enough to say that it was dead flat, battle scarred, and water-logged. The difficulty of finding any point where one could get a view over the enemy lines was immense, and of course to erect any sort of tower was to draw the attention of every enemy gun within range (not to mention the blasphemy of all the troops in the neighbourhood). Billeting was also a great difficulty under these circumstances, because shelter that might have been made passable for temporary occupation was not suitable for the men of the Groups, who had to spend all their time, except when on leave, in the area. On the other hand, under other conditions, this sector would have been well suited for Sound Ranging, but, as things were, Sound Ranging could only be carried on with the greatest difficulty. Finding a dry spot to house the instruments, getting a habitable spot for a site for an Observation Post, and, above all, keeping the microphone lines working were never-ending worries on this front.

Coming further south, the country still remained flat,

but it had not been fought over to the same extent, and it was always possible to find buildings or other objects that provided excellent Posts. In addition, the French population were to be found quite close to the line, and, as they were only too glad to take in "lodgers," the men at the Posts and with the Sound Ranging Sections could always find a certain amount of comfort and some of the amenities of civilization. Sound Ranging could be carried on in this area without any special disadvantages.

These were the conditions as far south as Lens, and then they began to deteriorate again. From Lens to Arras there were few buildings suitable for Survey Posts, but the ground-level was more broken and no difficulty was found in getting suitable sites for Posts. Billeting accommodation varied in this area, but, whether the billets were in houses or in dugouts, they were fairly good of their sort. Sound Ranging was on much the same footing.

From Arras to the southern end of the British Army front was a stretch of rolling country, but this was what was known as the devastated area, where living conditions were primitive. Ground Posts were almost universal in this area, and nearly all living accommodation was below ground. On the whole, Sound Ranging Sections did not find conditions too bad, although they varied a good deal from place to place. It was not difficult to find sites for Posts in this area, but it was more difficult to find Posts that would cover more than a limited section of the front.

In Italy things were quite different again. The operations were commenced in the Montello district. When the British Army was on the Montello front the Observation Posts were excellently situated, and billets were also of the best, as the country had hardly been touched and was well supplied with villages, shops, cafés, etc.

At Work and at Play

When, in the spring, the British Army moved to the Asiago Plateau, things were very different. There the Observation Posts were on the top of the mountains about 5,000 feet high, and they looked down on the plateau which was occupied by the Austrians. The view from these Observation Posts was really wonderful. Here, of course, there were no billets, and the Survey men had to improvise their own camps and billets.

On this front the Sound Rangers met with some difficulties that were almost unknown elsewhere. One difficulty was caused by the sound echoing round the mountains. As they could not shift the mountains, they had to make the best of that. But the other difficulty was due to the thunderstorms burning out the microphones. For this, after much trouble, they managed to devise a remedy.

So that it can be seen that if one tries to describe, say, a billet, the description must be looked upon as only a sample of the conditions, and not as typical.

The underground type of accommodation was much the same everywhere. A hole in the ground may be well suited to moles, but for human beings it could never have been anything else than a makeshift. The degrees of comfort that existed in different dugouts depended to a certain extent on the "forthcomingness" of the local R.E. dump, but more, perhaps, on the "scrounging" abilities of the men themselves. As these billets were only changed at long intervals, the men had more incentive to make them habitable than men of other units who were here to-day and gone to-morrow, and on the whole, these dugout dwellings were as comfortable specimens of their kind as were to be found. But if anyone "knew of a better hole," you could bet your boots the Survey men would find it out.

Although one would imagine that the men would have been more comfortable when housed in billets with civilians, they, themselves, always chose to live in semi-ruined houses if such were available. Sometimes they would get an empty château for themselves, but as a rule they were satisfied with something much less pretentious. A good deal of ingenuity was often used in rendering habitable a house that seemed to be hopeless as a dwelling, because practically everything used in these reconstructions had to be picked up from discarded material. It was not possible to get building materials from the R.E.s, except in very limited quantities, for this work.

At one Post, where the men were billeted a very long way from their work, they determined to adapt a ruined estaminet which was situated conveniently for themselves and another Post. It was not in too bad condition except for the fact that there was no roof, so they set about scouring the country for discarded tarpaulins, odd sheets of corrugated iron, etc., and set to work. When the job was finished, they felt that it did them credit, and they settled in with much satisfaction. As time went on, they executed sundry other repairs until the property was what a house agent would describe as a "desirable villa residence with a distinctive character of its own."

Unfortunately, they had reckoned without mine host. It appeared that the proprietor of the estaminet had been living in a village about three-quarters of a mile away, and that he had been watching operations with considerable interest because, once reconstruction had reached a stage when it was safe for him to return without the risk of getting rheumatics, he came back and claimed possession. Every effort was made to prevent eviction, but nothing could be done, and the Post had to start all over again to fix up a home. But it is credibly reported that some of them were sufficiently forgiving to patronize the estaminet under the new management!

But the men were not always as unfortunate as that, and the experiences of the men at "Gladys" Post are a pretty fair sample of how they could look after themselves.

No. 11 Group was in process of formation, and a small party set off "hiking" from La Targette in charge of a Corporal. Their objective was St. Laurent Blangy, a suburb of Arras, and their task to start off a new Post.

The site for the Post had been chosen previously, so their first task was to fix up a billet. It was not long since this area had been in German hands, and the best available accommodation for a few days was a borrowed tarpaulin fixed against a lone brick wall. From there they moved into a reinforced concrete Nissen hut, which was discovered by some adventurous souls on the prowl.

But this was hardly up to Survey standards, so they kept their eyes open for something more suitable. In the whole of the suburb only one room remained intact, and this was occupied by some officers. A watch was set, and when these officers moved on the Survey men moved in *toute suite*.

As may be imagined, this was rather a remarkable room. Once upon a time it had formed part of the out-buildings of the château, but as it had been reinforced time after time, it had become a miniature fortress on its own. The roof was 2 feet thick and the walls 1½ feet through. On one side it was protected by kerbstones piled to the roof and 3 feet thick. The room measured 40 feet by 25 feet and was in two parts, one of which was reserved for cooking. Round the walls were wire cots arranged in two tiers, and twice the number could have been accommodated with ease.

To add to the amenities, they managed to "find" a

stove. Photos from home adorned the walls, and a library
of about a hundred books gave an "air" to the scene, as
well as providing solace for the mind. Water was laid on.
Truth compels one to admit that the tap was 50 yards
distant, but this was not excessive for a French château.

The grounds were well wooded, and provided pleasant
shade in warm weather, and three ornamental lakes
provided hygienic, cultural, and sporting facilities. Bathing
was indulged in daily, and a punt, with half a bell tent as
a sail, provided an outlet for the sporting spirit. Those
who preferred more intellectual amusements could study
the gold fish in the pond, but, unfortunately, a bomb put
an end to the gold fish, although it spared the intellectuals.

As can be imagined, other people cast covetous eyes
on this "home away from home," and "orders" were
frequently received by them to the effect that they had
to find what has come to be known as "alternative
accommodation." But the people who tried this on (not
French civilians in this case) did not know the stuff that
Survey men were made of. Getting tired of these constant
"orders," the men appealed to Battalion H.Q., who took
the matter up with Army H.Q., and after that they were
left unmolested.

Unfortunately, they were not so successful with the
Germans, and when the enemy approached the garden
gate—as it were—they deemed it inexpedient to argue,
and got out. The Germans never actually got near enough
to leave their cards, but the men never saw the happy
home again.

With all these amenities at their disposal, it was not
to be expected that men in such a billet would waste
their time tending the garden, but some of the billets
were brightened up in this way. In his letters home one
officer makes several references to the fact that his dugout

is enlivened by flowers of his own growing. But one Post had no need to raise vegetables, as one of the observers was an expert on the use of common weeds as table delicacies, so they never suffered for the lack of something to help down the bully beef.

Before leaving the subject of billets, reference must be made to exploits of a Sergeant. This Sergeant was neither a Flash Spotter nor a Sound Ranger, and there is no need to indicate the particular branch of the Survey to which he belonged, but it was in Italy, and the Section was established in a good-sized country-house which boasted a billiard-table which the men were allowed to use in the evening. The men had to billet themselves, and this enterprising Sergeant billeted himself at the castello of an elderly lady of title. He was a man of good standing and manners, and, in due course, it came about that he had dinner with his hostess in the evenings. One night a very high officer in the Italian Army came to dinner, and a few days afterwards a discreet inquiry came from Intelligence as to who the Sergeant was, and in what circumstances it came about that he dined with General —— at —— on such and such a date.

This same Sergeant had the effrontery to come on parade one day with an open umbrella! It sounds incredible, but it is a fact! True, the parade was to march away for demobilization, and he explained that, as he had a week's journey in a horse-box in front of him, he saw no reason for starting off wet and arriving home ill, which was so eminently sensible that he got away with it!

Although the men had to be changed about at times, it was usual for them to stay at one Post or with one Section for quite a long time. In this way they all got very intimate with one another, and lived a real communal life. For the most part they were men who could make their own amusements by reading, writing, sketching, etc., but some of them spent much of their spare time in tramping about the country and visiting their pals at other Posts. They also used to put in week-ends with one another, although this was not officially recognized, and probably was not known to the Group officers.

When there was a Y.M.C.A. hut close at hand, the short services and the facilities for recreation were much appreciated. There was nothing like a sing-song now and then for driving away dull care. One of the Survey men, who used to officiate at the piano in one of these huts, was very much flattered by the close attention the Portuguese soldiers—who were in that area—gave to his playing. As soon as he opened up the front of the piano—so as to make plenty of noise—the "Ports" used to crowd round so that he had barely room to play. But, alas, he discovered it was the actions of the hammers in the piano that interested them, not his exquisite technique.

After these sing-songs it was usual to wind up by playing *God save the King* and the *Marseillaise*. The first time the Portuguese appeared in the hut the pianist was very much embarrassed, as he had not the haziest idea of the Portuguese National Anthem. But he remembered a waltz—*Sobre las Olas*—which happened to be by a Portuguese composer, and tried that. It was an instantaneous success, and, thereafter, was adopted as the Portuguese National Anthem.

Every officers' mess that could boast of a pianist in their company used to beg, borrow, or—what shall we say—"scrounge" a piano. The chief claim to fame of one officer was that he never had to leave his piano behind, and actually succeeded in getting it into a dugout 30 feet below ground in the Hindenberg line. At one Group one of the officers—who has since achieved considerable popularity as a composer—had a bundle of "modern" music sent out to him. He was so smitten by this that he took to composing at the piano at all hours of the day and night till the others struck. Eventually it was arranged that if he had to make these hideous noises he must get up earlier and get them out of his system before breakfast. This was known as the "morning hate."

Of organized games there were none—their numbers were too few—but there were exceptions. A certain football match took place in the early part of 1918 in a field by the side of the La Bassée canal, near Lacouture. The one team consisted of some enthusiastic Survey men from Larkspur and Heather Group H.Q., reinforced with two or three R.E. linemen. On the other side were something like twenty Portuguese with the haziest notions of the rules of the game. The match was, of course, a glorious farce. The second half was enlivened by two or three "77's" falling near the field of play—a German sausage balloon may have had something to do with this—and causing the players to beat a hasty retreat. Only just in time, for Fritz scored the only goal—a beautiful shot right in the Portuguese goal-mouth!

Sketching was always a favourite pastime both in the Posts and in billets. It may be wondered what business an observer had to be sketching whilst in the Post, but, of course, there were often occasions when mist, fog, or rain blotted out all the front, and there was nothing to do but wait. Some of the work done by these men was of a high standard artistically—the panoramas were a case in point—but most people confined their efforts to copying the rather voluptuous pictures from the current French magazines.

On the purely literary side, most of the writing done

was letter writing, but at least one man has confessed that his letters home were really magazine articles. Perhaps he, too, got his inspiration from the current French magazines, but he is silent on that point!

There was a popular war-time idea that all letters home consisted of "Dear Mother, send me some fags. This leaves me in the pink hoping you are the same, Love John," but this was far from true. One of the great difficulties of a conscientious officer, faced with the task of censoring a hundred letters in half an hour, was the fact that many letters had so much substance in them that it was not possible to just pass them with a glance.

But, of all the routine jobs that fell to an officer, this was one of the most distasteful, and one that every officer dodged if he could. It had its funny side too, and this was the side of censoring of which so much has been said. But gems of humour were few and far between. Grumbles were much more frequent, and there is little doubt that some men took this indirect method of grousing to their officers, knowing that either nothing more would be heard of it, or that they would be hauled up to explain, and that this would give them a heaven-sent opportunity to get it off their chest.

With no parades to worry them, the men at the Posts dressed more for comfort than for show. At Group H.Q. and at the Sound Ranging Section H.Q. they had to be more particular. But sitting in an Observation Post was a mighty cold job except in the very warmest weather, and most men going on duty resembled scarecrows or Christmas trees more than soldiers. After their transfer to the R.E. many of the men managed to retain some of the uniform of their old regiment, so that many of them had still their kilts, spurs, breeches, etc., with which to brighten up things.

At Work and at Play

One young officer, who felt that he could improve things in this respect, soon found that it was not too easy to make changes in the well-established customs of the Survey. He arranged to hold a parade of all the men off duty, together with a kit inspection. The billet was close to the road, so that when he drove up in the car and found only the Corporal waiting, he felt that something was amiss; because it was not usual to fall-in the parade after the inspecting officer arrived. So he inquired where the parade was, and was told that he, the Corporal, was the only man off duty. Different men that were seen hovering about in the vicinity were, it was explained, just going off duty, or just going on duty. Somebody else was just going to draw rations, and somebody else was just going to help him. As not much change was to be got here, he decided to inspect the billet.

Entering the doorway, the first thing that caught the officer's eye was an unmade bed in the corner. He strode across and with his stick made what was meant to be a contemptuous gesture with the untidy bedclothes, but, once again, the biter was bit, for out popped a head of curls and a sweet voice murmured, "Bon jour, M. le Capitaine." As he was only a "2nd Loot," what could he do?

This incident illustrates to some extent the rather curious relationship that existed between the men and officers in these Groups. It was quite possible for a man to go for months without ever seeing one of his own officers. Such a case was, of course, very unlikely, but it was possible, and it is certain that there were many men who would have had difficulty in recognizing their own Commanding Officer. (That is the C.O. of the Field Survey Battalion—not the O.C. Group.) When an officer visited a Post there were only two men on duty, and if he went to the billet, apart from any old soldier tricks, he was not likely to find any more. Unless an officer had the knack of getting on terms with people quickly, it was very difficult for him to get to know his men at all intimately. But there does not seem to be much evidence that anyone suffered thereby, although, perhaps, there were cases where individuals took advantage of circumstances to dodge unpleasant duties. After all, plenty of the men were accustomed to accepting responsibilities in civil life, and it was evident to most officers that the men would rather be left alone to work out their own salvation than be fussed over, or, as they themselves would have expressed it—"mucked about."

At their work both officers and men met with many of the escapes and adventures that were the common experience of all who worked near the line, but one Group C.Q.M.S. had an experience that was unusual for a Survey man. He took a prisoner!

This was on the road to Valenciennes. The Group had halted for a meal, and the C.Q.M.S. had seated himself on a doorstep to brew a dish of tea. Suddenly a shout rang out, "Quartermaster! Look behind you!" Which he did. There stood a large German infantryman, but as he looked much more frightened than the C.Q.M.S. felt, he decided that he was harmless, but what to do with a prisoner was a problem. It was not one of the many eventualities for which the Groups had prepared. Popular opinion rather favoured taking him back to Field Survey Battalion H.Q., and it is rather a pity that they did not do so. It would have given the Compilation Officer something really fresh for his daily report! But in the end a man of the Canadian Military Police relieved them of their somewhat embarrassing souvenir.

Up at the Posts and with the Sound Ranging Sections

At Work and at Play

the most dangerous and strenuous work was on the telephone and microphone lines. Most of the Posts were pretty safe against all but a direct hit, and casualties to observers in the Posts were, fortunately, rare. In addition, men were not expected, except under special conditions, to remain in the Post if it was likely to get hit. As every part of the front was under observation from more than one Post, work was not interfered with seriously if one Post was out of action temporarily, and most Sound Ranging Sections had two forward Observation Posts, so that it was always felt better to prevent the loss of personnel rather than risk lives for problematical results.

On the other hand, when a Post was getting flashes or a Sound Ranging Section "breaks," both observers and linemen were expected to take any risk to get them through. It was in carrying out this order that most of the casualties in the Groups and Sections occurred, and, it might be mentioned, that most of the decorations were won. As the war progressed, artillery concentration became more and more intense, and it became increasingly difficult to keep the lines up even if the Posts were left alone. Much good work in this job must have gone unrecognized because much of it was undertaken entirely on the man's own initiative, and would never come under the notice of an officer.

Naturally, with so few people concentrated at any one spot, casualties were not on the grand scale to which the infantry and artillery were accustomed. Even when things were at their worst, it was rare to have more than one or two men reported as casualties in one day. One of the worst disasters that befell the Groups and Sections was when the H.Q. of No. 9 Group and U Section were gassed. Over forty casualties (officers and men) were suffered then. How this tragedy occurred was never fully determined. The Group and Section were housed together, and the house where they were billeted had been shelled with gas shells for some time. It is known that they had been wearing their gas masks continuously for some twelve hours or more, but how they *all* came to discard them too soon has never been fully accounted for. A patch of the liquid from a gas shell was found in one of the lofts, and it is supposed that the gas had worked its way down after they had turned in, and that they had become insensitive to the smell after such a long time in their helmets.

Then, of course, the Groups and Sections suffered severely when they were with Carey's Force in 1918. But, on that occasion, they were engaged on a task that was not really their own.

Certain enemy gun positions seemed to be invulnerable, and as locations were frequent at these positions the observers used to call them by pet names. Instead of reporting a flash on such and such a bearing, the observer would report that "old so-and-so is active again." Officially, all known hostile battery positions were numbered, but it was more usual to talk of "that battery at so-and-so that you got last week" than "A123."

Nothing pleased the Survey Post observers more than when they were able to locate an enemy battery that was firing on one of our own, and, if the battery asked them to range for it whilst they tried to silence the offender, they felt that they were really winning the war. The Sound Rangers, likewise, always welcomed these chances. This is how an observer describes one such incident.

"Close by the Post was a battery commanded by a very able officer, whose ambition seemed to be to silence every Boche battery that opened up within range. We had a direct line to this battery and were able to deal promptly

with anything in view. On one occasion we were engaged
with this battery in quite an exciting duel. They were
firing with two guns on a German battery that was
shelling our trenches, when another '5·9' opened on his
gun pits. We spotted this battery, and our own battery
engaged it with the second Section of two guns. But a
third German battery of '5·9's' opened up, and once
again we managed to spot it, and another Section of two
guns took it on. This went on for about half an hour, when
the Germans ceased fire."

Incidents such as this were only of secondary importance
from the point of view of the work of the Group or
Section, but they had a very stimulating effect on both
officers and men. Because in dealing direct with the battery
instead of their own H.Q. or the Counter Battery Office,
their work became much more real to them. They often
felt like a ghillie who spends hours trying to hook a
salmon, and who, just when he gets it on, has to hand the
rod over to his master who gets the fun of playing the
fish.

Throughout this book it will be noticed that the word
"target" is used, as often as not, in describing anything
that engaged the attention of an observer, whether it was
a man, a gun, or a house. This is partly accidental, but
it is also partly deliberate, because the attitude of mind
of the observer to all that he saw was to consider it in the
light of an abstraction regardless of what it might be. If
he located a working-party it was a "target" that he saw.
That it was a group of human beings hardly entered his
mind unless something unusual occurred to remind him
of that fact. When that something did occur, as likely as
not any satisfaction that he had at seeing his "target"
attacked soon evaporated. The following incident illustrates this.

Flash Spotters & Sound Rangers

An enemy ammunition column was located in the distance, and its position reported to one of our batteries, which opened fire. The column broke into a gallop, but another shot hit one of the limbers, which blew up. The driver of the limber which was in front drew up and ran back to see if he could help anyone left. After sorting about for some time, he ran back to his own team, which then galloped off.

The observer writes, "I am afraid that I was guilty of a breach of duty on this occasion, as I gave no more directions to our battery until the limber was well down the road."

In case it should be assumed that Flash Spotters were people who sat aloft in safety and egged others on to do the dirty work, an account of an attempt to establish a special Survey Post will act as a corrective.

Puit 16 was only a few hundred yards from the line, but the O.C. Group was of the opinion that some hidden batteries might be observed from this position. The position that he suggested was on top of the winding gear—not at the bottom of the pit. Two observers were detailed to have a try, and they set off amidst expressions of regret from their pals that they would not be able to come in on the poker game any more. It was also suggested that they should hand over their remaining five-franc notes there and then.

The start was easy and led up to a communication trench. Leaving this, they had to do a sprint over some open ground, and they arrived at the tower breathless. To climb the tower was no easy task, as many of the rungs of the ladder had been shot away, and they had all their gear with them, but there was no time to loiter, and soon they found themselves at the top and congratulating one another that all was well. This condition of affairs did not last long, because a machine gun opened out and the shots rattled away in a most distressing manner amongst the ironwork. This was nasty, but apparently the machine gun could not get sufficient elevation, as the shots passed harmlessly below. Just as that danger passed, a field gun joined in, and the shells bursting in the engine-house sent the wheels and shafts humming around in close proximity to the men.

Despite this unnatural accompaniment, they located the gun and sent through an approximate location, and then—oh, joy!—the line went "dis," and a salvo of gas shells ruled out any prospects of further locations that day. They were free to light out for home, which they did *toute suite.*

Gathering together their gear, they scrambled down as best they could, falling flat in the mud in their unseemly haste. Then followed a race back to the trench and a sigh of relief that "that was that." So the poker school went on and the five francs continued to circulate.

A word should be said about the "attached" personnel —the A.S.C. men (both H.T. and M.T.). The H.T. men were typical "horsey" men, and some of them were inclined to give a little trouble as they were not of the type that could appreciate the form of discipline that existed in the Groups. But most of them settled down quite well, and, as a rule, the A.S.C. people would always take back the really "hard cases" amongst them. On the whole they had a fairly easy and safe job, and this always had a restraining influence on the wilder spirits amongst them, as they knew that any misdemeanours on their part might land them in some much less pleasant job.

Nevertheless, it was one of these selfsame drivers that enabled the Survey to be represented when first the

Allies set foot on enemy soil. This was in Italy, and came
about in this way. One of these lads had got into trouble
and had been handed over to a neighbouring unit to
undergo Field Punishment. It so happened that this was
just at the time when preparations were being made for
the push that was to carry the Allies on to enemy soil.
When the day of the great push arrived, this illustrious
fellow was given a rifle and bayonet and told to go to it.
This he did, and he did it so well that he found himself
one of the small band that were the first to find themselves
on enemy soil.

The M.T. drivers were of a different type. Originally,
they had come up with motor cycles and side-cars, and
then, as now, motor cyclists, as a class, were rather dare-
devils. When, later on, these side-car outfits were replaced
by light cars, most officers (who had to ride in the side-
cars) heaved a sigh of relief. But when these men took over
the light cars, they proceeded to drive them as though
they were motor cycles, and they thought nothing of
taking one round corners on two wheels.

Towards the end of the war an altogether different
type of man was sent as a driver. They were mostly low
category men who, after a week's tuition in England, had
been, to use a very inelegant but expressive phrase,
"bunged out to France." The ineffectiveness of some of
these men was a constant source of annoyance, but at
other times one felt rather sorry for them.

An officer was being driven back to H.Q. one night and
one of these men was driving. They ran into a light mist
which made driving uncomfortable but not difficult.
But the driver got the wind up, and eventually lost his
head and landed the car in the ditch. No bones were
broken, but the officer poured forth the vials of his
wrath.

At Work and at Play

"What the —— do you think you're doing?" quoth he. "What do you think you are, anyhow?

"I'm a draper's assistant," was the meek and innocent reply.

Possibly it was because they were so much in the company of officers, that most of these drivers were experts at the soft answer that turneth away wrath. One driver came back late one night and reported that the car would have to go into workshops the next day.

"How long will it be there?" inquired his C.O. anxiously, and thinking of a long list of visits that had to be made soon.

"I don't know, sir."

"But surely you know what is wrong with the car?"

"Oh, yes, sir. The crank case is cracked."

"And how the dickens did you manage that?"

"I ran over a church steeple, sir."

"You mean that you ran *into* a church steeple, don't you?"

"No, sir."

"Then, how on earth could you run over a church steeple?"

"It was lying in the middle of the road, sir."

It is so usual to make jokes and jibes at the expense of the men of the A.S.C., that it is only fair to say that these M.T. men were, probably, the hardest worked men at ordinary times. If they were not driving someone somewhere they were dashing off with messages somewhere else, and, in their spare time, they had the car and motor cycle to keep in running order. No light task. Their meal hours were erratic, but they generally got the night in bed—or at least its equivalent.

One word about the "old" men—that is, the men who were over age when they joined up. There were a good many of these men with the Survey, and, far from being a burden, they were always an inspiration and example to the younger men. Many cases could be cited of how these men "stuck it out" when every avenue was open to them to get transferred to an easier job or even to England. Not much has been heard of these men who in 1914, under no form of compulsion, either moral or otherwise, risked all to serve their country and live up to an ideal. Now that the "young men" of 1914 are, in turn, becoming the "old men" of to-day, they can appreciate still more what these men did. In the Survey, at least, they will always be remembered with respect —and affection.

To conclude this chapter it might not be out of place to relate the adventures of the men of Laurel Post in the early days of Flash Spotting. This is no tale of battle, murder, and sudden death, but of experiences that were not likely to have come to men in more conventionally organized units.

In February 1916 a little band of men were assembled at the H.Q. of the First Army Topo. Section to be tested as to their suitability for employment as Survey Post observers. They had all come out of the line, and were delighted to find themselves in the pleasant atmosphere that pervaded Bethune at that time. The mornings were spent receiving instruction in the use of the theodolite, but those of them who were already *au fait* with this instrument wandered around the field engaging the local M'selles in light badinage. For the rest of the time they were free to do pretty well as they chose, and the only fly in the ointment was that a certain number had to act as cook's mate each day.

But the week sped past in a very pleasant manner, and when orders to proceed arrived they were as happy as a

At Work and at Play

Sunday School treat. One afternoon they were bundled into a box-car and were told to follow up a car in which there was an officer who, it was expected, would see them settled in their new home. They had not gone very far when a dixie fell off the back of the box-car, and whilst this was being retrieved the car got lost in the distance. The driver of the box-car had only a very hazy notion of how to get to their destination, and he obviously felt very uncomfortable when nearly every turning he took led them nearer and nearer to the line, but, whenever the driver felt inclined to stop and turn back, he was greeted with ribald shouts of encouragement to carry on. (Perhaps it is needless to remark that the shouters were quite sure that their advice to press on would not be taken.)

Eventually they landed outside the Château of Bouvigny Boyeffles just as some French infantrymen were being dismissed from parade. Describing what occurred, one man writes: "I really believe that this was the most thrilling moment of the war to me." The French swarmed round the car with shouts of "Les anglais! Les anglais!" "Bons camarades!" etc., and soon the Allies were swopping cigarettes, whilst the Frenchmen vied with one another in giving advice as to the best estaminets and other less reputable establishments in the village.

The party were now in the best of spirits, and decided to try to get through to Topo. H.Q., and report progress. This they did, and great was their joy when they discovered that they had arrived at their destination, and that the French Army authorities would look after them.

They were given a building to themselves in the château grounds and a French Sergeant—a resident in Jersey in times of peace—was detailed to look after them.

As he spoke English fluently, everything went smoothly. For a day or so they were rationed by the French, and even after they started to draw their own rations the French kept pressing theirs on them, and the morning coffee was ever welcome.

The French remained in the village another fortnight, and during this time our little band of heroes devoted themselves to cultivating the good graces of their Allies. In the evening they used to foregather with the Frenchmen and "swop lies." Amongst other things, they learnt that the Frenchmen had heard from the Germans about a fortnight before they rolled up, that the English were taking over that part of the line!

A Gascon, who was known to them all as the "Prisonnier," was a well-known character. His failing, apparently, was overstaying his leave, for which he blamed the generosity of the English in Bethune, who had supplied him with *beaucoup stout et bierre*. But he bore no ill will, as he considered *Les soldats anglais* as *très bons camarades*.

All too soon the time arrived when they had to start into the job. They moved up to Marqueffles and took up their quarters in the cellar of a miner's cottage. An officer came along and instructed them in their duties and they were told to carry on.

All went well for a day or two. If it was fine one or two of them would take a turn up to the Observation Post and enjoy the view through the fine telescope provided for their enjoyment. They really felt that if they had been members of the War Cabinet they could not have been treated with greater consideration. It was rather a nuisance having to send a report to H.Q. each day, but as that was the Sergeant's job, it did not worry the others a great deal.

But after the lapse of a few days they received a visit from the C.O. and Adjutant, and the illusion that an Observation Section was a home of rest for tired troops was rudely shattered. The unfortunate Sergeant was sent packing and the remainder took up the white man's burden.

There is no moral to this story, but it is satisfactory to know that every one in this party made good, and received promotion sooner or later.

10

OFFICERS AND MEN

FLASH Spotters and Sound Rangers were picked men in the sense that they had need of some special qualifications before they were considered for the work at all. Both officers and men, with few exceptions, were obtained from units in the field, and, as they all had to serve a period of probation before they were finally accepted, it was only natural that there were very few duds.

The original Flash Spotters of the Ranging Section were highly trained surveyors, and it is not at all surprising that they were very soon diverted from Flash Spotting to their own job of surveying. These were all regulars, but in the subsequent experiments regular and temporary personnel were both used. For the most part, the regulars were artillerymen, and the temporaries were men with civilian experience of survey, but it was not very long before nearly all the regulars, both officers and men, were withdrawn to their own units. By 1917 there was only a handful of regulars left amongst the rank and file, and, with very few exceptions, the only regular officers were the C.O.s of the Battalions.

Before the formation of the Depot Field Survey Companies, each Company got its personnel where and when it could. This usually meant that the Army authorities asked units for returns of men with certain qualifications, and the results were most surprising. As far as the Observation Groups were concerned, the qualifications were purposely made as few and unexacting as possible, as it was always realized that only training in the Posts could make a good observer, so as a rule, all

We see neither this —

nor this —

nor this —

nor this —

nor this —

nor this —

nor this —

What we see now-a-days, is mostly this.

Drawn by E. M. May

A SKETCH MADE BY A FLASH SPOTTER IN FEBRUARY 1918
A month later he was too busy to sketch the sequel

that was asked for was some experience with survey instruments, and the ability to read a map.

Recruiting men for the Sound Ranging Sections was not so easy. As far as the forward observers were concerned, the qualifications were not very different from those for a Survey Post observer, but the computers and instrument makers were in a different category. Men who were to be trained as computers had to have at the very least, "a good head for figures," but it was not sufficient qualification for an instrument maker to say that he was "handy with tools." There are not many properly trained instrument makers at any time, and, latterly, the Depot had to fall back on watchmakers and similar tradesmen and put them through a course of intensive training.

Although these appeals resulted in a very mixed bag, this form of recruiting served quite well in 1915 and 1916, but it was astonishing the number of men that rolled up with absolutely no qualifications of any sort or kind. They must have known that they were bound to be sent back to their units as soon as ever they were tested in any way, but some men seemed to be prepared to clutch at any straw to get away from their units if only for a few days. One man confesses how, after being torn from his "old" Battalion and posted to about three other Battalions in as many months, he became absolutely fed up, and determined to get away from the infantry at any price. He applied for a job as an interpreter, but, whilst waiting to hear the result of his application, he heard some men talking of the Flash Spotters.

"Are they much bothered by their officers?" he queried.

"No," was the reply. "They hardly ever see them."

This decided him. He promptly applied for transfer to the Survey, and as he was a well-educated man, who could tell the difference between a theodolite and a telescope, he was accepted.

But the only qualification of others was a spirit of optimism. Nevertheless, some of these men did manage to get kept on. If a man appeared to be clean, intelligent, and willing, he often made a better cook or orderly than the men who were sent up from the base for these purposes, so that no man who reached a certain degree of intelligence was sent back until he had been tried in some job or another.

A very good example of how a man of this sort made good is the case of a man who was sent along as a lithographer. Actually he was only a boy, and very little questioning soon made it clear that his knowledge of the trade was of the scantiest, in fact, he finally admitted that his knowledge of the trade had been picked up in the works where he had been employed to clean the windows and sweep the floors. Nevertheless, the boy's whole manner and general bearing made such an impression on the C.O. that he decided to fit him in somewhere, although there was no actual need for an orderly at the time. So he was put in the Litho. room to clean and sweep up. It was not very long before he was promoted to be a machine hand, and at that job he soon proved himself as good as the best.

Strictly speaking this incident relates to neither the Groups nor Sections, but it was in much the same way that the Groups and Sections got some of their best men. One Category "C" man, who had been sent up from the base as a cook, turned out a first-class observer, so a man who had turned out rather a dud as an observer was made into a cook to take his place. He, in turn, sent up top-hole meals, and everything in the garden should have been lovely if it had not been for the matter of pay. The cook who had become an observer was receiving his modest bob a day as a pioneer, whereas the sapper, who had become a cook, was getting Corps pay on top of his pay as a sapper. The cook who was now doing skilled work thought, naturally, that he should be paid accordingly, but the observer who had qualified for the higher rate of pay did not see why he should give it up just because people preferred his cooking to his observing. As only one of them could draw Corps pay as an observer it was an impasse to which there was no solution.

Very often men who were sent along for the Topo. Section, or perhaps as draughtsmen, might not have come up to the standards required by these Sections, but they were first-class material for the Observation Groups. For example, when draughtsmen were required for map drawing a good many artists were sent along, but there is very little relation between drawing maps and drawing, say, a comic strip, so that these men were of no use in the Maps Office, but as they were well-educated and intelligent men, the Observation Groups were only too glad to take them on.

Some of these artists turned out panoramas showing the view from the Posts. These were very useful for familiarizing the observers with their ground and enabling them to identify landmarks, and also to know what was "dead ground" for observation purposes. Moreover, Posts were usually very proud of these works of art which adorned the walls of the Observation Post.

One might think that as the war went on, and experience was gained, that it would have been possible to state just exactly what qualifications were required of a man to make him a good observer, but, actually, one found that qualifications made little difference and that character was what made or marred an observer. That is true of both the Survey Post and Sound Ranging observers. As one officer put it, a first-class observer was a man who kept himself clean and said "Sir" when spoken to by an officer. To put this in another way, what was needed was a man who could look after himself and play the game.

Curiously enough, good eyesight was not an essential. In fact one experienced N.C.O. with a long experience in the Posts, claims that the best observers were men who were accustomed to wearing glasses. He claims that men who normally used glasses found it less irksome to use binoculars or telescopes for long periods, whereas the man with good eyesight was inclined to trust over much to his own faculties. The disadvantage was that, when the second observer went to the instrument to confirm the first man's bearing, if he had to take off his glasses, he had to readjust the focus of the instrument. This wasted time, and might mean losing flashes. Whether this was a true estimate of the relative advantage of poor eyesight or not, it was certainly true that no one ever worried about it at the time, and observers were judged by other things.

In the early days, before it was quite clear what was required of an observer, a good deal of emphasis was laid on recruits having some knowledge of survey, but when it was found that too much insistence on this one qualification would make it a very slow business to gather together all the personnel required, attention was directed to other trades and professions that might supply likely men. One of the most interesting suggestions in this line was that poachers and gamekeepers should make good observers, as they were men trained to study the lie of the land. It is not known whether any poachers came forward, but some gamekeepers were taken on, although their previous experience did not seem to make them any better observers than others whose previous vistas had been bounded by rows of chimney-pots.

But they did sometimes show their special capabilities in other ways. Down in the devastated area of the Somme, where it was difficult to buy any little luxuries to vary the monotony of the rations, one of these gamekeepers, who had charge of a Post, used to send in a hare or a bird of some sort to the Officers' Mess about twice a week. As one had always to be very careful in all matters that might infringe on the rights of the civilian population, tactful inquiries were made as to the source from which this fountain of plenty arose. It would have been dreadful if the gamekeeper had turned poacher, but there was no need to worry. Assurances were forthcoming that the game had been found dead in the adjoining wood. There was a battery of 8-inch howitzers there, and the game-keeper observer "thought that the birds must have been killed by the concussion."

The officers for both the Groups and Sections were got together to a large extent by a series of personal recommendations. When the first Flash Spotting Sections were forming, many of the officers were men who had attended courses in Survey, and in this way their capabilities had become known to the officers who were forming the Observation Sections. These officers, in turn, were often able to recommend others with whom they had served. It was not always possible to get sufficient officers in this way but, on the whole, it proved a reliable method of preventing the Groups from being landed with too many misfits. With only two officers in each Group, it was very difficult to know what to do if an officer proved unsuited for the job. It was not possible to try him in some other job, as was done with the men, and to have him returned to his own unit was an action that was liable to be mis-interpreted. But there was little room for passengers, and for this reason most Battalions liked to know something of the personality of an officer before they were landed with him.

The great majority of the Group officers had been surveyors, architects, etc., in civil life, although there was a good sprinkling of men from other professions. It was very desirable that an officer should be familiar with the principles and, to some extent, with the practice of survey, but this did not necessarily mean that they must be surveyors. For example, one officer had been a ship's officer and another a Church of Scotland clergyman. The first, of course, was technically qualified by his knowledge of navigation, and the second—presumably—from his experience as a "sky pilot." Of the latter, it was rumoured that he was accepted for the Observation Groups because at the interview the C.O. could not understand what he said on account of his strong Scotch accent.

Personal recommendation played a large part in getting together the first officers for the Sound Ranging Sections. With very few exceptions, they were all trained scientists, many of considerable standing in the world of science, but all young. One very awestruck artillery liaison officer was asked how he got on with the C.O. of the Sound Ranging Section that he was in the habit of visiting. "Oh," he replied, "D—— is a very good chap, but I am sure he bathes in binomial equations and dines in the fourth dimension." Most of these officers had been research workers or lecturers in different universities. As Sound Ranging developed less highly trained men were required, but a sound knowledge of mathematics and a scientific training of some sort were always essential.

Schoolmasters and lawyers were two professions that were well represented.

To be a "good mixer" was a qualification that was a tremendous asset to both Group and Section officers. A great deal of their time was taken up with interviews and discussions with all sorts of people. In their contacts with other people they had to work with men of varying experience and rank, so that an officer who could make himself liked personally found many a rough path made smooth, whereas another officer, who might have been just as efficient in his own way, had an uphill struggle with prejudice and indifference.

With very few exceptions, none of the rank and file of the Groups and Sections were granted commissions that would have enabled them to continue to serve with the Field Survey Companies. This was a distinct misfortune as, when the period of rapid expansion came along, it would have been possible to get plenty of men suitable for the position of officers from within the units themselves. But it was a matter of high policy that men applying for commissions must be posted to fighting units and it was a policy with which most people were in sympathy, but it bore hardly on the men of the Groups and Sections who had already served a year or more in the line, and who were deserving and fit for promotion.

Most of the officers and men came from infantry regiments. This is, perhaps, not quite so true of the Sound Ranging Sections, as the artillery seemed to have had a great attraction for the scientifically minded. But it certainly did apply to the great majority. Whether their experience in the line was of any great use to them as observers is doubtful, but it undoubtedly imparted a sense of responsibility to the individual that was invaluable to the Group as a whole. Whatever reasons for complaint might attach to individuals, slackness on duty was seldom one of them. Even when Posts were badly placed, and results were hard to get, there never seemed to be any slacking.

As already noted, very few of the men who were sent along for trial had any idea of the nature of the job they were going to, and it is interesting to note their reactions when they found out what it was. The great thing that impressed everyone was that squalor and dirt were a thing of the past. However primitive their accommodation, it was always possible for the men at the Posts or with the Sections to arrange for regular baths. Once the newcomer discovered this fact he no longer bothered about anything else. The thing that made the deepest impression on another man was when he walked into the billet and found the men sitting down to a meal at a table covered with a white table-cloth and waited upon by a smiling French *bonne*. All questions of safety, interest, pay, etc., receded into the background when contrasted with the joy and relief of regular baths and decently served food.

There were baths *and* baths. In billets it was usually possible to have a tub in front of the kitchen fire in the good old way, but when living in dugouts and such-like places less luxury had to serve. A sample of this less luxurious accommodation was the bathroom—for "officers only"—on the Somme. A hollow had been scooped out of the bank alongside a sunken road near Beaussart, and lined with roofing felt. From the sink a pipe led out to the sunken road—a most convenient arrangement, as all the water had to be carried some distance, but this device enabled the same water to be used over and over again. A screen of hessian on sticks preserved some of the modesty of the bather. The procedure was to step behind the screen and raise an old petrol can filled with water above the head. After a few preliminary shivers, the can was inverted and the water allowed to flow over the body. Then one dashed for the hut to complete the towelling. This was the only bathing accommodation all one winter.

And beds! Most beds consisted of some wire-netting stretched over a wooden frame. With some brown paper or old newspapers laid on the wire these made comfortable beds. But think of the bliss for a man who had been sleeping with all his clothes and equipment on, in the bottom of a trench or in a rat-infested dugout, if, by chance, he had been sent to join a Group in some inhabited village, and was shown into his billet with a real bed—and blankets, and—good heavens—clean sheets!

It was not until 1917 that permission was granted to transfer the personnel to the R.E. Up till that time everyone was "attached" and the complications arising out of this were many. Nearly every regiment in the British Army must have been represented in the Groups and Sections at this time. They ranged from Life Guardsmen to Able-Bodied Seamen (R.N.D.), and a visit to an Observation Post would possible have shown one a kilted Highlander sitting, cheek by jowl, with a breeched R.A.M.C. orderly, or, perhaps, with an "Aussie" with shirt-tunic, "wideawake"—and drawl.

This sort of thing had its amusing side, but it also led to many awkward situations, the most usual of which were spy scares. Although there was nothing very secret about the work of the Observation Groups, the nature of Sound Ranging was kept as secret as possible, and everyone was strictly forbidden to talk about the nature of their employment, which made things more difficult. A man is seen leaving an empty church about midnight,

and, on being challenged, he answers "Topo. Section,
R.E." Nobody—and least likely of all an infantryman—
has ever heard of a Topo. Section. It should be noted
that many of the men went on describing themselves as
belonging to the Topo. Sections long after these had
become Field Survey Companies. But even the dullest
infantryman does know that the Royal Engineers do not
wear kilts nor sport Red Cross badges, so the man is
detained for further inquiries. This was just the sort of
situation in which the average man delighted, and he
seldom went out of his way to clear things up.

It did not take long to put things to rights, but sometimes
there was quite a fuss before things could be straightened
out. It all served to break the monotony, but after a
time the joke began to pall, and to show that these men
were engaged on special duty they were supplied with a
little badge with the letters "F.S.C.," which they wore
on their right arm. The effect of these badges was almost
magical. Instead of being constantly suspect, both officers
and men found themselves being treated with a sort of
solemn awe. This was a great improvement, as it became
possible to move about freely almost anywhere. In
addition, when one wanted things done, the little badge
seemed to have a "gingering" effect.

The letters "F.S.C." (short for Field Survey Company)
always aroused great curiosity in estaminets and similar
resorts of the sociable. Very few people came into contact
with the Field Survey Companies, and so even the name
was almost unknown. When the curious were invited to
have a guess at what it stood for, "Field Service Company"
was usually the nearest attempt. But when, in turn, the
Survey men were invited to solve the mystery, they could
not resist a little bit of leg-pulling, and all sorts of
imaginary units were invented. Probably the brightest

improvisation—because it had just that little possibility of reality that is so necessary for a good leg-pull—was that "F.S.C." stood for "First Serving Conscripts!"

In another case an officer was approached by a very young subaltern and asked to supply some forage.

"Forage?" queried the Survey man. "Who do you think I am?"

"Well, sir," nervously answered the sub., "I thought from your badge that you must belong to the Field Supply Column."

But usually the infantryman, with his sublime contempt for everyone who did not share his discomforts and risks, did not worry himself about what these letters stood for. He dismissed the lot as "These Y.M.C.A. blokes."

It must be admitted that the immunity that these badges conferred was not always used legitimately. Down on the Somme a party of observers were engaged in what was known as "scrounging" some timber wherewith to add to the amenities of their temporary home. The good work was proceeding merrily when a rude voice demanded to know "what the ——" they thought they were doing. They found themselves confronting an irate Staff Officer, but the N.C.O. in charge, with great presence of mind, brought his left arm to the front and replied "Field Salvage Corps, R.E., sir." Possibly, being on the Staff, the officer did not care to acknowledge that he had never heard of the Field Salvage Corps, for this reply seemed to satisfy him, and the N.C.O. got away with it—and the timber.

The Survey men were always on the look out for any unconsidered trifles that might add to the amenities of life. In fact, this was the principal hobby of many of them. Their ingenuity in turning everything to account is shown in an incident of the Italian front. The Group were putting up a corrugated iron hut. One misty morning sounds of hammering were heard, and on investigating an Italian soldier was found trying to "scrounge" parts of the hut. To put the wind up him, he was placed in a tent and two men with fixed bayonets were placed on guard. Later on the Survey officer interviewed his C.O., who, apparently, also got the wind up as the Survey officer returned with eight ingenious iron and canvas cots in exchange for the "prisoner."

Which just goes to show that even "picked" men are just as capable of picking up unconsidered trifles as others.

But although Flash Spotters and Sound Rangers were very much like other men, it was noticeable how little trouble the rank and file gave in matters of discipline. Court martial offences were exceedingly rare and even petty offences were quite out of the ordinary and looked on as nuisances rather than as part of the daily round. It would be very nice if one could attribute this immunity from "crime" to the superiority of the personnel of the Groups and Sections over that of other units. But, except for the fact that the general educational standard was higher than in most units, they were a pretty "human" lot. The real reason seems to have been that the nature of the work and the conditions under which they lived bred a high sense of individual responsibility. The attitude of the rank and file towards defaulters is shown by the remark of one man when talking of another man who had been giving a lot of trouble. "Oh, yes. He is always ready to take full advantage of all the privileges of the Survey, but he never seems to think that he has any responsibilities."

It might be suggested that one reason for the absence of defaulters was the facility with which infringements could be kept from the notice of the Group and Section officers, but charges even from the Military Police were rare, and even these seldom merited more than a reprimand. If, say, drunkenness had been usual, but blinked at by the N.C.O.s, some of those sinners were bound to have fallen into the hands of Military Police.

The working unit of the Observation Group was the Post. On the Western front alone there must have been a matter of eighty to ninety of these little detachments, and each of these little detachments was more or less self-contained and self-administered. The Sound Ranging Sections were not split up in this way. All the little details of army life such as billeting, rationing, discipline, etc., that are usually carried out, or at least supervised, by an officer, were, as often as not, done by the men at the Post themselves. Of course, the ultimate responsibility still lay with the Group officers, and, through them, with the C.O. of the Field Survey Battalion, but undoubtedly the most successful Groups were those in which the maximum trust could be placed on the N.C.O.s and men.

At times these little Groups would carry on for quite a long time without even one N.C.O. to take charge. From an administrative point of view, it would not have been difficult to arrange that at least one N.C.O. should be at each Post, but from the point of view of technical efficiency the continual movement of either N.C.O.s or men from one Post to another, or, for that matter, from one Section to another, was disadvantageous. So that when the men were to be trusted, and this usually was the case, it was generally better to leave a Post without an N.C.O. for a short time, rather than sacrifice the technical efficiency of the Group on the altar of convention.

At one Post that found itself without an N.C.O., the senior Sapper was an old soldier who was an excellent disciplinarian but "no scolard." He could have been trusted to keep his mates in order, but the reports, indents, etc., would have been too much for him. The "old soldier" was popular with his mates and they did not wish him to be superseded, so, in the best Soviet manner, they suggested to the Group officer that if this man was put in charge for discipline, one of the others would be made responsible for all the paper work. This solution was adopted and worked well for the three weeks that it lasted.

There is nothing very exciting about a little incident such as this, but it is typical of the continual shifts and absence of red tape that was a feature of the Groups and Sections. In this way the men got so accustomed to assuming responsibility, and the officers to delegating their duties to responsible men, that it became quite a matter of course to let the most suitable man tackle a job without reference to convention. An instance of this occurred in one Group, when a battery rang up to arrange a shoot. As it had been very quiet, both officers were away from Group H.Q., and the N.C.O. in charge of the office was, for some unknown reason, not to be found. The telephonist on the Flash and Buzzer Board did not feel up to calculating the bearings, and, after a frenzied search for someone to do the job, the carpenter volunteered. True to his craft he made his calculations carpenter's fashion—on a piece of planed deal! And there was no mistake about them.

This habit of self-reliance was invaluable in the hectic days of 1918 when the Posts suddenly found themselves cut off from their H.Q., and the best-laid schemes went all askew. They proved well able to look after themselves and were able to connect up again without being a burden on anyone else. In the same way, when the time came to advance, a Post could be sent forward without the necessity of making any detailed arrangements for rations, etc.

After the Armistice this spirit of independence had its disadvantages. When all the Groups and Posts, together with the Sound Ranging Sections, were brought together at Battalion H.Q. they were rather inclined to resent their loss of independence. This applied to officers and men equally. Whilst the fighting was on nobody had time to concern themselves with all the details of each Group and Section. As long as they kept out of trouble and got results, everyone was satisfied. Naturally this resulted in considerable differences as between different Sections in the amount of direct supervision exercised by the officers over the men. Some officers followed as closely as possible the traditional Army ways, whereas others were only too eager to throw off the yoke and work in their own way. On the other hand it was often more circumstances than personal choice that decided these matters, so that, when all the Groups and Sections were gathered together at Battalion H.Q. and some common standard became necessary, both officers and men were inclined to feel aggrieved.

For example, when the Groups were called in to one Battalion H.Q., after the Armistice, all arrangements for billeting, etc., were made beforehand and, naturally, these arrangements were made to keep each Group and Section together as much as possible. But the Groups and Sections had not been in the village more than twenty-four hours before each Post had started out to find fresh billets wherever they thought best. The village or small town was devoid of civilians, troops, or even a Town Major at that time, but, obviously, to let the Battalion spread itself all over the town was inviting trouble in the future. But in the meantime, many of the Posts and other little detachments had found the billet of their dreams, and as they had moved in with the sanction, expressed or implied, of their own officers, they felt that it was a case of unnecessary interference when they were told to clear out.

As things turned out, it was difficult enough to retain suitable billets after the civilian population started to return. It always seemed to be the owners of the cleanest and most suitable properties who returned first, and to clean up and make habitable many of the houses in this village was a mighty task. It was incredible the state of filth and muck the Germans left behind them. In some cases the men had put in many hours of most unpleasant labour making a billet habitable, and no sooner was the task completed than up would come the owner of the property and claim it, and out the Survey men would have to go. It was suspected, but never proved, that these people fixed themselves up temporarily in another part of the village and waited until the time was ripe to claim their home.

But these little difficulties were soon straightened out, and once again scope was found for their self-reliance and initiative. It must be remembered that for two or three years these men (of all ranks) had been cut off from all the usual routine of army life. In most units, parades, fatigues, kit inspections, guards, pickets, etc., absorb a good deal of time even when reduced to a minimum, but when the Groups and Sections went out of action there was nothing of this sort to engage their energies. It was felt that something had to be done and a certain number of parades, etc., were instituted, but the thread had been broken and there was an air of unreality about it all. Besides, both officers and men had come from different branches of the Service and there was no guarantee that they were all conversant with the same drill. Others again,

such as some of the M.T. drivers, had never had any
training at all except in a car or lorry. These, if they were
to take their place in the ranks at all, required squad drill,
and there was something a little ludicrous in teaching a
man who had been some time on active service how to
form fours, slope arms, etc. So parades were kept to a
minimum, and the men were left very much to their
own resources, and they seemed to get along pretty well
without any nursing. At least they kept out of mischief,
which was the great thing.

Within a very few days of the Armistice they had (in
co-operation with the other Sections of the Battalion)
arranged a syllabus of lectures, debates, classes, etc., which
kept the days and evenings from dragging, and sports and
sketching clubs made the most of the short days. Football,
of course, was king. All these activities were arranged
and carried on by the men themselves, subject to the
ordinary necessities of military life. Classes in Maths.,
Languages, Law, Economics, Shorthand, etc., were
started and attended with much enthusiasm for a little
while, but very few of them made much headway as there
were no textbooks available, or, at least, they were very
slow in arriving.

What upset arrangements more than anything was that,
contrary to expectations, some of the other Sections of the
Battalion found themselves busier than ever. The Mapping
and Printing Sections, if they had taken on all that they
were asked to do, would be working still, but this unwanted
activity threw out of gear all the arrangements for inter-
sectional contests that would have given vitality to many
of these efforts and ensured their continuance.

It was only after the Armistice that the Survey Bats. had
an opportunity to parade for the first time as Battalions.
The 1st Battalion determined to celebrate the great

occasion with a church parade. But in spite of the fact
that at one time the strength of the Battalion had been
over a thousand on this auspicious occasion they could
only get about a hundred and fifty men on parade. And
the service itself was hardly any more inspiring. Some
difficulty was met in getting a parson to officiate, and the
man who eventually offered his services was a "Wee Free"
from the Orkneys. He delivered a discourse under
thirteen different "heads" in the best Scottish tradition of
seventy years ago, so it was decided that church parades
were not a strong point with the Survey, and after that
the churchgoers were sent off in small parties to worship
with other units that had been better brought up.

Another Battalion—stationed at Lille—also celebrated
the occasion with a church parade. Swinging along the
Boulevard, marching "at ease," there suddenly came the
order to "march to attention." Before the command had
been passed back more than a few files a car sped past
flying the Royal Standard. It was the King. Imagine the
chagrin of the men at being caught out in this way. No,
church parades were not a strong point with the Survey.

It has been remarked that there was something absurd
about teaching squad drill to a man who had been some
years on active service. But what can be said about
enlisting a man who was actually at the front, and who
had been there for nearly three years? This was what
happened to two of the observers in No. 10 Group. These
two men had joined the R.N.D. in 1914, and had been
attached to an Observation Group since 1916. They were
rated as Able-Bodied Seamen. In June 1917 all the personnel of the Survey Bats. were transferred to the R.E.,
and the names of these men were included in the lists of
those to be transferred. What nobody realized was that
there was no machinery whereby a person could be trans-

ferred from the R.N. to the Army. So these two men were discharged from the Navy, but nobody was informed of that fact. It was only when the question cropped up about pay or something of the sort that this fact was discovered. For some months they had been free men—but they had not known it! So they had to be invited (they claim that they were ordered) to enlist "for the duration." They make the claim that they were the only soldiers in the British Army to have been enlisted whilst actually serving in the face of the enemy.

Then there was the case of the man who was sentenced for desertion, who had never been away from some unit or another at any time. It appears that this man, whilst serving with an infantry battalion, had been put on road control duty. Fritz started to shell the road and he got shell-shock or something and eventually he found himself in hospital. From there he was sent down to the base, where he was picked for the Survey. Apparently his absence from his Battalion was never explained, and during his absence his Battalion was sent to Italy. In due course this man arrived with a Group in Italy, and finding his old Battalion billeted close at hand he popped over to look up his old pals, little thinking that he was posted as a "deserter." A short time after this an order came through to arrest him, and in due course he came up for trial. He received one month's Field Punishment, and on release resumed duty with the Group.

But the most remarkable muddle of all occurred during demobilization. A man who had enlisted as a volunteer in 1914, and who had fought throughout the war, first in the infantry and then in the Field Survey Company, was found by the Record Office to be—a German! It turned out that his father, who had lived most of his life in England and married an Englishwoman, was a German and had been interned. This never came out until the boy (as loyal a British soldier as there was in the British Expeditionary Force) began to agitate, when the war was over, to get back to his civilian employment. It was all straightened out somehow, but only after a good deal of trouble.

Little difficulties of this sort were of frequent occurrence when each unit got its own personnel when and where it could. Fortunately for the peace of mind of those whose business it was to deal with these matters, all questions of recruitment and training were taken over by the Depot Field Survey Company, and newcomers arrived at their units as full-blown Engineers.

One good thing that the Depot did was to arrange that men who were likely to become due for leave soon, were sent off before being sent up to join a Group or Section. An extraordinarily high proportion of these newcomers seemed to have been without leave for a very long time. Consequently, it was no unusual occurrence for these newcomers to go on leave only a few weeks after joining the Group. This not only interfered with their training, but was apt to cause ill-feeling amongst those who were "sweating on leave" and who found that they would have to wait a bit longer for their turn.

It might not be out of place to say something about leave here. There is no need to say what leave meant to officers and men alike. It was the one thing that kept alive the hope that one day it would be "Good-bye to all that." Everyone as he joined up was asked for the date of his last leave, if it was not already marked in his pay book. This date stood until it could be verified and, in one Battalion at least, not a single case came to light where this date was mis-stated by even a few days. It can hardly have been a fear of being found out and punished that led to this accuracy, because men who otherwise led a blameless existence used to tell the most atrocious fairy tales about their balance with the Paymaster. What this condition of affairs seemed to indicate was that no one was inclined to take the slightest chance of jeopardizing his chance of leave.

On the other hand, when special leave could be had at times, there was no doubt that many men resorted to subterfuges of a not too honourable nature in trying to make out a claim for it. When it was ordained that special leave had to come out of the places allotted to the unit for ordinary leave, and that, on returning from his special leave, the individual had to revert to his old place in the roster, applications of this nature ceased almost at once. There was little doubt that special leave was out of place under the conditions that existed, and it was a good job when it was done away with.

It is not improbable that Survey men were not the only people to think that they were harshly treated in the matter of leave allotments. It was a common subject of complaint that the complainant "knew as a fact" that the men of such and such a unit got leave far oftener than the men of the Survey. Sometimes the report was true, but generally the discrepancy was temporary. Even when well substantiated the anomaly was not due to favouritism, but to causes that it was not easy to adjust. On the whole, judging by the leave records of men when they arrived at the Survey, leave was much the same everywhere in France.

A strong feeling of esprit de corps permeated all ranks, also a strong competitive spirit. Posts eagerly vied with one another to get the most "flashes," and each Group felt that it was—if all the circumstances were taken into account—much the most efficient. The same spirit permeated the Sound Ranging Sections, but, in addition to rivalry in getting "guns," there was a wide field for competition in devising technical improvements. The same thing applied to the different Battalions but, generally speaking, a man's first loyalty was to his Group or Section, and then to his Battalion. This was understandable, because the Group or Section was to all intents and purposes the unit, and Battalion H.Q. was remote in every way from the men at the Groups and Sections.

Finally it can be said without qualification that there was no "happier" branch of the Service in the British Expeditionary Force than those of the Flash Spotters and Sound Rangers. They no longer exist as Royal Engineers, but they are carrying on the good work in the Royal Artillery, and those who have come in contact with the present-day Flash Spotters and Sound Rangers know that the traditions that were built up in the field are in safe keeping.

11

LETTERS FROM "SOMEWHERE IN FRANCE"

*These letters were written by Lieut. Claude L. Penrose, M.C.,
R.A., and we are indebted to Mrs. H. H. Penrose, his mother,
for permission to use them here. Lieut. Penrose was a Regular
Officer, and so had to return to the Artillery in 1917, when the
authorities decided that no Regular Officers should be employed
with these units. On returning to the Artillery, he soon attained
the rank of Major, and was awarded a Bar to his M.C.
He was wounded on July 31, 1918, and died in the C.C.S. on
August 1st.*

It is possible that the impression made on the reader's
mind so far is that Flash Spotting and Sound Ranging
were jobs that involved very little danger and only minor
discomforts. But this would be a mistake, for there was
not an attack or an operation of any sort on the whole
front where the Flash Spotters and Sound Rangers
were not involved.

But once they got involved in general operations of
any sort, their experiences were not much different
from those of any others in the front areas. And that is
why, so far, attention has been directed mostly to conditions when the line was fairly stable, because it was
then that the life of the Flash Spotters and Sound Rangers
was most differentiated from that of others. It was also
at these times that the work of the Groups and Sections
was of the greatest value. It was in the preparation for
an attack, or in the consolidation of a position, that the
Groups and Sections could make their greatest contribu-
tion to the whole effort. So that in dwelling on what

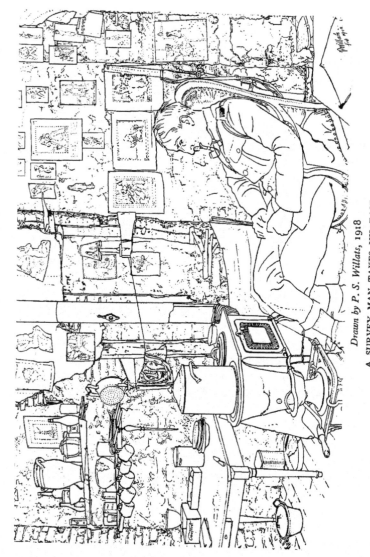

Drawn by P. S. Willats, 1918

A SURVEY MAN TAKES HIS EASE

This picture shows how the men of the Survey managed to impart a "homely" air to the most unimpressive surroundings

happened at these times, one is only emphasizing the most useful and distinctive side of the picture.

But to make the picture complete, it is necessary that some account should be taken of the experiences of the Groups and Sections under "battle" conditions. To do so for all the Groups and Sections would involve a work of several volumes, so that it is proposed in this, and in the following chapters, to give some personal accounts of the experiences of different officers and men on different fronts.

Nevertheless, when one tries to reconstruct all the happenings and incidents of these fateful days, it is curious how it is the happy recollections that come floating to the surface of one's memory. The dangers and horrors of these times seem to be tucked away in the deeper folds of the mind, and only by deliberate effort can they be brought to the fore. Sometimes one thinks that this is the effect of time, but contemporary documents show that this is not so. We have been fortunate to get permission to reproduce extracts from some letters written to his mother by one of the very first of the Flash Spotters, and these are reproduced here, so that the reader may see how life in a Group appeared to a Flash Spotter in 1916.

This officer was sent on a Survey course in September 1915, just at the time when the question of forming Observation Groups was being discussed. Apparently he had made an impression on the O.C. Topo. Section, for he was sent for at the beginning of November to take charge of one of the new Sections that were being formed in the Third Army.

The first specific reference to the Survey in his letters is in one dated November 14th: "The day before yesterday I went with Major W. down to the four southern stations and took all day on the job. The Sappers being a bit slow, owing to the press of work, but they are very good as far as they have gone. But every day the prospect of leave becomes more remote, as this show is taking the deuce of a time to get in working order. I shall enjoy it all the more when it does come, as I shall be able to tell myself that there is nothing to worry about, which is by no means the case at present. . . . The mud is like nothing I have ever seen."

He was getting things going by the end of the month, as he writes: "I am in my hole in the ground now, for better for worse. . . . My dug-out and the men's are awfully good; but we have no cooking utensils yet, except what we can steal, and are still in the throes of starting. To crown all, the frost stopped last night and it has spent the day raining. I have sent frantic messages to the local Sappers to come and shore up the neighbouring trenches, as the approach to our kitchen—which, by the way, leaks like a sieve—is rapidly filling in. . . . My men are all wet to the skin, and I have been lending them my under-clothes—I having had to change once a day; so we are having 'some' time! However, everyone is very 'merry and bright' in spite of it all, or at least much merrier and brighter than any one could reasonably expect."

In December he writes: "If you saw this now you'd just think 'How cosy.' Nice board walls; maps and pictures on them; pigeon holes; gramophone on the table (I can do maths. to a musical accompaniment better than without!) and your 'birthday fuse' as a paper weight; bed tilted up against the wall; waste-paper-basket; shelves round the walls, with clothes, knives, forks, jams, etc., in more cobby holes—and a nice oil lamp to light it all up."

"This has been the first clear day of the last four or five, and I have been down at my other post, going over the country with them. It is pretty tiring, as the only way to get there is to dismount and leave horses at a certain farm, and then walk on to it—a matter of two miles across country with a stretch of knee-deep trench at the end. Then back. Altogether about five miles to walk, and ten to ride, exclusive of 'incidentals' such as getting from the road to one's own 'house,' which puts on another couple of miles to the total. But it's a very good life, and one isn't going to turn into a white rabbit, or die for lack of exercise. . . ."

"We have had a merry day here, starting with the total collapse of the men's dug-out this morning, owing to the heavy rain last night. One man is to sleep under my bed to-night, with another on watch; and the rest will be at a farm about a mile and a half away, but a mile and a half here is 100 yards in peace time."

"All my records [gramophone] have come at last; but now, as the men's dug-out caved in on Christmas Eve, there is no one to play them to at present, even if there were time to do it, which, until the new dug-out is made, there emphatically won't be."

So Christmas celebrations were a wash-out, but a week's leave early in January made up—to him at least—for this loss. Shortly after his return from leave he writes: "Ever since I last wrote, I have been running about like a dog in the city—or the devil in the world; also at times playing the roaring lion, as people won't do always what one wants them to. However the new No. 3 [Post] is now well on towards being built; No. 4 men's dug-out is quite done; and now, just for something to do, I am strafing about kitchens."

"They gassed us this evening, but no harm done. . . ."

"What a life! My corporal went sick this evening with trench fever, so I am doing his duty for him—unfortunately a night duty—till I get a man to replace him to-morrow. It is not so very cold, but it is exceedingly dull, as the Boche seldom shows any signs of life at this time of night. At present I'm on the telephone and the other chap on watch. We take it in turn, two hours about, from 8 p.m. to 8 a.m. . . . We got just a little gas, but it wasn't the bad kind, and was rather thin by the time it arrived at our house!"

"The weather here is shocking. Yesterday it defeated us completely. My O.P. slit was half choked up with snow, the instrument had to be covered up all day, and the whole interior of the post itself was about eighteen inches thick with drifted snow, several inches of which, in some mysterious way, had managed to blow through the door into the passage. The dug-outs are still 'bon,' but I fear much there will be 'some' leaks after the thaw. The mice, driven in for warmth, are more than ever a plague."

This brings the story to the end of February, when the Topo. Sections became Field Survey Companies and the Group system was introduced in the Third Army.

On February 29th he writes: "I'm frightfully busy just now, and in the throes of becoming a slightly bigger person than heretofore —taking over five posts instead of two. . . . Only three of my posts are active, but five will be shortly, and I have been out in the side-car (a new game) looking people up and arranging things. Now I must see to cleaning up the trench which fell in during the thaw. It always does!"

About this time the Fourth Army was formed and took over part of the front held by the Third Army, and in this way Lieut. Penrose found himself transferred to the 4th Field Survey Company.

On March 12th he writes: "Up to my eyes in work. I have now changed ownership, and one McLeod is my boss."

Flash Spotters & Sound Rangers

"Still as busy as possible. I shall be going to live in a real live house to-morrow. I was out all morning to-day, walking, and by the time I got back it felt about 96. In reality, I suppose, it was about 65; pretty hot for this time of the year anyway. I'm really having a great time now."

"I don't live at No. 4 now, but in a house, and I have another officer—one James, from the 31st Battery—to help me. I liked him, so I asked for him and got him! Side-car-ing is quite a good way of moving, though a little bumpy sometimes. I haven't had time to learn to ride yet, so have to be content with sitting still."

At the end of the month he went down with German measles, but on April 7th he writes: "I arrived back yesterday, and have been busy ever since. I was out all morning to-day, looking at new posts, and everything goes well. . . . I have quite a lot of stuff about the hospital to put on paper when I have time—so many amusing people there."

" . . . as I was still hard at work on yesterday's flashes. They are giving me a third officer now, so I shall be a bit better off. . . . I think there is quite a lot to buck one. Things seem to be going excellently. . . ."

"Still busy and likely to remain so. All leave was stopped the day I last wrote. I am living in a house that formerly belonged to a tailor. There is a loft, a kitchen, a store (clothing etc.), an office, a mess and a bedroom. There is also accommodation for horses, carts and mobikes, and a back garden with a tortoise! Also an Armstrong hut which we put up ourselves for extra officers. . . . Also I have a second officer now, who has just gone to learn the job at No. 4, with Norris as preceptor! I'm so sleepy I can hardly write straight. . . . Getting new posts made, strafing signals, etc., without end. . . . We are starting a vegetable garden here."

"Somewhere in France"

"Still no time. . . . However, I thrive on the work. . . . One of my posts got blown to blazes a couple of days ago, so I'm busy building a new one. No one hurt!"

"Just as busy as ever. . . . James goes on leave to-day and unless I get Bishop at once I'll have the whole Group on my hands for ten days. I cannot get the Field Companies to work as I want them, and just at present life is one continual bicker. However, I expect things will settle down again soon. . . . We grow lettuce, peas and nasturtiums round the Armstrong hut."

"I have five out of the six posts working now, but am still busy as ever."

"The garden is getting on well, and we nearly always can manage a pot of flowers to decorate the mess table. . . . Both my motor-bicycles are in hospital! . . . I must be up betimes to-morrow, and hie me to one of my posts—the one that is being rebuilt."

Then came another week's leave, and on his return he found that he would have to shift the Group H.Q. Preparations for the Somme offensive were proceeding apace, and the French were taking over the village of Bray, where the Group were located. They moved Group H.Q. to a little dell on a ridge to the west of Bray.

On June 1st he writes: "Since I last wrote we have moved into our new Headquarters, but are still getting it ship-shape. James spends a lot of time making himself 'an house.' I sleep in a tent, and our mess is an Armstrong hut. They have built us a very nice office and the whole place is really ripping. . . . The weather is perfect. I was out all yesterday morning, and part of the afternoon, and am so busy there is no time to be tired."

On the eve of the attack he writes: "Everything is going excellently. We had a very good dinner last night in honour of Brownjohn, who is leaving us . . . and got to bed about 1 a.m. When we got up we found enough flashes to keep us busy till lunch time, and after."

The attack was launched on the morning of July 1st, and from that time till about the end of October the line was continually shifting, with the result that the Group never got a chance to settle down to routine work. Nevertheless, as Lieut. Penrose and some of his N.C.O.s were trained Gunners, they were able to do some very valuable work at this time in sending back general information to the artillery.

On July 5th he writes: "All going well. . . . I have moved one post already—in fact, am finishing the move this morning."

On the 10th he tells of how he watched the attack from one of his Observation Posts, and now goes on: "I have moved Group Headquarters three miles forward, but so far have moved only one post (the one that I used to live at all winter), owing to the scarcity of high ground which is healthy enough to allow of keeping up communications satisfactorily; but I hope to have the others moved in two or three days."

"Much fun. On the 14th I got up at 3 a.m. and, as I was mounting my horse at our new H.Q., a shell came into the copse 15 yards behind me. Then I moved off in the dark. . . ." He was setting out "as I wanted to lose no time reconnoitring the ridge for O.P.s, which, by the way, was a wash-out, as we weren't far enough beyond it to put posts there safely. However, we had a most interesting day! Brownjohn had a piece of shell land flatways on his thigh, just above the knee, which fortunately didn't do any damage and only smarted a bit. The next day I moved both posts and H.Q. on to 'German soil,' where we are still, the posts being now about 3,500 yards in front of where we were before, and H.Q. about

"*Somewhere in France*"

6,000 yards in front of the old place at the Dell. I must not
at present describe our H.Q., but suffice it to say that it is
impregnable, or practically so. To-day I was talking, just
outside it, in the open, to the Colonel of a neighbouring
R.F.A. Brigade, and his orderly officer and Bishop were
with us, all four in a bunch, as close as could be. Suddenly
the Boche started 5·9-ing about 500 yards away. 'By
George, dam' good bursts!' said the Colonel. Then another
salvo, one of which was a little closer. I was just going to
suggest coming in out of the way and having a drink,
when one dropped a hundred yards off and there was a
'Whang!' and the Colonel toppled over. A piece had
caught him on the side of the jaw, or, rather, just below,
in the neck, and split it open for five or six inches—only
a flesh wound, but the deuce of a gap; so we tied him up
with one of our field-dressings, and took him down to the
office dug-out. The orderly officer and I fetched medical
aid—nearly getting bowled over by another shell for our
pains—and eventually got him off, well on his way to
Blighty! This is a jolly fine game. . . ."

"I got up at 1 a.m. this morning . . . and went up
front . . . to look for new sites. We had a huge time. I
took Norris and there were ten of us altogether stuck in
a 4-foot trench for an hour's bombardment, the only
casualty being this child hit on (not in) the leg with a
lump of H.E. and I've frequently had much worse at rug-
ger. Then we wandered about country, looking for things
and signalling . . . James has split into a new group of
his own, and I have Bishop and three posts. We are getting
Sapper pay from July 8th."

"Two days after my second 'outing' with Brownjohn, the
Boche took it into his head to throw 8-inch and 5·9's at
us for four hours on end. Having two very excellent dugouts, no one was hurt, but I got another scratch on the

same old shin while trying to fall into the dug-out! I have had to send one of my men back to the waggon lines with shock . . . Stringer, my waggon line N.C.O., came up 'all in a muck of sweat' with the news that a 4·2″ had come and killed the little mare, hit one draft horse (our best) in the stomach, and wounded three more. . . . I went with Brownjohn yesterday, and succeeded in seeing the 'Promised Land' from the high ground that we couldn't get to the last time. This time a hunk of 5·9″ that burst about fifty yards off cut my boot (left as usual) after slicing Brownjohn's coat skirt! But now I know where to put my posts when the time comes. . . . We're having a tough job right enough, but I think that we will get through all right."

On August 31st he writes: "The weather has been awful until this morning, and we have been struggling with new dug-outs and posts—everything flooded etc., —but it is fine to-day and that will give us a chance to get on a bit. . . . Since we've been up here, I've had (in posts and H.Q. staff) five casualties—one killed, three of my own and one of Brownjohn's wounded—which is not so bad, all things considered.

"Weather much improved. Leave is open on some parts of the front, but we're still busy here—digging and making posts."

September 10th: "We have the Group working again now more or less properly, and things are going well. . . . Parcels are arriving all right. . . . We have had a dug-out, 9 feet by 24 feet, with a kitchen joined to one side by a tunnel 5 yards long, made for winter quarters, mess and office. . . . I have a Singer now instead of the sidecar, but it burst its driving axle as soon as it arrived, so at the moment I am worse off than ever."

"We are all working in the open, and are having a

ripping time—real war for the time being, at any rate. I am about 200 yards from the Boche at one point, and am getting on very well. Everyone is quite pleased, and my chaps are playing up well. I got complimented by the Army Commander, together with Norris and another man, the other day for a job—not very hairy, though it might have been. . . . I'm learning to drive the Singer. . . . The last few nights I have been sleeping rather too close to a very mort Boche and several morts Frenchmen; but one gets used to it after the first few hours! We dug one out of the post where I am when the side of it fell in yesterday evening. . . . But we have made ourselves very comfy—as long as it doesn't rain too much."

September 21st: "I have been out of sorts so retired gracefully to 'Maps' two days ago. . . . I had a man hit just after I left—the sixth, I think, since the start. . . . I shall drive the Singer myself, but have only had time to try once so far, and traffic is rather thick these days."

The "out of sorts" was an attack of dysentery, but despite this Lieut. Penrose filled in his time at H.Q. by making visits to see how things were done in other Armies, and by making visits to the line to try and find new positions for Observation Posts. He got back to his Group in the middle of October.

"Imagine how busy I am: since coming back to the Group, I have not been once in to lunch! But things are going excellently now. . . . Rafferty, my other sergeant, has just got a Military Medal. That is the second. . . ." (The first was Norris.)

"Things still going strong, and our work is once more excellent in spite of difficulty in keeping up communication. We have a topping little camp here now, and are even enclosing it with rabbit-wire fencing."

November 6th: "All my men are getting special leave,

but I haven't an outside chance until I get another officer—and one who is some good, at that. . . . I am having a new Headquarters built, as this is a bit far away—also very muddy and un-get-at-able."

"I got hit on the right leg the other day, but am quite all right again now. I fact, I was hobbling for a couple of days, but nothing more than that. It was like a hack on the shin that bruised and broke the skin considerably, but did not even cut my riding boot! So far I have had Old Nick's own luck. . . ."

"It's damp, and it's muddy, and one's life is a continual strafe about oil stoves, drawing paper and broken lines; but still, somehow, I'm feeling cheerful in spite of the fact that two out of the three posts have been dis. for twenty-four hours, and likely to be so for another twenty-four or thereabouts. Also I have a man going on leave every day, and who knows but I may be back before the New Year? This time I think I really require leave. . . ."

November 19th: "I am now in a new place—very cosy —and with the much longed for second officer. . . . Please send plum-pudding enough to feed sixty men."

"We have a big hut—corrugated iron outside, with a matchboard lining—which we have divided into two parts. One is office, mess, and Goodwyn's sleeping place; and the other is store for instruments, etc., and my sleeping place. A big stove, in which we burn wood (there being plenty at hand), is in the middle of the first compartment, but the heat penetrates to the other half, as the partition is only canvas. Before I go to bed, I light an oil stove for half an hour in my little canvas cubicle—luxury indeed!"

The plum-puddings must have turned up all right, for on December 27th he writes: "I got here on Christmas Eve, so we had a proper 'Group Christmas.' Norris nearly got killed on Christmas Day. There was some heavy crumping at a certain well-known corner, and he was going to meet Rafferty to bring him to Christmas dinner. He helped to hold some restive water-cart horses, and the team and drivers of the next cart got chawed up by an almost direct hit. . . ."

"I went in to the Company yesterday after McLeod had rung me up and congratulated me" (on his M.C. gained in September 1916, which was gazetted January 1st, 1917) "and we went all the way in the Singer on top and first, as the second went west about half a mile after starting. Coming back the brakes wouldn't work properly, and just as we neared 'home' we failed to stop her until we got fair and square across a light railway and got rammed square on the port side by the light train. (It was port in more senses than one, as I had two bottles of it, as well as several of plums, between me and the engine, which, though they weren't broken, insinuated themselves between my ribs.) Marvellous to relate, nothing but the side step was hurt, though I felt a little joggled. Of course it heaved us off at an angle of 45° into the ditch alongside, from the depths of which I used the most awful language about men on point duty, driver of light railway train (poor devil, it wasn't his fault!), brakes of Singers and— quite a lot of things. However, the car can't run to-day, and is going sick to get itself mended. . . . The weather has given me rheumatics, but I walk 'em off—12 miles a day with two wretched men puffing behind me. Norris, short as he is, is the only one of the Group who isn't terrified of a walk with me."

The next three months included a spell of leave, and plenty of hard work, but little incident. But when the Boche retreated to the Hindenburg Line in March, things livened up again. He writes on the 23rd:

239

" . . . but I often go miles for 'picnics' these days, and it is a blessing to see green grass again. . . . We are having a lot of rest just now, but will probably have to work all the harder later on."

On April 10th: "We moved our Headquarters and the whole Group on Friday, and are now living in tents— right up to the neck in it. I'm putting out my people in the most weird positions, but it's all right, as this is not trench warfare. Norris, in the forward control, had a man hit yesterday, but only very slightly. I'm about $2\frac{1}{2}$ miles further back, but of course do a good deal of wandering around in front. In spite of the weather, which is erratic in the extreme, we are having a sporting time of it."

"Absolutely no time for the last four or five days . . . I ride most of the day, visiting all posts, eat like a horse between-whiles, and sleep like a log. . . . The Boche is certainly wanton.

"Still very busy. One leads a great open-air life here, and I'm feeling more fit than I have felt for a long time."

"I went up to see Norris this morning. As usual, when left to himself, he has been overdoing it, and collapsed yesterday after getting out of bed and going for some R.A.M.C. man to doctor up some men who had been buried in the next dug-out. Stacey, one of my line men, and Thomson, one of 'the family,' both distinguished themselves fishing these chaps out under fire, and have been recommended accordingly. Norris would not tell me how many nights on end he had been up. He's the limit! . . . It's pretty good sport here as long as the weather keeps decent."

"I'm still where I was, but expect to be moving a couple of miles north in a day or so. . . . It is being really quiet here just now. I was going to send you a box of wild flowers in moss, but there wasn't enough moss."

"I have just been moving—a couple of miles due north of where I was before. We have a topping little camp, and the weather is perfect."

"I went in to Headquarters the other day—it had just moved a good distance—and found them nearly all in their shirt-sleeves, making flower-beds! *We* have tulips, narcissi, and lilac in our vases."

"Don't write again till you hear from me, as I am going to change my address. I heard quite suddenly last night that all regimental gunners had to go back to the Regiment."

On June 2nd: "I am now in the 132nd Heavy Battery. . . ."

And so the entries relating to the Survey Groups end. The recollections that these extracts will arouse in the reader must vary with his or her personal experiences. But to all who served with the Survey, they must recall vividly the mixed emotions of these far off but not too unhappy days, and the memory of many good companions who made the great sacrifice.

12

AN OBSERVATION GROUP IN NORTHERN FRANCE

By way of contrast, let a Sapper in one of the last Groups to be formed in France relate his experiences. The last chapter covered the long-drawn-out agony of the Somme; and this, the tragic days in the spring of 1918 and the strenuous, but triumphant, days that followed. Although conditions were so different, the reader will note the same keen spirit of loyalty to the Group and to one another that was so noticeable in the early Group.

A little before Christmas, 1917, representatives of nearly every infantry regiment, with a sprinkling of other arms of the Service, assembled under a Corporal in the ragged shadow of the battered tower of Vlamertinghe Church, and the 23rd Group was born. It was a merry party. Destined to perform good work along that much battered ridge from Kemmel to Mont des Cats, which probably saved the Channel ports for the Allies.

Certainly we had every right to be merry in the busy days which followed, for was not the comparatively dry mud of Vlamertinghe a welcome change from that of the liquid variety of the old front line, and the mild thunders of the instructors as nothing to the thunder of guns? We were only too happy to make the acquaintance of "graticules," and to manipulate the gentle director in preference to the bucking Lewis gun. Were other advantages asked for did we not have the Presbytery next door, as an inexhaustible source of firewood? Furthermore, we had our regular Sunday holiday, the only condition being that we should find someone to conduct a short service in the morning. But some of us eventually decided that a holiday could be purchased at too high a price. After calling upon the services of all available authorized "pilots," local talent was resorted to. We mustered one who in civil life was a real local preacher, but there were others. We could understand why the Ironsides were so fearless—what was death in battle to compare with life enlivened by amateur preachers?

It was poor old Bill—he had a somewhat walrus moustache, too—who next tried his hand at conducting service. The rest of the Group were not enthusiastic, but it required something more than implied discouragement to deter Bill in anything pertaining to religion, in which he was extremely interested. Well, he gave that service, and he gave the sermon. The natural politeness of Britishers where religion is concerned kept us serious—with difficulty—for the first ten minutes or so, but for the next fifteen or twenty minutes—well, we stuck it out with the traditional sticking qualities of the British Army. The last fifteen or twenty minutes were a sort of evil dream.

Our tortures, however, were not over yet. Bill was wholehearted in his methods, if nothing else. He insisted—yes, absolutely insisted in the face of very real disapproval—on singing a sacred solo. It was no half-hearted sort of song either. It had ten verses or so, droned out in Bill's inimitable style with a ruthless slaughter of aspirates and a gasping "er" inserted in place of every full-stop in the good old canteen style.

Yes. A Sunday afternoon holiday can be purchased at too high a price!

There was practical work as well as theory. Favoured ones departed at intervals for tours of duty with established Groups and in January, the Group, now fairly well grounded in the theoretical work, removed to the village of St. Jean. We eventually discovered that we were billeted on the site of the village cemetery, if old leg-bones and occasional skulls were any criterion. With one of these skulls the one actor of the Group used to enliven the proceedings with a spirited rendering of Hamlet's soliloquy when things were dull.

In this insalubrious locality we settled down and proceeded upon the British soldiers' inevitable job of clearing up the muck. There was plenty of opportunity for us to exert our powers to dig among mud and brick-bats with a vague idea of making an Observation Post, and this was varied by organized rat hunts.

It was with some satisfaction that the whole Group got into action in conjunction with an old Group, and the three Posts experienced between them the varying conditions possible in Flash Spotting. One Observation Post, for example, was in the front line above Zonnebeke with a fine view of Daisy Wood, its attractive name being entirely spoiled by its unattractive appearance and odour. On the other hand, another Observation Post was established on the Menin Road quite near to Ypres, where the observers could go home to dinner and tea. The third Observation Post was in a half-way position on a steel tower, usually referred to as the Christmas Tree owing to the efforts of the humorists in camouflaging it as a battered tree.

It was at Zonnebeke that the 23rd had the first casualty —young Hunt being killed in the Observation Post by a stray shell, on a perfectly quiet night when a thick fog made observation impossible, and when he had only gone above the ground for a breath of fresh air. He was "sweating" on leave at the time. He was not unavenged.

On April 13th, at a moment's notice, the Posts were bidden assemble at H.Q., and found themselves directed

244

A Group in Northern France

to make their way to Locre. It was the first of those "Swiss Family Robinson" treks for which this Group was famous, though at this early date the menagerie of dogs, cats, pet jays, and various other animals had not been collected. The Posts, however, set out with their household goods stacked on home-made trucks which broke down at inopportune moments—such as crossing Ypres Square with high shrapnel falling.

It was a glorious—if quite premature—summer dawn when the 23rd reassembled in the grounds of Locre Château, and made themselves comfortable in some well-built huts. All the world was shining. The air was warm. Not a shell-hole was in sight. A rumour was current that the Group would remain there all the summer, and optimists were arranging fishing and swimming excursions in the château lake.

A few days later the front line ran through Locre, and snow was falling.

The first intimation of trouble was the growl of guns growing louder and more insistent, and literally battalions of walking wounded. Then came the order that one had to carry his rifle everywhere. Then certain observers, refreshing themselves in an estaminet, suddenly saw the landlady leaving with her clothes tied up in her bedding.

The 23rd found themselves waiting for the foe and destroying superfluous and incriminating maps and documents.

Presently the word came to fall back, and accordingly the 23rd started off, assisting their transport up the steep path which crossed the ridge behind—with an occasional shell falling uncomfortably near. The shelling grew more brisk on the far side of the ridge. Worse still, the roads were crowded with the panic-stricken civilian population.

It was decided to take a cross-country trip to Westoutre, the carts being hoisted bodily over the ditches. Eventually the Group halted at a deserted farm-house.

Matters were looking serious. The bombardment was general, a furious battle was raging, and evidently our people had had to retire.

To complicate matters, a cart that had set off from Rieggersburg Château with special instruments for the Group was found to be missing. It would be pleasant to relate how volunteers were called for to go back and seek for the missing instruments, but what actually occurred was just as effective, if less romantic.

Turning to the man at his side, the officer in charge demanded:

"Chapman. Are you a brave man?"

Chapman, with the sure instinct of an old soldier that there was some dirty work on foot, replied modestly and briefly,

"No, sir."

"That's a pity," quoth the officer, "because you will have to go back along the road we came and find that cart."

So he and a companion set off along the road from La Clyte to Locre. The two, having seen nothing but dead men and horses, eventually reached Locre. They were shelled out of the château, where they had gone on the scrounge, by what was probably the British artillery; and sat down to sup contentedly in what was probably the German front line. After nearly being demolished by a great howitzer, which was fired at the moment they were just under its muzzle, they reached Westoutre again and found that the cart for which they were searching had already arrived.

During the next few days the Group's movements were

erratic and uncertain. Wippenhoek was presently reached in a sleet storm. The 23rd possessed themselves of some leaky tents, after raiding a straw stack, to keep themselves out of the icy water underfoot.

Posts had been thrown out in the meanwhile. One, the band of heroes on Kemmel, having been burned out of the windmill, fixed up a post on the ground, from which they enthusiastically, if vaguely, carried on observation. One night an officer happened along and asked them if they knew that the French had been driven off Kemmel, and the front line was a good many hundred yards in their rear. The Post did not know this and hastened to repair the matter. They were lost entirely for about a week, as H.Q. had moved in the meantime, and they could not get into touch again till they had gone right down to Company H.Q. at Cassell. In their wanderings they had added a motor-car and a motor cycle to their outfit—they were celebrated for acquiring unconsidered trifles.

Matters were running to a tragedy on Mt. Noir. A shell dropped in the inadequately protected huts where the Post was billeted. Poor little "Eustace" Miles was killed, and Capt. Yarwood, the popular O.C., had his leg taken off. It was in getting him to the dressing station that Clem Hartley won his M.M. Shortly afterwards, Cpl. Brown and Wyrell, the linesman, were wounded, from which they both died.

There were shifts and changes with the beating back of the fighting line. Every available man was put on to line work in an endeavour to keep telephonic touch with the Posts. The shelling on the hillside was steady and pitiless. Telephone wire was blown to fragments, to be painfully pieced up only to be shot away again. There was the night when within view there was, apparently, only one

French field gun and an Australian howitzer left in action. All else had been systematically knocked out. How those Diggers fought their gun—with the assistance of rum—till their charge dump also blew up and left them helpless!

How many adventures there were in those vain endeavours to keep the lines in repair? Nobody was sorry when the Group was pulled out of action and sent down to a farm between Abeele and Sandvorde, where we were joined by our new O.C. From this place after a while Posts were thrown out, presumably ready for further German advances, but Jerry had reached his limit in that quarter. Once more the Group was on the move and H.Q. was fixed at Godewaersvelde, and remained there till the day of the forward movement in August.

It was during the next few months that the Group fully justified its existence. The chief Posts were Surrey on Mt. Noir, Kent on La Mountaine, and Derby on Mt. des Cats. At times there were two other Posts which came into being at intervening points. Work became regularized. Surrey and Kent found themselves comfortable billets on the outskirts of Boescheppe. Surrey had a picturesque mud cottage called "The House of the Mountain Ash Trees," while Kent annexed the cellars of the local château. Derby Post billeted near H.Q.

Surrey were given a lively reception. There was little cover across Mt. Noir to reach the Observation Post. It was a case of making for a wayside shrine, then a dash along a woodland track to the Observation Post, which would not have stopped an airgun pellet. On several occasions the observers spent the day stretched out on the floor, expecting the next shell to make a direct hit. Eventually the Observation Post was temporarily abandoned to the attentions of another Section of the ubiquitous R.E., who strengthened the structure and also constructed a dugout. Communication trenches were also eventually dug over the hill.

In those blazing summer days we watched desperate battles fought round Mettern; saw Bailleul crumble to ruins as the salient narrowed; and eventually found ourselves picking up the flashes of our own guns behind the German lines. There were dawns when we slipped out and raked for potatoes in the abandoned gardens below the Observation Posts; mornings when there was a deadly, uncanny stillness and Surrey observers watched anxiously for their luck fetishes—the woodpigeons. There were days when the Observation Posts were reached only by mad dashes between shell bursts, and when we had to creep out to repair telephone wire under fire.

There was the hectic morning when Surrey picked up two big guns right in the front line, and registered a most accurate shoot upon them. There was the occasion when Kent picked up a pillbox and dealt with the occupants who attempted to rush for safety—after which a cat was observed to stroll leisurely out of the building. There was another time when Kent discovered the endless train of transport along the camouflaged road, and there was excitement which trickled down to the "Great Ones," till it was discovered to be nothing but a strip of camouflage flapping in the wind.

The lighter side was not absent. There was our local preacher friend, with mild voice and inoffensive bearing, who was the prize scrounger of the British Army, and who could, at an hour's notice, be trusted to find for you anything from a case of bully to a blacksmith's shop complete. There was the Sapper Company Director, whose spare time was occupied in making "Heath Robinsonian" inventions. Then there were the pets—

those gallant comrades of our adventures. George, the wolf dog, soldier, and gentleman; Little Bobby, the canine Cockney street urchin; Nell, the scatterbrained society lady, who divided her domestic responsibilities with the futile but optimistic pursuit of magpies.

Then came the German retirement from Bailleul, when the Group was able to see something of the effects of good work done. It was at this stage that Surrey found themselves on Hill 63. It was the sort of place where the telephone was never kept in action for longer than fifteen minutes at a stretch, and the observers crawled out to repair the wire with the certainty of having the doubtful distinction of being sniped by whizzbangs. Surrey removed to Scherpenberg, and Kent took over from them on Hill 63. By this time it was not nearly such a lively spot, but Jack Austin was killed there.

It was from Scherpenberg that some favoured ones saw, between the rain squalls and crystal sunlight of a certain autumn morning, the grand advance. That was the moment when every British gun from the sea downwards spoke out, and the German lines flared up like a volcano; while wave after wave of infantry went over in the irresistible advance which finally pushed the Germans out of Belgium.

The Group was left high and dry. A move was made first to Wulverghen and then to Hollebeke. It was from this point that we had the inspiring experience of marching up the whole length of the epic Menin Road, past the utter desolation of Hooge to Gheluwe, where green fields commenced again. We tried to get into action, but the German retreat was too rapid, so we had to reel up our wire again. We regretfully left the Ortz Kommandateur's billet, which we had annexed, piano and all, and marched through to Coyghem. A regular triumphal progress it was, too, with enthusiastic welcome all the way from the lately released Belgians.

We were soon to find that we had still serious business in front of us among the swampy land, where Jerry was making his last stand. The land was so flat that cover was absent and observation extremely difficult. We got one battery and curiously enough were commended for it by the powers-that-were—our other good work had apparently gone unrecognized. Then the Spanish influenza caught us and a fair proportion of us were out of action when the Armistice was declared. Even then, it may be remarked, we celebrated the great event exactly twelve hours before it happened, and at 11 p.m. on November 10th were quaffing an assortment of liquors which were hastily decanted from the stores and officers' mess. Still we all lasted out safely till 11 o'clock next day.

After that we felt as if the mainspring of our very existence had been cut short. For about three days all we did was to play football. The dance given to the troops by the good citizens of Dottignes, at which we distinguished ourselves, helped somewhat to attune our minds to a new condition of affairs; but the old days were at an end with all their good fellowship and the jolly times—all the more jolly for the strenuous intervals. In addition, the Group was reorganized and some of us went off to Douai, where we felt lost amidst so many strangers all intent on their own business. The Group as a whole, however, went up to Roubaix and finally to Wahn, where the story of the 23rd quietly closed with gradual demobilization.

F. O. STURGEON

13

IN ITALY AND ELSEWHERE

No. 26 Group was known to its members as the "Tourist Group." Formed at the Field Survey Companies Depot at Mirlemont in December 1917 it travelled to Havre, the Rhône Valley, the Riviera, Genoa, Milan, across the plain of Lombardy to the River Piave just north of Venice. Withdrawn in April 1918 it returned across northern Italy to Marseilles and took ship to Salonika, spending five days at Malta on the way. After the Armistice with Bulgaria various members went to Sofia, Constantinople, the Dardanelles, Black Sea, Georgia, and Armenia.

In the Group was a strong nucleus of experienced observers contributed by various Groups on the Western front. These men after a continuous spell in the line, and finding themselves in the Base Camp of Havre awaiting entrainment to Italy, naturally hoped for passes into the town. These were rigorously forbidden by the camp authorities in spite of the O.C.'s efforts to obtain them. But the natural aptitude of the Survey man showed itself in the following amusing incident. One evening a message was received from the Assistant Provost Marshal that a certain Sapper had been found in Havre without a pass and was in the guard-room under arrest. At "Orderly Room" the next morning the "charge" was duly investigated, when it transpired that this Sapper, with other "veterans," had marched out of camp under the Group's then one and only Corporal, as an "R.E. Working Party," past the guard into the town to freedom, estaminets, etc. Falling in at a rendezvous they had marched smartly back. This simple plan had been worked successfully whenever required until this Sapper failed them at the rendezvous.

The weather was bitterly cold and the ground covered in snow when our seven-day train journey to Italy began. At St. Germains just north of Lyons was a rest camp at which troop trains stopped for a few hours—a very welcome change after two days in a railway carriage. We were sorry our horses could not also have the change. We fell in on the platform—a mixed crowd, "26" was the only unit, the others being drafts and details of all arms. Under the officer commanding the train, we marched the half mile or so to the camp. There in delightfully hilly and, to our eyes, gorgeous surroundings, although under snow, was a large canteen with a wide verandah. The programme at this "Rest Camp" was either (a) a short route march or (b) a bath. "26" stepped back two paces as one man in favour of (b). (b) was likely to take less time than the route march and to allow scope for the enjoyment of other attractions that might be available or were to be discovered. The few hours of freedom passed too soon and when the time arrived to fall in for the train the marchers had not returned, having lost their way!

The next morning, Christmas morning, broke clear and bright, the sun shining warmly, birds chirping, lizards flitting over the stone walls, the Rhône flowing blue alongside the railway—snow, frost, bitter cold all gone in the night! Our spirits rose with the temperature. What about a Christmas pudding all alight! The matter should be investigated when we arrived at Arles. As the result of a conference with the manager of the station restaurant a rum omelet was produced in a flaming dish and was rated an excellent substitute in all the circumstances.

While travelling over the plain of Lombardy, there

was a stop for lunch, which was served to all officers in the restaurant on the platform. The Railway Transport Officer informally presided. The repast was most welcome and we were about to commence the second course when our train was perceived to be very slowly drawing out of the station. The R.T.O. assured anxious questioners that it was merely clearing the platform and would be found in a siding, so all was well again and the Chianti was particularly good. But, alas, the train was not to be found in any siding, but had resumed the journey and without an officer on board! Much gesticulation ensued between the worried R.T.O., our very anxious O.C. train, and the excited Italian stationmaster. There was nothing to be done, however, but to follow in a subsequent train hoping to catch up. Some hours later, we arrived at a town and pulled up. Hurrah! Two British Sappers wearing Field Survey Company badges on their sleeves were on the platform. Everybody got out. "Where is our train?" asked the O.C. "Gone on an hour ago, sir," said our Sappers brightly. "Then, what the hell are you two doing here?" demanded the Colonel. "Please sir, as there were no officers on board, we didn't like to stay so we all got out and let it go!"

Our final destination was Padua, but No. 26 continued to occupy their coaches in a siding surrounded by numerous store trains. These were guarded by Italian soldiers. At dusk we were interested to observe the fine lanterns with which each sentry was provided. Presently we heard the drone of aeroplanes approaching and bombs were soon falling about the station and in the town. Our Allies dropped their lanterns under the wagons and faded away. It was curious that some most excellent lanterns were afterwards found in our horse boxes when we eventually detrained at Montebelluna.

In Italy and Elsewhere

The line held by the Italian Army followed the River Piave across the plain to the sea and included one of the foothills of the Alps known as the Montello. This hill and some few miles of line in the plain were taken over by the British, and No. 26 Group established a left Post on the Montello and three other Posts in buildings on the plain.

The Montello was a geographical curiosity. Kidney-shaped, about 8½ miles in length east to west and about 3½ miles wide, it rose smoothly to a height of 1,200 feet, being separated from other hills by plains on the north and south, the Piave ravine on the east and another river valley on the west. A circular road ran all round the foot of the hill and it was crossed from north to south by no less than 22 approximately parallel roads. Why this particular hill should be so amply provided with means of communication was a problem we had not time to investigate. Group H.Q. was in a farm-house at the south end of Strada 6. In the surface of the Montello were numerous craters, many quite 50 feet deep, the sides being grass covered, others with fruit trees. These were plain basin-shaped sinkings in the surface. They did not suggest volcanic origin. None held water. They formed excellent positions for howitzer batteries.

On the plain a village usually comprised a quite small group of houses clustered round the church with its inevitable campanile or bell tower.

The view from an Observation Post on the plain, generally sited under the tiles of a roof, was a perfectly flat country as level as the sea, the line of horizon being broken only by farm-houses and trees which in the telescope seemed to join up to close the view. The peasant farmers lived on their farms and their houses were dotted all over the countryside. Those near to the line were occupied by our troops, for there were far too many for any one house to become a particular mark for gun-fire.

The campaniles were obvious sites for Observation Posts, but were they not likely to be too obvious to be of real service? Thinking so, our preference was for more prosaic roofs.

We were especially pleased with our right Post in the roof of the railway station at Spresiano, where the line runs on an embankment, but the attraction of the campanile as an Observation Post was, however, too strong for H.Q. and we were instructed to move into the campanile of Ludovina, an adjoining village. The Post itself was in the belfry and open to view on four sides, any movement being visible in silhouette. Every precaution to prevent signs of occupation was taken, but the enemy must have suspected something because he commenced to shell the tower one morning and was not content until it was reduced to ruins. They achieved a direct hit on the Observation Post, and pieces of the instruments, watch, telephone receivers, and other equipment were afterwards picked up on a farm and in a field nearby. Most fortunately our two observers were not included in this disbursement, as an early shell had severed the telephone line, and the Post being, therefore, out of action both had descended to repair the defect. Some few days later, when complete new equipment had arrived, we resumed our old Observation Post in the station roof.

On going into action we found that no counter battery work had been done, and that the enemy had his guns well advanced and took little trouble to hide flashes. Then we Flash Spotters got to work and very soon had most of the gun positions located and confirmed by R.A.F. photographs. When the 11th Corps Artillery came into position each location was carefully plastered with 400 rounds of 6-inch howitzer shell. The enemy retired further and further and soon rarely fired after dark. The corresponding relief from shell fire in our back areas was most noticeable. In the hills direct flashes were almost impossible to obtain as the gun pits were in gullies and ravines.

The small town of Nervesa on the bank of the river had been evacuated by the civil population and was constantly shelled. One night an observer who had been there with rations came to the mess. "Would the Captain like a chest of drawers and a wardrobe?" He had seen them in a house which had been seriously damaged and considered they would be safer at H.Q. and had brought them in on the ration cart. Other articles continued to arrive until our originally poor farm-house became a sumptuously furnished dwelling. A few weeks later two peasant women looked in one afternoon; we surmised they might be the owners of the place; they obviously knew it well. The expressions on their faces as they glanced in the various rooms were funny.

When we moved, all these nice things were left behind. Did these good people find them there when they resumed occupation? Did the Nervesans realize that their missing furniture might be found in the nearby countryside and attempt to recover it? Could they prove it to be theirs when found and would our landlords give it up were questions which have occurred to us many times.

For no apparent reason that had to do with the conduct of the war, No. 26 was transferred from the Italian front to Macedonia in April, returning across northern Italy to Marseilles. A pleasant fortnight was spent there awaiting a transport with no difficulty about leave out of camp, then another fortnight on board under convoy.

Macedonia was a barren land. Even Salonika we found

burnt to the ground and there was nothing to scrounge. The reason was simple. There had recently been two wars here before ours. Never before had we been so dependent on R.E. dumps, and things were—well, they weren't.

The portion of the front allotted to No. 26 Group was along the Greco-Bulgarian frontier opposite Guevgeli with one Post east of the river Vardar. The country was hilly with deep ravines and grew the very finest Turkish tobacco.

We were sent up the line from Salonika in lorries by night with lights out and were guided to an H.Q. site which had been chosen for us in a mulberry plantation. When dawn broke it was discovered that our heavy guns were in the ravine behind us and our field guns in a ravine in front, and it seemed likely we would make the acquaintance of all enemy shells which fell short of the former or over the latter and our telephone lines would be continually severed. Altogether different from the nice quiet well-furnished farm-house which we had been accustomed to!

A ride before breakfast to find another site was therefore urgent. In this country the climate was more to be feared than the action of the enemy and in choosing a site for a habitation, babbling brooks at the bottom of valleys, however good for guns, were not ideal for Flash Spotters on account of mosquitoes who gave you malaria.

An open breezy space reasonably level, out of sight of the enemy, with spring water and conveniently near to our heavy guns was our immediate objective. We therefore explored the high ground behind the heavy-gun line and were fortunate in finding a site which served us excellently for the whole of the summer, until the war in this theatre ended, and gave us a health record which was a credit to the camp.

In Italy and Elsewhere

The war here was mostly of a desultory character enlivened by occasional raids. One night we definitely located a new gun position. The next day Corps H.Q. telephoned that plotted on the map the gun was in the middle of the river Vardar. We suggested the river might be shown incorrectly on the map, which was not too accurate, but we were not believed. After the Armistice we searched for this gun and found it in an embrasure cut out of a cliff overhanging the river. It commanded a wire entanglement constructed below water-level to prevent our people sending a naval expedition up the river. The map was wrong after all.

When the Bulgars retreated, before the Armistice on September 30, 1918, No. 26 Group concentrated at H.Q. ready to advance, but no more Flash Spotting was required, and, for a short time, we were left to our own devices. We took the opportunity to explore the old enemy lines, to clear up doubtful locations, and to check others. While engaged in this work the writer found some deserted Bulgar dugouts in the form of caves cut into the face of a cliff, each with a door at the entrance. Opening one of these he found the whole of the floor strewn with paper and, peering in in the dim light, he presently noticed a slight sound like raindrops; the sound seemed to come from the floor yet there was nothing to be seen to account for it. Then the patter seemed to be at his feet; he looked down. It was fleas. Thousands of them hopping on the paper and hopping on to him! They must have been starved for some days and were not a bit shy. He hastily retreated and shut the door, but found he had already collected several dozen under putties, breeches, tunic, etc. Here was a predicament. He could not advisedly ride in the car much less would he be welcomed at the mess. To reach the dugouts from the road, it had been necessary to cross a

259

stream and this suggested a solution of the difficulty. He undressed, shook out and carefully examined each garment and threw it over the brook. Finally, throwing himself over, he redressed and returned to the car having had the novel experience of hearing fleas on the march!

And so to home. Once a year members of the Group who can get to London attend the parade of the re-union of the Salonika forces, and afterwards forgather with their C.O. in his home at Hampstead to retell the old tales and remember departed comrades.

CHAS. STRACHAN

14

AN APRIL MORN: OR HOW LARKSPUR WAS EVACUATED

THE bombardment which of a sudden shattered the uncanny stillness of an April night at Lacouture, blew into smithereens on the instant a state of tranquillity which in the Lys sector had lasted for an incredible two years.

In the steeple of Lacouture's ruined church was Larkspur, B Survey Post of No. 8 or Heather Group. Most favoured of all Survey Groups on the Western front, Heather had, since the Posts were first established in 1915–16, lived a comparatively quiet life. Despite its proximity to the line at Neuve Chapelle, Larkspur and its neighbouring Posts, Lavender, Birch, and Forget-me-not, had been "homes from home" for the men stationed there.

In 1916 and 1917 from the Somme to the Salient, save for that sanctuary in the valley of the Lys, battle had flared up in sector after sector: always (since the battles of Neuve Chapelle and Festubert) that strip of the line between Laventie and Annequin, which happened to be under the observation of the Posts of Heather Group, had been spared any serious attention by the opposing armies.

The new year of 1918 had dawned on this charmed Group peacefully enough, with work on the Posts done efficiently and without fuss, and life in billets all that could be desired. Most of the sector was held by the Portuguese troops; and at Laventie their warrant officers paid calls on the village maidens sporting the glossiest of silk hats, well-groomed tail-coats, lemon gloves, and silver-headed canes.

At Lacouture in the snug estaminet next to the Mairie, which they shared with mine host, genial white-moustached Abram Chavatte, the men of Larkspur continued to make life endurable with occasional champagne supper parties to which favoured guests from Group H.Q. and the neighbouring Posts were invited.

After two years of agreeable residence at Beuvry, an N.C.O. of Birch was the accepted suitor of the charming daughter of the billet. Feminine society was appreciated by the men of Forget-me-not, too, at their billet at Sailly-la-Bourse, as a distraction from the annoyance of the close proximity of a battery of field guns to their Post on the smouldering Fosse. And Group H.Q. at Zelobes, not to be outdone by the Posts, went swimming in La Bassée canal and made merry o' nights with comrades of Z Sound Ranging Section at a noted house of call at the cross-roads at Les Lobes on the Bethune road.

Disquieting rumours there were, naturally, in those early weeks of 1918; and these received a big stimulus when the shock of the news of the March offensive down south disturbed this Elysium. Talk there was of a forthcoming enemy "push" in Heather's sacred sector; of special orders for Posts to meet unthinkable contingencies; of a secret rendezvous in the event of a forced withdrawal. Drivers of ration carts brought in news of vast trench systems under construction miles away in the back areas: rumours of mighty siege guns coming up by rail; and to show all was not rumour one actually appeared in position at Laventie.

First-hand evidence of an approaching change in the situation on the immediate front of the Group was furnished not so much by increased activity of the enemy's artillery as by the fixation by our Post observers of many new battery positions. Flashes having been observed and reported in an unfamiliar quarter and the battery located by cross observation, it was noted as significant that it betrayed no further sign of its presence.

"New batteries registering!" grunted the war-wise Field Survey Company observers in their eyries.

Such signs of artillery concentration were common in those tense days of early April. From the spire of Lacouture church the unusual sight of enemy working parties began to be reported whilst, on April 7th or 8th, observers on that Post actually picked out German gun teams openly hauling their pieces into position at no great distance behind their own front line.

How eagerly Larkspur put through word of this impudence to Group H.Q., itching to see our Counter Batteries get on the tempting target. But alas! nothing happened, and the reason was only too clear. Between Lacouture and Laventie there was, it was whispered, only one battery of 60-pounders; and this news the observers nursed with such philosophy as each could muster, and hoped for the best.

Such then was the situation at Lacouture on April 8, 1918. The Post, mustering eight men, was in charge of a Corporal, one of the "old hands" of the Field Survey Company, known to the Posts far beyond the limits of Heather Group as "Bom," in deference to his rank previously in the R.F.A. With "Bom" were "Ginger," an old cockney sailor; "The Gunner" (ex-R.G.A.); "Sowerby Bridge," whose West Riding speech was translated to the Londoner by "The Scribe," a Lancastrian; "Pat," who wasn't an Irishman, but talked like one; Derbyshire "Charley"; a loquacious Welshman, and the inevitable "Jock." In short a typical Field Survey Company detachment.

Two men went on duty that night as usual, leaving the others sleeping peacefully in the billet a few hundred yards along the village street.

Up in the Post it was a dead quiet night and a night of pitch darkness unbroken by moon or stars, gun flashes, or even the usual trench fireworks. The first wan light of early morning came filtering through a sea of mist. "Misty in the distance" had for long been a stock joke at Larkspur, having more than once caused the rising moon to be reported as "Big fire behind the enemy lines." But now the mist was right up to the observers' peep-hole.

At 4.15, by the Post chronometer, suddenly out of the mist and the silence surged a roar like a hurricane. The crazy steeple rocked. The air was filled with a mighty rushing, and the next moment a pandemonium of bursting shells crashed into the universal uproar.

On the instant the man at the telephone yelled to Group H.Q.

"Heavy bombardment just started. Shells dropping all around."

From all the other Posts in the Group similar reports were coming in simultaneously, and H.Q.'s reply to all was:

"Same here and all along the line," adding on a note of cheery optimism, "What about flashes?"

"Flashes be ——! It's like pea-soup," must have reached H.Q.'s telephonist in a five-mile chorus, for, as at St. Quentin three weeks earlier, the enemy's hammer-blow on the Lys was favoured with a mist as thick as an old-time "London particular."

That was the last Larkspur heard that day from Group H.Q., for the lines were blown to pieces there and then by the barrage. So there was the Post out of action through the mist, and the two observers cut off from communication with both their H.Q. and their billet and Post Commander. There was nothing for it but to seek such shelter as they could find behind the massive stone walls at the lower part of the tower.

Their plight was indeed unenviable, for not only was Lacouture steeple, a conspicuous object in that level landscape, an obvious Observation Post, and, therefore, target for the enemy gunners, but it was actually at the very centre of a redoubt, which had long before been constructed all round its graveyard. The church building itself was a roofless ruin, with nave and aisles littered with the debris of bombardments of 1915. The churchyard was chiefly remarkable for overturned gravestones and yawning vaults. Rats ravished the desecrated tombs, and, littered with human bones, the weedy burial ground was an open-air charnel house. Not a pleasant place to linger in at the best of times, but excessively gruesome under the flail and harrow of drum-fire!

Down at the billet, chez Chavatte (which Abram in his wisdom had evacuated a week before) the crash of the barrage had sent seven sleepers leaping in a frenzy from their beds, under the confused impression that an earthquake, a volcanic eruption, and a tornado had all struck the place at once. The floor under them trembled. Down from the ramshackle roof rattled its remaining tiles. The roar of gun-fire, the crash of explosions, the rushing of shells overhead clouted their eardrums.

A shell bursting on the *pavé* immediately outside shook the walls and shattered the windows, raining broken glass on the hapless crew who had had the good sense to fling themselves on the floor like a well-rehearsed troop of acrobats. Two more narrow shaves were to test their nerves, and at first probably all were seized with the notion that their billet was the vortex of this storm that had so suddenly been let loose. It soon, however, became obvious to the seven men struggling into their clothes, steel helmets, and equipment, that not their humble cottage nor even the village itself was the main target. Many as were the shells bursting on all sides close at hand, the unceasing screaming overhead told of countless messages of hate speeding farther afield.

So, of course, it proved. While at first Lacouture was actually under the curtain of the barrage, the terrific bombardment was, at one and the same time, battering the unfortunate Portuguese infantry in the line behind their hopelessly inadequate breastworks, cutting off with an impenetrable barrier any possibility of reinforcements reaching them, hammering every British and Portuguese battery position, searching out all divisional and brigade H.Q.s, churning up every cross-roads, and making an impassable inferno of every bridge over La Bassée canal —*which lay across the line of retreat from the line and Lacouture.*

The first surmise of Bom and his anything but merry men (and also, as it later proved, of the two men on the Post) was that nothing more serious than a big trench raid was afoot; and their immediate thought was, of course, to seek shelter from the storm which threatened every moment to engulf them.

Fortunately for his small command, Bom had a cool head and a steady nerve. He also lived up to a precept which was a favourite of his: "Always keep a little bit up your sleeve." The first of these "little bits," which was now forthcoming just when required, was the result of a piece of forethought which had at one time proved a bit irksome to his men when off duty.

When in the early part of 1918 talk of dark future

possibilities was rife, this resourceful N.C.O. had either indented for, or scrounged, a small "elephant hut." This contraption of corrugated iron was, under his direction, assembled against the back wall of the cottage, and was strongly reinforced on both sides and at one end with a triple wall of sandbags. Heavy beams laid across the top were roofed over with further courses of sandbags, and two half-walls of sandbags cunningly built at the front with a passage between, protected the entrance to the hut and gave a well-shielded means of access to it.

By the time this miniature strong point was completed, even the grousers (there were no shirkers) were mightily proud of it. They had cause to be; for without a shadow of doubt it saved seven lives on April 9th. And—to make a brief digression—what is more after that day's retreat and after three months of bombardment by our artillery, in turn, of the positions the Germans came to occupy at Lacouture, some of these same master builders of Larkspur had the curious satisfaction of finding that hut, during the final British advance, intact and as snug as when they had left it. It had served the enemy right well as an ammunition store!

It was to this refuge that the seven men of Larkspur turned gratefully after being so rudely awakened on the morning of April 9th, and there was held the council of war at which Corporal Bom announced his decision that every preparation should be made to retire, but that no move should be made, except under express orders from a superior officer, till the two men returned from the Post, and till either the refuge received a direct hit or the enemy actually arrived in the village. Meanwhile, there they would remain to await any orders that might (miraculously) come through from Group H.Q.

It was a long wait. Hour followed hour and the bombardment showed no signs of abatement. The hut bore a charmed existence. In the yard close by, a shell fell plump in the hen-house, filling the air with feathers as though a feather bed had burst. Again one fell in the midden, and the air was filled with something worse.

All this time—it was now eight o'clock—no word had come from the men at the Post. The Gunner gallantly volunteered to run through to find out how they were faring, and at the same time to take the two men their breakfasts. So heavy was the shelling of the village that it hardly seemed possible he could accomplish his mission, and there was a long and anxious wait till at length he returned with the news that the two others were safe at the base of the tower and the Post itself was as yet unhit, although shells were dropping unceasingly all around.

The Gunner had carried with him Bom's authority for the two men to return to the billet at their discretion, but they had preferred the shelter of the stone walls to the chances of a dash through the open while the bombardment was still at its height.

To the Old Larkspurians, waiting behind their sandbags and corrugated iron for something to turn up—or fall down!—the deafening hours that slowly passed were a waking nightmare. The thunder of the bombardment rolled continuously, and all around the air seemed filled with bursting shells. It seemed incredible that the hut should escape a direct hit much longer; and every man knew that a 4·2 or anything bigger must crumple it up like an old can and write "finis" to the adventure.

Heavy as was the elephant, but with its three layers of sandbags, again and again the whole contraption was lifted bodily as a shell landed particularly near. The houses on each side were brought down with a roar; and three or four shells actually fell in the small yard in which the hut stood.

Conversation was desultory. Fatalists all, the little garrison whiled away the time as each thought fit. What had needed to be done had been done. All Post records, maps, and written orders had been brought together, and a can of paraffin stood handy. Every man wore his full equipment, and loaded rifles were within arm's reach.

The Scribe acted as a self-appointed sentry at the entrance: neither he nor anyone else knew why! Bom, Gunner, Jock, and someone else grimly played nap and pontoon. Number Six kept on softly saying his prayers, till this getting on the nerves of the others, number Seven had the happy inspiration of starting up the gramophone and putting it through the whole of its repertory, which kept him busy, drowned the prayer meeting, and cheered everyone up. Never will anyone who was there forget the incongruity of hearing Caruso's passionate "O Sole Mio" raised against that tumult of bursting shells and the roar of the barrage.

Noon brought no abatement of the bombardment, but The Scribe peeping out now and again reported that the mist was lifting. Of a line of poplars that stretched across the meadow from the billet yard, the first, second, and third could now be made out.

Perhaps an hour later there was at last a perceptible slackening in the intensity of the shelling nearby, though the screaming of shells overhead was continuous.

Bom pricked up his ears and took his eyes off his "hand." "Lengthening their fuses," he remarked with professional interest. "See, they're shoving the barrage farther back!" This new phase encouraged debate. Its significance was plain. The trench system had been carried and the enemy was closing on Lacouture.

Still no orders, no word from the Post, no signs of reinforcements. All strained their ears for the first sound of machine-gun fire heralding the approach of the German outposts. Meanwhile pontoon gave way to nap.

One memory deserves to be set down. The mass challenge of the German artillery had not gone entirely unanswered. Our 6-inch gun at a farm beyond Vielle Chapelle had been silenced within the first half-hour; but in an orchard just outside Lacouture village two British 60-pounders played David to the enemy's Goliath with the greatest gallantry: though without David's luck. One gun was fought till knocked out by a direct hit or wrecked by a "premature," while the other barked away magnificently, hour after hour, a lone British voice amidst the enemy's thunder, and, miraculously almost, was eventually hauled out and got back into safety just in time to escape capture. A gallant achievement!

At two o'clock the rat-tat-tat of machine guns announced the German infantry's approach, confirmed a minute or so later by the tardy return of the missing two men from the church. Yes, the Germans were at the farther end of the village. The Post? Everything had been deliberately destroyed to prevent it falling into the enemy's hands. The observation of fire instrument had been pitched from the top to the bottom of the tower, being too heavy to be carried away.

Again Bom had "a little bit up his sleeve." From some secret hiding-place appeared as if by magic a jar of rum which (regulations or no regulations) he poured into the men's water-bottles. The paraffin was poured over the heap of records in the yard and a light set to it.

And as the bonfire blazed up the party of nine, with such goods and chattels on their backs as they could

An April Morn

lump along, at 2.15 p.m. said "Good-bye" to the old
billet and sallied forth in good order into the shell-pitted
and debris-strewn village street. Impossible for everything
accumulated in the course of a long residence to be
rescued. One strange find for the enemy "Intelligence"
would be a dozen copies of the *Humanitarian Review*: who
was to know that these had been used by one fond English
mother for packing the parcels sent fortnightly to her son?
Another literary discovery for the German searchers
would be the manuscript of an unfinished novel which
one of the outgoing tenants had been writing in leisure
hours.

Although now out of the billet, the nine companions
were by no means out of the wood. A hundred yards or
so down the village street they passed a group of Portuguese soldiers sheltering behind a garden wall. The
officer in charge of this party called upon the Survey men
to stop and join him and lent emphasis to the order by
flourishing his revolver. Since it was quite obvious that
no attempt was being made to hold up the enemy, and
since the Field Survey Company personnel were in no
sense under the authority of the Portuguese, this the
Larkspur detachment refused to do point blank, in-
forming the officer that they were making for their headquarters.

Strange to relate, as they hastened through that street
of ruins, they were joined by terrified villagers emerging
from hiding-places in cellars and old dugouts. "Les
Boches!" they screamed as they fled down the street,
"Les Boches sont ici!" Oddest sight of all, one young
woman well known to the Larkspur lads was in her
Sunday best, a bundle in one hand and in the other a pair
of smart high-legged boots which she dropped every few
yards. "Come on, Marie," called out Ginger, cheerily

picking up her boots, and Marie, sobbing with fright, fell in beside them.

Bom's line of retreat had been carefully planned to avoid such points as the enemy might be expected to make for. The main problem was how best to cross the broad La Bassée canal which cut across country at a distance of two kilometres between Lacouture and the comparative safety of the "back areas." Of no use to follow the road to the main bridge on to Vielle Chapelle. The probability was that it no longer existed. The little band left the road at the end of the village and in single file struck across the open fields towards a small foot-bridge a kilometre or so farther along the canal. And suddenly they came under a desultory rifle fire from the direction of some farm-buildings faintly seen through the thinning mist at a distance of perhaps three hundred yards.

Marie screamed but was told she would get smacked if she didn't behave, so suffered herself to be bundled over the canal bank to a narrow footpath that ran alongside the water. The troops followed and, thus sheltered by the bank, all covered the remaining distance to the foot-bridge without mishap, except for one man who got entangled in telephone wire and slipped into the water, from which he was quickly fished out.

And now they were heartened by the sight of British troops coming into action across the canal. A kilted regiment, the Liverpool Scottish as it later appeared, was doubling up and getting into firing position in extended order at a distance of fifty yards beyond the further bank.

Larkspur's final dash for safety was the most hazardous part of the whole adventure. As each member of the little band clambered up the bank to get to the footbridge he

Drawn by P. S. Willats, 1917

ARRAS CATHEDRAL

The Survey men manned a Post on top of the wall to the left near to the
small opening seen on the drawing

was met by a burst of machine-gun fire at such short range as to make a hit certain had it not been for the mist which still clung to the ground. However, their luck held—the Germans on the one side of the river continued to fire and miss, while, on the other, the Scottish infantry, who might have been excused for mistaking the fugitives for the enemy's scouts or advance guard, continued to hold their fire. Their footsteps speeded by these individual attentions, all the nine together with their terror-stricken girl friend bolted across the bridge at decent intervals and, reaching the other side, immediately felt that they had made good their escape.

Passing through the lines of the kilties they were called upon by an officer to give an account of themselves; but a Brigade Major coming up at that moment and perceiving their Field Survey Company badges gave them authority to proceed; first, however, demanding news of what was going forward on the other side of the canal. The news that Lacouture had only just been occupied by the enemy took the Staff officer by surprise, as it had been understood that the village had fallen into the hands of the Germans before noon. It was then about a quarter to three.

The knowledge that, as Survey men, our fugitives had of the surrounding country, gained in many peaceful walks, stood them in good stead. The roads were, of course, crowded with troops and military traffic, and with refugees hurrying away with such poor household goods as they could pile into farm wagons, handcarts, or even bassinets. Larkspur's band cut straight across country for Hinges, the secret rendezvous assigned by Group H.Q. long before, but arrived there to find that village in the process of being evacuated and a party of Engineers already preparing to blow up the bridge across the canal.

A minor incident of the party's adventures was the

chasing of two of them round a haystack by an enemy aeroplane flying low.

By this time British artillery was in action in prepared positions and giving a good account of itself, and a noted division was hurrying forward to stop the gap in the Allied line.

Beyond Hinges our nomads from Larkspur were fortunate in being hailed by an officer from Field Survey Battalion H.Q., passing in a car, and were told they would find Heather Group assembled at a farm at the village of Lannoy. And there, in the early evening, they were uproariously welcomed by their comrades, who had long before given up all hope of seeing them again, assuming Larkspur Post to have been taken prisoners when Lacouture was captured. Group H.Q. at Zelobes and Lavender Post at Laventie had retired early in the morning, while reports had been received that Birch Post at Beuvry and Forget-me-not at Annequin were still in possession. Thus, Heather Group kept up its lucky reputation, not a single casualty being sustained that day by any of its scattered detachments.

The later adventures of this Group belong to another story; but it may be said here that within four days the Old Larkspurians were again in action, manning a Post at the top of the massive tower of Bethune's ancient church. That once populous and busy town was empty, its public buildings, shops, and streets silent as the grave, save for the spasmodic outbursts of shell fire directed by the enemy into its midst. For fourteen days the Survey men were the only inhabitants of the town, except for occasional artillery officers going up the church tower to direct the fire of their batteries.

Their Post, with the redoubtable Bom still in charge, had three addresses in that fortnight. The first "billet" in a cellar opposite the church lasted two nights. Instinct dictated a change of quarters: a direct hit on that house the following day made the move a wise one. Another cellar gave shelter for three nights till a shell knocked the roof off. On April 18th the Germans renewed their attack all along the line and made a determined effort to capture Bethune, but were stopped in Gore Wood on the outskirts of the town.

A laconic diary entry for that day reads "Hot time on Post." It was! The following day the billet was removed to safer quarters, and a diary entry for Saturday, April 20th, reads, "Spent birthday in cellar furnace room of Bethune Church." That was their third and last billet while manning the Post on the church tower.

What made life so exciting in those days was the fact that, apart from the sporadic bombardment of the town which was making a shocking mess of the place, as early as the second day of occupation by the Survey Post, the church had been palpably "registered on" by 8-inch batteries firing from directions about ninety degrees apart, one battery somewhere around La Bassée to the north and the other somewhere in the middle of the new salient which the Germans had created by their break through on April 9th. The only thing the Survey men did not know was when the "shoot" was dated for. . . . And to make things yet more comfortable they learned that the tower had been mined by our demolition engineers' ready to be blown up with dynamite by an electric spark if the town should be captured!

During those fourteen days splendid results were obtained by the observers, the new positions of the enemy's guns being located with ridiculous ease. Curiously enough, the telephone lines back to Group H.Q. at Fouquereuil held good throughout. It was, of course, only a matter of days before such a magnificent Observation Post, dominating the country for miles around, was put out of action. It lasted till April 27th, when the two suspected batteries opened fire with deadly precision and deliberation. Both were on the target in half a dozen rounds, and nine men, late of Larkspur, having got news through of the batteries that were engaged, cowered on the spiral staircase below the belfry while the interior of the ancient church was battered into tumbled masonry, and a mountain of debris and great stones came crashing down from the top of the tower.

It was time for this sorely tried band to make another bolt, which they succeeded in doing after first, at some risk, climbing up to the belfry, dismantling the Post and carrying down the crazy ladders and the spiral steps all their instruments. They fled, one by one, according to plan, in the half-minute intervals between the fall of the shells; and, with a white terrier which they had rescued some days before barking at their heels, they never stopped running till they had placed some hundreds of yards between themselves and the particularly unhealthy spot which they had left.

This time all their personal belongings were left behind them—in the furnace room, below the church tower, the entrance to which had been effectually sealed by the fall of some tons of masonry. And (though this loss was not reported) in the furnace itself they left behind them three dozen bottles of choice wines which had certainly never been placed there by the caretaker of the church!

And so back to Group H.Q. at Fouquereuil with the news. That was Saturday. On Sunday came through orders that at all costs a Post must be maintained in Bethune. Sunday saw a dejected party on a G.S. wagon, complete with the paraphernalia for equipping another

An April Morn

Survey Post, clattering once again into Bethune—now a mere travesty of a town with most of its well-known buildings in ruins.

Old Larkspurians with Bom again in command drew up at the Convent of St. Vaast; and this time probably all said their prayers. "Third time unlucky," said a lugubrious voice. There was a little pinnacle above the roof and in there a Post was set up. A billet was established in the spacious basement refectory. Twenty-four hours passed uneventfully, with no results to speak of. The following day was May Day and H.Q. marked the occasion by sending up seven or eight reinforcements, men new to the Survey just up from the base.

That same night heavy shelling started, and continued. Mixed with the high explosive were many gas shells. The men down below were warned and put on their masks, and kept them on for some hours. When it seemed safe to do so and the shelling had ceased the masks were removed. And, to cut a long story short, in the hours that followed one after another (beginning with the new recruits) went down, and at ten o'clock that night the last two were led away by rescuers from Fouquereuil blinded. The whole post of sixteen men gassed, and away off, some to hospital at Etaples and some to Blighty. . . . That was the last of Larkspur.

W. Bently Capper

15

THE SURVEY POST OBSERVER AS A
FIGHTING MAN

THE Posts and billets of No. 24 Group were in the devastated Somme area, and there were no villages or towns in close proximity. There were the usual ration dumps and isolated canteens but the country was most depressing after our experiences in the north. However, the men made the best of it and life was very pleasant in spite of the drawbacks. Great friendships were formed, and the mail arrived promptly and with it the usual number of parcels including gramophone records. The chief recreation in the evenings was cards, reading and chess coming far behind.

Pettie and another observer took over from the writer at dusk on March 20, 1918, and the night was quiet until between 3 and 4 a.m., when Pettie reported (there was a telephone line to the billet) that a heavy bombardment had started. Two minutes after the line was "dis" and the wires were found absolutely shot to pieces. The men in the billet—who had not undressed—got ready. The billet was situated in shallow reserve trenches and was now under heavy fire (high explosive) and gas.

There was a thick mist blotting out everything beyond ten yards.

There was an S O S 18-pdr. battery about fifty yards to the rear of the billet and as this had not opened up it was thought that the attack had not again developed.

It afterwards transpired that the battery had pulled out without firing a round and as the billet was a small isolated one it would appear that the artillery officers had not troubled to let us know—or had forgotten to do so.

The firing died down at dawn and it was decided to snatch a meal. All the open food had been contaminated with gas, so tins of bully beef and biscuits were opened.

The mist muffled most sounds, but suddenly and most unexpectedly there was a burst of machine-gun fire right over the billet, and there was no mistaking the steady beat—it was a Jerry gun.

The N.C.O. hurriedly stuffed maps and papers into the Canadian type stove and, having doused it with petrol, set it alight. He told the men to follow him with loaded rifles and went up the half-dozen steps, climbed through the barbed wire and headed towards Group H.Q. One man who forgot his steel helmet went down the six steps and on returning was captured. Another—the cook—who made a detour in the trench was also captured.

The party had only travelled about fifty yards when they saw through the mist the new British front line and our infantry were lining a trench and aiming at us. Just in time the writer yelled that we were British, and we were allowed to pass through on stating our destination.

By this time the enemy guns had been pushed forward and were putting down a barrage, which, more by luck than judgment, the party got through and arrived at Group H.Q. at Jussy.

A word of the two men at the Post. They had orders to retire on the billet in an emergency, but did not get the chance. The attack was so sudden and severe that they found themselves in the middle of a scrap. The Observation Post was hit and they were wounded. There was an Aid Post in a dugout next door and they managed to get there and were taken prisoners after the dugout was bombed by the kindly Hun. The men returned home after the war.

Back at Jussy there was much excitement. The even tenor of their way was rudely shattered by the arrival of high explosive and gas shells. Congdon was standing at the door and was slightly gassed. He was put in charge of the Group cart and evacuated the equipment, another gassed man being put on top and taken to a dressing station.

All telephone lines were out of action, and by nine o'clock it was known the situation was serious and it was decided to evacuate the Group, Banes-Condy being in charge of this whilst Bishop waited for the Posts to come in.

Nos. 1 and 2 Posts got in safely, except for the two men from No. 1 who had been taken prisoners, but Nos. 3 and 4 were not yet in touch.

It was known that No. 4 would be in bad case as Fort Vendeuil was a strong point and nobody would be allowed to leave even if found to be possible. This left No. 3 unaccounted for and Bishop and the writer set off to try to get up to this Post. Arriving in the vicinity they found it in no-man's-land. They crawled through our infantry to the Post and found it had been safely evacuated and all instruments, etc., removed.

On regaining our lines they told the infantry to help themselves to the Post larder as soon as it was dusk and set off back to Jussy.

The old H.Q. had been evacuated and it was decided to rest the night there unless the Group's old Ford turned up. It did arrive later, fortunately, as Jussy was in enemy hands early next morning.

For the next few days the Group retired by long marches, the O.C. being in touch with the higher command and presumably expecting to get into action again as soon as the enemy were brought to a standstill.

The roads were thronged with troops and transport, enemy planes circled overhead dropping bombs and machine-gunning. One plane was brought down by bullets from one of our planes, the pilot and observer fell and landed some thirty yards from the road, the machine bursting into flames on hitting the ground. The men were searched for papers and their hands folded upon their chests.

On March 26th in the village of La Motte the party (about fifty strong) were resting in a billet, lying on the floor and hoping to get a night's rest, when the cheery word came that Uhlans were approaching the village. Bishop ordered the party to fall in, those without rifles to retire behind the village in charge of Railton and the remainder to join other oddments for a scrimmage.

Railton marched his party of about thirty to a cross-road, adjoining which was an aeroplane hangar and machines. Halting the men he explained the position to a R.F.C. officer, who was fuming because he could not get his planes away and would have to fire them.

Transport was dashing down the road and civilians were screaming and retiring in great disorder.

The R.F.C. officer was told that the men wanted to assist in the defence of the village, but had neither rifles nor ammunition. This sportsman then assisted by pulling up lorries which had slowed down and insisting on their occupants handing over any rifles and ammunition. If any objected he threatened them with his revolver, until at last everybody was equipped, some with long rifles and short bayonets and others vice versa. Dashing back to the village it was found to be a false alarm and the men had their night's rest after all.

For the time being the excitement was intense; civilians hastily pushed off with barrows laden with a few things, Chinese from labour units were waddling along with bundles on their heads, transport was getting mixed up, and in the midst of it the Field Survey Company transport was seen charging gallantly rearwards.

Here again the Field Survey Company did good work in helping to calm down the agitated civilians. In one case an N.C.O. was asked to stay with an elderly lady through the night, being regaled with bottles of champagne.

The trek terminated at Marcelcave—a village on a plateau—where the Field Survey Company got into touch with the local command. Here we learnt that we were to form a part of what came to be known as "Carey's Force."

The honour of forming this mixed unit at a time of crisis really belongs to General Grant, 5th Army C.E., who handed over to Carey when he came back from leave.

There was some discussion as to the line for the trenches, and whilst this was being settled Bishop instructed Railton, who was an old infantryman, to try to improve his unit's musketry practice, and there was much activity on the village green. Some of the men had never handled a rifle, except for early instruction on joining up.

It was thought the scratch force would take up position in a day or perhaps two, but in the afternoon, after returning from inspecting the proposed trench positions, Bishop called at the H.Q. and was told the position was most serious and that he would have to move in right away. This would be about March 28th.

Parading his Group of fifty to sixty men, Bishop stated the position was serious and that the O.C. had volunteered on their behalf to go into action as infantry.

The Flash Spotter as a Fighting Man

He knew some of the men had no experience in the line and if any thought they ought not to go in he could stand forward.

To the credit of the Field Survey Company only one man came forward—a cook—and he was told by Bishop to get back into line and that he ought to be damned well ashamed of himself.

It was early evening when we moved in, occupying some old trenches, which we proceeded to dig deeper and string out some concertina wire (not barbed) which someone had found.

The only rations were those we carried in our pockets.

We were not in contact that day except that a gun was dropping shells from three-quarter rear in the afternoon. The writer suggested to Bishop that he should send word back that our artillery were firing short and was told "you damned fool that's a Jerry."

That night the troops were withdrawn to a new position behind the village and again dug in. The writer, who had been digging a machine-gun post—in anticipation of getting three Lewis guns from a Canadian unit— was forgotten, but eventually got in touch with another Field Survey Company unit.

There was a supply of water in petrol tins guarded by a sentry. Knowing No. 24 Group did not have any water he asked for a tin, which was refused, so when the sentry's back was turned he "Knocked one off" and managed to locate No. 24 Group just before dawn.

Some rations had been got up, so the tin of water was boiled up, all the tea, sugar, and milk put in, and passed round to the men in the isolated escarpments. (There had not been time for a continuous trench to be dug.)

The bread and jam was eaten and the meat destroyed.

All through the night the men had taken turns on

guard and all were feeling thoroughly fatigued, some dropping asleep while standing.

On the previous afternoon Grant strolled up, without a tin hat, to have a look at us. He stopped some infantry-men who were retiring through us, and on being told they were not wounded told them to get into the trenches with us and the "R.E.'s will show you how to fight." The fact is that these infantrymen had been through a hell of a time and were *in extremis*. Many of them were covered with blood and their faces were yellow and green from powder and exposure, but this was no time for sentiment and anybody who could possibly fire a shot was invaluable.

As soon as dawn broke enemy planes came over the trenches, flying about thirty feet above ground, and dropped white ranging lights on us. This was the signal for the barrage and it was merry hell while it lasted.

There were one or two direct hits on the bays, but otherwise the damage was not extensive.

Bishop had passed the word that it was understood there was to be no retirement from that position unless *written* orders were received from H.Q. Otherwise it was to be fought out.

If instructions were received to retire, we were to crawl through some old barbed wire and form a position immediately to the rear of a main road some two hundred yards to rear.

Looking over the parados the writer saw from the barrage that we were at the apex of a horseshoe, and that it was only a matter of an hour or so before we would be surrounded.

There was not a single reserve behind us and it looked pretty bad. The writer and others in the immediate neigh-bourhood shook hands, believing it to be indeed farewell.

When the Germans appeared on the scene most of us

were devouring snacks of bread and jam and had our rifles ready with clips of ammunition. We were a very mixed crowd. Some had old rifles, some had odd bayonets, and others had none. We could see the enemy advancing and trying to take cover behind some mounds in the fields as they advanced. We held our fire and then let them have it.

One man near the writer yelled, "Pass the word my rifle's jammed." The reply was most crude.

Presumably on account of the encircling movement written orders arrived to retire to the road position and the writer had been told to lead the way with four other men, the rest coming on in small numbers.

On leaving the trench we could see the whole line scrambling out and making for the road. We had to get through the old barbed wire to the accompaniment of shell and machine-gun fire, which increased in intensity when our move was spotted.

A most unpleasant quarter of an hour ensued. Men were hit, limbs were hurtling through the air, and the whole neighbourhood seemed an inferno.

The men were rallied in a rough line. By this time the units were well mixed. Apart from the Field Survey Company there appeared to be members of nearly every regiment.

There was a Staff Captain who did yeoman work with great coolness. He led a party up a bank through a coppice and this commanded the advance in the valley below. The spot was enfiladed by machine-gun fire, but our fellows held it. One man was unwounded, although he got a couple of bullets through the stock of his rifle and one through his gas-mask. A field battery eventually got the range and he was put out. In an adjacent spot Bishop was seeing red. Waving his long rifle with short bayonet he yelled, "Watch my bayonet, boys." This gallant officer was hit several times until, getting a hit in the abdomen, he was put out and was evacuated with great difficulty.

He was in hospital for many months, but eventually recovered and came out again.

During the next few hours there was much hand-to-hand fighting, and marvellous feats were performed by this scratch force, fighting with the knowledge that they must hold on at all costs in the hope that somehow, somewhere, reinforcements would arrive. The writer later heard yarns of the fortunes of the men, but the incidents related above give a fair indication of the conditions.

Up till now everything had been much in favour of the enemy, but the tide was turning. There had not been a single gun firing for us and there were no men in support. Towards noon reinforcements arrived in the shape of a contingent of Australians rushed up from the coast where they had been on rest.

The first intimation we had was to see batteries of 18-pounders galloping into action on a plain behind us. What a magnificent spectacle! They swung round and unlimbered and at once opened up, firing over open sights over our heads.

This was followed up by the arrival of infantrymen brought up in lorries. They came on in open order through us and knocked hell out of the enemy. "Let's get at 'em!" they shouted.

This was the end of our activities for the moment.

I formed up about fifteen of our men and marched them to our rendezvous—a village about five hundred yards to right rear, where we prepared a scratch meal of boiled bully and biscuits (scrounged), which was eagerly eaten by the men now arriving.

Villers Bretoneux was on our left rear and the Group

marched there in the late afternoon, being accommodated in an old prisoner of war camp on the outskirts.

There was a large aerodrome nearby which had been ignited by shell-fire and was burning furiously. Nearby, wonderful work was being done by the R.A.M.C. in evacuating the wounded. A hospital train was steaming away from the line at walking pace and stopping every few minutes to allow the cases to be taken on board whilst the shells were bursting around.

Next morning we marched back a few miles to more healthy quarters, and on the roll being called it was found that about half our strength were casualties.

The Groups were therefore amalgamated and it was whilst refitting that the Company had a very pleasant surprise.

The Company was paraded and General Rawlinson arrived. Addressing the Company he thanked them for the way they had stepped into the breach at a most critical stage of the battle. He understood that many of them had had no experience in the line and thought their conduct the more praiseworthy. On behalf of the Army and country he thanked them from the bottom of his heart.

It is important to note that with the relief by the Australians outlined above there was an end to the retreat which started on March 21st. The battle continued to wage around Villers Bretoneux, but the Australians finally held it until the great advance in August.

Observation Posts were again manned and normal observation work went on. The sector became very unhealthy as the enemy artillery outnumbered ours. There were many narrow escapes.

But our artillery strength was steadily increasing until in August it was clear that we were going to take the offensive.

Flash Spotters & Sound Rangers

We were kept very busy calibrating and ranging with the new type of bursts. The writer was taken down to our lines by a Counter Battery officer just before the attack and was amazed to see the line upon line of guns of all calibres practically wheel to wheel.

The attack opened on August 8th and by 10 a.m. the Australians had reached the 1 o'clock objectives. The writer went up with observers, linesmen, and a ration cart ready to go into action. He stayed the night with the commander of a 6-inch howitzer battery at one end of a village, with Germans at the other end.

The successful result of the advance is well known. The defeat of March was wiped out with a vengeance.

The things that made the deepest impression on my mind during these days were:

1. The rapidity of the German advance on March 21st, and the immediate destruction of telephonic and other communications.

2. The pluck and audacity of our airmen in flying low and harrying the enemy, simply parking their planes in a field for a hasty meal and going up again.

3. The wonderful pluck and tenacity of men who dug, marched, and fought long after they were absolutely "dead to the wide."

4. The coming into the action of the Australians when we were almost out.

5. The complete success of the August offensive, and last but by no means least the treasured companionship of officers and men of the Field Survey Company with whom I had the honour of working through these most difficult times, and of whom one cannot do better than quote our national poet—"Here was a man."

W. J. RAILTON

16

THE SOUND RANGER AS A FIGHTING MAN

In early February 1918, I returned to France and R Sound Ranging Section, from which I had been separated after an encounter with a shell at Ypres a few days after the opening of the Third Battle.

I found the Section's new base in the village of Grand Seraucourt where a French Sound Ranging Section had recently handed over its duty. We used our apparatus successfully on the long irregular microphone base connected by an earth-return line system, but this is only a point of technical interest. My chief impression on approaching Grand Seraucourt was the clean dry country and the comparative absence of signs of warfare. The village itself was indeed somewhat ruined. It was branded here and there with the red hand of Ulster. I had never seen in France such smart clean infantry as those of the 36th Division in Grand Seraucourt. Paradoxically they strengthened the impression of peacefulness. The weather was cold, crisp, and sunny. You breathed more freely in the spacious undulating territory, and the ground was firm beneath the feet. The sound of the guns was rarely heard. This was a delectable spot for R Section, veteran of the Somme, the Ancre, and Ypres.

I returned to Sound Ranging to find great changes afoot. Fresh Sections were being formed. The great feature of our map was St. Quentin. The trenches skirted it to form a small German salient and our microphone base extended on each side of it. My wanderings towards the front soon roused suspicion of the peacefulness. Staff officers were seen reconnoitring on the Roupy ridge to the north, in front of Grand Seraucourt and at Essigny to the south. Every night men were digging hard. Every day it became more difficult to negotiate a broad line of defence works 4,000 to 5,000 yards behind the front line, until we proudly said to each other that the Germans themselves had never built anything so trim and formidable. We crouched into newly prepared machine-gun posts and laughed at the thought of men attempting to enter the field of fire. Tales were told of what experienced Lewis gunners had said they could do in such posts. In front of our village we found two big trench mortars already in place. Field-guns were "ringed" with wire and provided with Lewis guns—a precaution adopted after the Cambrai retaliation which on the fateful day proved only to be a trap for the defenders.

We Sound Rangers also had a place in the scheme of defence. I had instructions to reconnoitre for a base on the assumption that the new trench system would be occupied. I studied a map of the defence scheme with Besley at his Flash Spotting H.Q. The existing front line, labelled "Forward Zone," was overprinted in blue, the new trench system roughly parallel to the front line was named "Battle Zone," and appropriately coloured red. A third zone, shaded in green, was not named. It was formed by natural defence features and was unofficially styled the "God help us" line.

Since returning to France I had noticed a very gratifying change in the artillery attitude towards Sound Ranging. Counter Battery wanted our information direct, quickly, and often. They pressed us to conduct the shooting of our own batteries, and so with their attentions and the measures to be taken to install a new system we were kept very busy in spite of the comparative inactivity of the enemy guns.

The Sound Ranger as a Fighting Man

About the middle of March, when our defence schemes had been laid out, all Section and Group Commanders had orders to attend at Company H.Q., which was still at Lamotte en Sauterre more than thirty miles behind the line. The C.O. received our reports about the preparation that had been made and then made a speech. "For the first time since 1914," he said, "the British Army is obliged to adopt the defensive—but only temporarily, for we shall soon assume the offensive again. The Army Commander says it must be our firm resolution to yield no ground to the enemy. It must be particularly understood that the opening of the attack is not the signal to withdraw to the Battle Zone. The attack will be resisted to the utmost in the Forward Zone and in case the Battle Zone has to be occupied, it is to be held to the last man."

The interpretation of this policy for Sound Rangers was that microphones should remain in the existing positions and that the new base should not be occupied until the old one was captured. The section was to be organized at the opening of the attack to repair damaged lines expeditiously. We went back to our units in no doubt about the imminence of battle.

Earnest discussions took place in the little Sound Ranging mess as to the probable course of events. One of the new officers had the gift of eloquence and he used it to expound his view that the enemy could now only have enough strength to bluff. As a test of his sincerity and a sign of my own difference of opinion, his coveted Colt automatic passed into my possession at a favourable price. The discussions were stimulated by the arrival of a document from H.Q. which announced the appearance of Von Hutier and his 18th German Army at St. Quentin. Von Hutier was a stranger to our front but he came with an awe-inspiring record. At Riga, we noted, he had brought all his infantry into action from seventy miles behind a quiet front, in a single night. We began to wish our front was not so quiet. It flashed on us that those unconfirmed gun locations in so many places near St. Quentin were really guns kept silent after only a round or two for registration. That problem film of a high-velocity gun firing from a position away to the south parallel to the front was explained now as a trick to register the gun without giving its position away.

Signs of nervousness on our side became more and more apparent. Gas parades and gas mask inspections were ordered, the observers were required to take rifles to the Observation Posts, and then a big black canister arrived. We placed it under the instrument board as instructed and called it "the bomb." It contained 30 lb. of ammonal and was intended to reduce our instruments and everything near them to smithereens if the enemy appeared to be likely to get possession.

The Summaries of Information which we received daily gave us plenty of news about the enemy activity. Officers had been impudently pacing the forward areas. The enemy was reported to have "Tanks" capable of a speed of nine miles an hour. The air photos which were passed on to us from "Maps" in order to confirm our locations and the accuracy of shoots were not otherwise very informative, but one day we had a surprise. In a valley north of St. Quentin and only about 2,000 yards behind the front, patches of ellipse-shaped objects appeared in hundreds. We all tried our utmost to make out what they could be. In every mind there was a great fear and a great hope. Could these things possibly be anything other than Tanks? Would Von Hutier expose precious Tanks so near the line? Could the Germans have built so many Tanks?

The Sound Ranger as a Fighting Man

Next morning the Wireless officer of 52 Squadron R.F.C., with whom we were collaborating, came in. He told us that the "Tanks" were causing great excitement and had been given the non-committal title of "maggots." On a wonderfully clear and sunny day we saw a further episode in the story of the "maggots." With dogged persistence three aeroplanes flew round and round in front of our north Observation Post, and then like birds spying out their prey they swooped across the line. At the same time the enemy waiting in readiness opened out a murderous "archie" fire which made the airmen dive and wriggle and beat a hasty retreat at a low altitude.

The Summary of Information began to get more exciting. The attack was actually expected at any moment. Then it was definitely promised for the morrow, but nothing happened. Undaunted, "Intelligence" again promised the attack in the morning and again nothing happened.

At midnight of March 20th I was working alone in the computing office. The silence was broken by the telephone bell and I was surprised to hear the voice of a Counter Battery Staff officer at that hour. I began to assure him that there was no activity on the front when he cut me short with an excited message, "I don't want to know anything about it," he said, "but I do want to tell you to drop everything now and go to bed. You will need all the sleep you can get because you have just four hours before the attack opens. Yes, it is quite certain this time— no doubt whatsoever." I did as he advised and was asleep in a trice.

The crash of shells in the village brought me violently back to consciousness. As I hastily scrambled to my feet, I heard "drum" fire on the grand scale between the crashes. It was still dark. How were the Observation

Posts faring? What could they tell us? The telephone line was already cut, but we buzzed on in hope, straining every nerve to hear. There was little else we could do. Day dawned mistily and the roar went on unabated. We breakfasted with all the composure we could muster and, still without news, held a council of war. I was to go and look for the observers of the southern Observation Post and collect a microphone on the way. With two men I started out and found the mist so thick that it was difficult to find the familiar route. We were obliged to follow the poles of our "air line" and where these came to an end we advanced singly so as to be within sight of each other and the terminal pole. I found myself in view of one of our Battle Zone trenches and on the fringe of a "whizzbang" barrage. In the trench I saw dimly the only sign of life that we had seen on our journey. A solitary figure was digging feverishly. We were in a futile position and had spent much time arriving there. A great anxiety came upon me for the safety of the Section and the apparatus and we returned with all speed. We found that news had come through about the progress of the battle and though it was bad news it came as a great relief. We had only been back with the Section a few minutes when a shell found one of the billets, blew off the roof, and wounded two men. One of them had just returned with me from the front. The observers had managed to get back from the Observation Posts. The two men from the north Observation Post had made their way through mist, gas, and shells, and turned aside to pick up a microphone on the south bank of the Somme. A German machine-gunner on the north bank covered them with his weapon but they pushed on until one had received a bullet in the shoulder. His companion came back suffering from gas.

The Sound Ranger as a Fighting Man

Hodgkinson, making a tour of the Sections along the enemy front from north to south, came in and arranged for our retirement. He said the Germans were advancing in full view all along his route.

All energy was now concentrated on the removal of our apparatus and the destruction of any evidence of our Sound Ranging activities. A tender arrived and took away the heaviest apparatus, and the men were sent back in parties along the bank of the dry St. Quentin canal to the rendezvous at Flavy le Martel, five miles to the south. Corporal Randall and I were left on the scene with the bomb. Should we wreck the empty house? It seemed pointless to us then, because we never dreamt that the Battle Zone would fail to stem the advance, so we chalked a message on the bomb "Danger, Explosive." "After all," I said as we left it in a ditch, "our office will make a fine billet for the infantry." The Corporal and I decided to take the road in preference to the canal bank. The mist had lifted and the road was full of traffic. Above the din came the roar of aircraft and the rattle of machine guns. A German aeroplane forcing one of ours to land almost came to earth, then wheeled towards us. We pressed ourselves against the bank on the roadside and cringed to think what havoc the victorious German was about to create along the road. He was so low I aimed at him with the newly acquired Colt automatic but I had forgotten the safety catch and by the time I had released it, the aeroplane had gone up and away and had mercifully missed his opportunity.

We arrived at Flavy late in the afternoon dog-tired. JJ Section had come in and told how they got their apparatus away but had been obliged to leave hurriedly without some of their personal effects with German infantry hard on their heels. Early next morning we heard machine guns announcing the arrival of the enemy at the Crozat canal. So we were back on the "God help us" line in one day! We now had instructions to retire to Army H.Q. at Nesle and the Sections were started early on the march. The village was deserted as our rearguard retired in the baggage tender. On the open road a horseman approached us. He was an R.E. Captain, responsible for blowing up the canal bridge at Jussy. He said he had failed to blow the bridge up and had no more explosive. He talked strangely. Without doubt he was demented. He left us, riding towards the bridge.

We halted at Ham, where the civilian population was going about its usual business apparently quite heedless of the oncoming enemy. We found in conversation that they had already entertained the German Army once during the war and the only difference they expected if it advanced again would be a change from khaki to field-grey customers.

In the evening, as we dined in a little restaurant crammed full of officers, the waiters and waitresses suddenly disappeared. The drone of aircraft and the boom of bombs reached our ears. We helped ourselves to food and in due course, following the example of the regular diners, left the money paying for our meal on our plates.

Next day we reached Nesle and eagerly awaited reports from the front, but an aerial battle at only two or three thousand feet close to the town seemed more significant than reports. The rattle of machine guns drew attention to four of our aeroplanes converging on a German who was doing some desperate evolutions in an attempt to get away. A spark appeared in the tail and flames swept quickly forward. Two figures began a cartwheel fall to earth and two French peasants who were standing by us breathlessly watching the fight dashed away at that moment. An hour later they returned triumphantly with a scorched flying boot and a leather seat. They demonstrated how they had kicked the bodies!

Our next move was to Lamotte, 20 km. east of Amiens. It was a tiring march. Near Chaulnes we crossed an area desolated by the Somme battle, and as we rested gloomily a smiling Chinese of the Labour Corps, wandering free, raised our spirits by attempting to sell us a tin of bully beef.

At Lamotte we found all the Field Survey Company assembled. My Section made its home in the hay-loft of a farm, the buildings of which adjoined the road and completely enclosed the dung-heap in the characteristic French fashion. I shared with Gillanders and R. F. Bishop, the Flash Spotter, the hospitality of an old peasant whose wife was bedridden. How the old man's eyes sparkled when he was offered the luxury of a cigarette and then a sip of whisky. We heard that the Somme had been crossed at Brie, but still we hoped that the lines of the old Somme battlefield would be held. Our hopes were rudely shattered in the evening when a wild-eyed breathless soldier burst unceremoniously into our little parlour and panted out, "The German cavalry are here." Under the silent disapproval which he faced the man lost his excitement and looked puzzled. Gillanders dismissed him savagely—"Get out," he said. Quickly we arranged to collect our respective Sections and Groups. I had to go across the village and was astounded as I entered the transport park where all the Field Survey Companies vehicles had been collected to see our last mule cart galloping away. The driver was standing in the cart lashing his animal wildly. As I paused to look round I heard a strange roar from the road. In a minute I was looking on a melancholy spectacle. The road was packed

297

tight with a mob in full flight. There were cars and guns and tractors and a road roller and agricultural machinery moving in the midst of a press of soldiers, civilians, and animals, and curses rose above the clatter of machinery.

I found my Section in the depths of the hay-loft calmly sleeping. The Corporal roused the men. In the farm-yard there were stacked boxes of small arms ammunition and we collected a few. When we opened the great gate of the yard, the noise of the road burst in on us, but I saw that only stragglers of the main body in retreat were left. A group of familiar faces marched by amongst them but one of the officers caught sight of us and, darting across, he said, "Where are you going?" "We have an appointment at the east end of the village," I said, "and we are taking this little find of ammunition along with us." "Then I'm with you," he said, and we marched to the rendezvous, where we were greeted with cheers from those already assembled. We deployed away from the road in front of the village, then two or three officers went forward along the roadside with ears strained and revolvers ready. The sound of hoofs brought us to a halt. It was quite dark and we listened tensely. We could not make out at first whether the horse was walking or trotting, but after minutes of waiting we decided that the cavalryman was solitary and leisurely. He had a shock when he suddenly found himself faced with revolvers on both side. From a rapid exchange of questions and answers we learnt that the horseman knew nothing of the retreating mob and was sure there were no German cavalry within ten miles. What then was the origin of the stampede and where had it ended? We heard next day. It had been stopped at Villers Brettoneux by shooting the horses of a G.S. wagon near the head of the stream. It had been started by an enemy agent and an order came from Army H.Q. saying that the ruse of entering the Allied back areas in Allied Army uniforms and stampeding disconnected units had already been practised by the enemy with disastrous effect on the Italian front and that any unknown person, no matter what his uniform, who gave orders to retreat must be shot at sight.

We left Lamotte next day and marched to Hangard, 10 km. south-west. Our route lay through Marcelcave, which presented a scene of joy and peace. The villagers were gathered in the market-place and a band played bright music. Little did the merry folks know of the swift doom awaiting the village. At the small, peaceful village of Hangard, destined soon to be the scene of bayonet fighting, we were billeted in the Mairie. Pre-war German prints hung on the walls of the corridors! We drank coffee in glasses at a little estaminet by the grand gate of a château. As I slept that night I was aroused in the darkness by an officer who asked all about us and departed with the news that he would be wanting us to fill up the ranks of the defending infantry. Next day I attended a conference of O.C.s Sections and Groups at Demuin where the C.O., 5th Field Survey Company, explained that the situation was grave, Amiens was threatened, and the Survey Company was now going to take over part of the defensive line. We were all to concentrate that day at Demuin. I returned to Hangard, and during the march forward to Demuin we saw the villagers of Marcelcave scattered along the road which dips into the valley of the Luce struggling with bundles or piled-up carts and wheelbarrows. It was a pathetic scene. The pain of the fugitives was intensified by the sight of their intimate treasures and the thought of yesterday's jollity. I was given the address of our billet when we reached Demuin and, proceeding to the house, the door was flung open as I put my foot on the lowest step. In the doorway a young woman stood defiantly barring the way. Her eyes blazed her contempt for the English soldiers. No word passed, for I retired until the house was evacuated. A wine shop was attached to it, and everything seemed to have been left undisturbed. It was left next day by us as we found it. In the clean and tidy bedroom where I lay down that night photographs of soldiers in French uniform seemed to regard us reproachfully. Refugees continued to straggle through the village. One pitiable old man showered blessings on me when I relieved him of a sack of potatoes and gave him money. A cow strayed into the backyard of our borrowed home with a distressed mooing—we milked her until she was happy again, but unfortunately she was still ownerless.

Next day we moved up to the positions we were to hold. We were armed with rifles, picks, and shovels, but we had no directions as to where we should begin digging ourselves in. We were near the crest of a ridge extending south-west from Marcelcave. I approached the C.O., who was watching our arrival, to ask for instructions. He greeted me, asked me what I knew of infantry work, promised me a chance of exercising my knowledge, and referred me for all details to Hodgkinson or Besley who had been given joint command of the improvised force. Besley was now the Flash Spotting counterpart of Hodgkinson and had been liaison officer for Fifth Army Groups for a few weeks. A much harassed Hodgkinson gave us our dispositions and we dug ourselves a series of posts to a south-east front when we were told the attack was expected. Opinions as to the direction of the attack changed quickly and before we laid down our tools our posts had become isolated units of a castellated trench line. Whilst we were busy digging some of our infantry came straggling back across country. They belonged chiefly to a Cornish regiment and still carried their arms. They joined forces with us, and with at least one Lewis gun added considerably to our powers of resistance. A Sergeant approached our post and said we might as well go home as the game was up. I remembered the order at Lamotte and raised the Colt automatic, telling him to join his comrades on the left without any more words. He obeyed only for a time, then turned again. Even in our isolated post all kinds of scandalous rumours reached us. They were aimed at the higher command, and the Army Commander in particular. I felt convinced at the time that enemy agents were again active undermining morale and regretted that I had not given the Sergeant more attention.

Before evening we had finished our labours and were waiting and watching for the enemy. His approach was signalled with a flourish, for during the night the village of Marcelcave on our left was set on fire. Next morning the roar of guns putting down a barrage came from somewhere to the north of Marcelcave. We heard later that the 61st Division had been heavily engaged at Lamotte and had counter-attacked through the village. Sadly I thought of the old man our host and his bedridden wife, for Bishop a day or two earlier had returned to Lamotte by motor cycle to recover something he had left behind. The village was deserted and he found the old man under the bed. He emerged overjoyed, only for a brief moment, to find a British officer instead of the German he expected.

Developments on the north flank redirected our front. A message was passed along to keep a keen look out between Marcelcave and Villers Brettoneux, where there was known to be a gap in the line. At the same time, however, we came under the fire of field guns from the opposite side of Marcelcave. The battery was seen to come into action and it was solemnly affirmed that it was accompanied by two elephants harnessed to low trolleys! The battery fired from an open position. We saw the gun flashes and in a few seconds the shells burst around us. We had been told that we had one field-gun battery with very little ammunition and one 6-inch howitzer as artillery support, but we were denied the satisfaction of seeing retaliation on the enemy guns.

On our right we looked over Demuin across the valley of the little river Luce and saw the enemy advancing on the opposite ridge. He occupied Demuin after it had been shelled and then shells of heavy calibre fell in the valley behind us. An infantry ration party was lost by shell-fire that night. Those who held positions on our right were well placed for firing at the advancing Germans. We climbed out of our holes and fired from where we stood but the effect of our fire at a considerable distance was negligible. The enemy swept forward so swiftly on the south side of the Luce valley that we on the north side found ourselves behind the line of his field guns and turned about to watch the bursting of his shells miles beyond.

In the late afternoon a German aeroplane made a reconnaissance over us. It circled lower and lower and, deciding that it would be well to make a display of strength, I ordered rapid fire from the Section and joined in the fun. The airman was very unperturbed by the fusillade which, it seemed, could not have failed to take some effect. He made another circuit still lower and returned our fire before flying away.

We were sure now that we should soon be attacked. As soon as night fell we had a fresh duty on the left flank.

The Sound Ranger as a Fighting Man

It was imperative that our defence line should be pushed out towards Villers Brettoneux and our plan was to dig a trench across the fold in the ground behind the ridge we were defending and opposite Marcelcave village. We dug hard in relays until in the grey of dawn we began to discern the outline of the village. The new trench was very narrow and shallow, but in the re-distribution of personnel which now took place R Section found itself displaced to the right of the new work, into wide deep trenches which were part of the permanent defences of Amiens.

With the improving light Germans were observed debouching from Marcelcave to occupy posts on the south side, and we opened fire with rifles from the new trench. A Lewis gun had been mounted at the end of a gap in our sector, which commanded a good view of the village. The gunners gave me instruction in its manipulation.

During the day we heard that a young infantry officer in the cramping trench had been shot through the head by a sniper. The space in the trench was so limited that those near him rolled his body out. Hodgkinson, on his way to reconnoitre an extension to our left flank, stepped out of the trench to examine the victim and take his papers for identification. Though the sniper missed an opportunity he had marked another target, for Hodgkinson showed himself again as he squeezed down the trench and promptly had a bullet clean through his body from pocket to pocket. An hour or so later he crawled painfully down the trench to a dug-out which also formed part of the Amiens defences.

The first excitement and effort in our new work was now on the wane and we began to take stock of ourselves and our position. We had not yet felt hungry, our beards began to add a shagginess to our grimy faces and though very weary the enemy had not yet directly disturbed our short spells of rest at night. We were ill equipped. There was no wire in front of our inadequate trench line except a few yards of single strand carrying tins to serve for an alarm. We had no support on our flanks. The narrow trench that we had thrown out towards Villers Brettoneux had not established contact with the defences, which we assumed would be extended from Villers Brettoneux towards us. There was also a gap on our right flank towards Hangard. Our communications were already seriously threatened by the occupation of Marcelcave and Demuin, and it was suggested that the enemy would probably avoid a frontal attack and work round us from the open flanks. Some argued that in view of our hopeless weakness it would be folly to throw away our lives, so when the attack came we ought to give ourselves up. But messages had also reached us telling us that the eyes of the world were turned to us as the saviours of Amiens, and perhaps the unity of the Franco-British Armies, so when day dawned again and "stand to" was passed along the line, there was hardly a man who did not spring to arms and stand patiently waiting to meet barrage or bayonet. The critical time passed again without attack.

News came from the right that two Flash Spotters patrolling in front of their trench during the night had encountered a German patrol and successfully disposed of them. At about ten o'clock in the morning a written message was passed along instructing us to retire to a ridge crowned by a wood about a kilometre behind the position we were holding. This move was evidently intended to close the gaps on our flanks but it was difficult to understand why it had been postponed till full daylight when considerable losses were bound to offset the advantage of the readjustment. As I was instructing the men where and how to go the cook came along the trench with a panful of bacon. "Put that down," I said, "and let us hope the Bosche is hungry enough to have his attention taken off us as we go up that slope." I sent the men off in parties. "Off you go as fast as you can," I ordered, "don't bunch and good luck to you." I saw Gillanders starting out with a resolute plod, refusing as usual to be hustled. As soon as the movement began, machine guns and rifles opened fire from Marcelcave whilst a barrage of light and heavy calibres was put down round the wood, the cover of which was instinctively sought. I descended our ridge quickly but on the opposite slope I found myself entangled in the rough earth of a ploughed field. My feet seemed to become heavy as lead. One of the men of R Section moved across to me asking where to go. "Follow me," I called, then "Down!" as a stream of bullets whizzed over us. I was now profoundly thankful for the cover of the furrows and I lay as closely to the bottom of one of them as I could but a bullet entered my right hand and ran down the arm. The gunner continued to sweep his bullets over us. They whistled by and pattered around. A memory of Gillanders's determined face and an overwhelming anxiety for his safety spurred me to take my chance and walk through the barrage of bullets and shells to the objective. So I scrambled to my feet and proceeded. A man in front of me seemed suddenly to spin round and then crumple up. A big shell landed on my left. At the root of the dark spout of earth and smoke that shot up several khaki figures toppled and were swallowed up.

I reached the crest and found men digging posts. Shells were still falling thickly in the wood. A Major whom I did not know told me kindly that I had better go back to a dressing station. Leaving him, I was surprised to see a line of our own cavalry prancing on the plain. They were drawn up to ensure that the new line was not overstepped, but I bitterly resented the sad misjudgment which led to their being ordered to flourish their naked swords.

9th April, 1918.

Dear ——,

I'm sure you'll be delighted to know that the Fourth Army Commander had the remnants of the 5th Field Survey Companies on parade and congratulated them on the firm stand they made and told them that they really did not know how much they had done. For untrained troops to stick it as they had done was splendid.

Of the officers four are missing—prisoners or killed. Eight are wounded and two sick. In your own R Section, besides yourself, eight of the men are wounded, three of them at the opening of the attack. Three of your men are missing, one is slightly gassed and one suffering from shock.

Yours sincerely,

P. Rothwell

IN PERPETUAM REI MEMORIAM

APPENDIX

NAMES AND APPOINTMENTS OF OFFICERS WHO WERE PRINCIPALLY CONCERNED WITH THE INCEPTION AND GROWTH OF SOUND RANGING AND SURVEY OBSERVATION

THERE are very few references to individuals by name in the body of this book, and the reader may wonder why. The reason is this.

In the "Survey" everyone prided themselves on the team work, and conferences and other meetings for the interchange of ideas were of constant occurrence. From the team spirit so engendered arose the feeling that the achievements of one were the achievements of all, and it is in accordance with this spirit that this book has been written. Nevertheless, it would be a pity if there was no mention made of those who by virtue of their positions and talents did so much to guide these Battalions to a successful end. It was no straightforward task they had to tackle; because most of these officers had to deal not only with the day-to-day affairs of units in the line, but they also had to create what was virtually a new arm of the Service.

Here, then, is a list of some of these officers and their appointments:

At Maps, G.H.Q.

(The Topographical Sub-Section of the General Staff, I.c.)

Officer in Charge: Colonel E. M. Jack.
Technical Assistant: Lieut.-Colonel H. St. J. Winterbotham.
Sound Ranging Adviser: Major W. L. Bragg.
Cross Observation Adviser: Major H. H. Hemming.
Map Supply: Capt. E. E. Field and Lieut. Whitby.
Personnel: Capt. G. Carlyle.
Equipment: Lieut. G. A. Allingham.
Geodosy: Lieut. G. T. McCaw.

Flash Spotters & Sound Rangers

Experimental Section, Salisbury Plain.

Officer Commanding: Major W. S. Tucker.

Commanding Field Survey Battalions.

1st. Lieut.-Colonel B. H. Wilbraham (who succeeded Major H. Wood).

2nd. Lieut.-Colonel C. S. Reid.

3rd. Lieut.-Colonel B. F. E. Keeling (who succeeded Lieut.-Colonel Winterbotham).

4th. Lieut.-Colonel M. N. MacLeod.

5th. Lieut.-Colonel F. B. Legh (who succeeded Major Keeling when he was wounded).

(NOTE.—Lieut.-Colonel Keeling died shortly after the war from the effects of the wounds he had received whilst serving with the Survey.)

Lightning Source UK Ltd.
Milton Keynes UK
UKHW022131070620
364529UK00009B/731

9 781783 313389